PENGUIN BOOKS

# LEONARDO DA VINCI

Kenneth Clark was born in 1902. He was educated at Winchester and Oxford and worked for two years with Bernard Berenson in Florence. He was appointed Director of the National Gallery at the age of thirty and remained there until 1945. During the war he organized the war

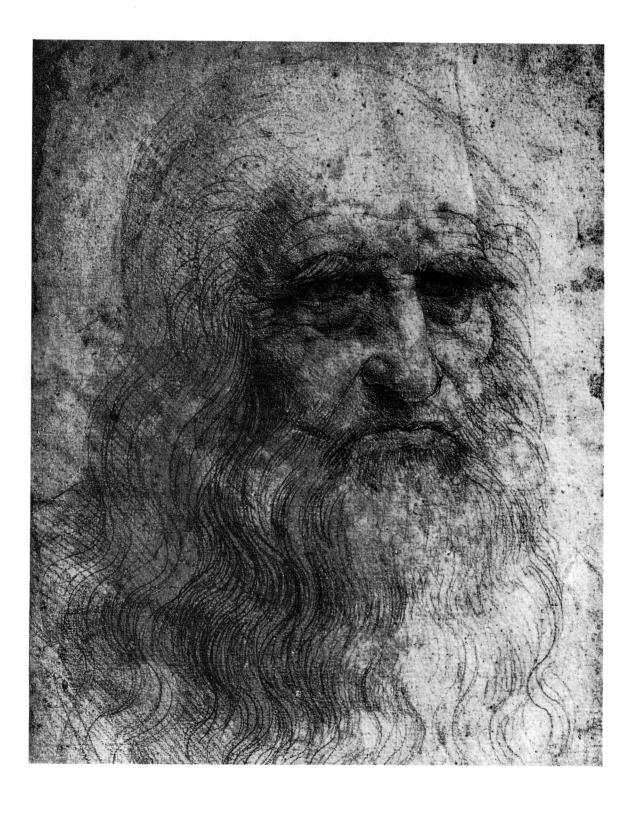

# KENNETH CLARK

# LEONARDO DA VINCI

*INTRODUCTION BY*
*PROFESSOR MARTIN KEMP*

Penguin Books

*Dedicated to*
DAVID BALNIEL

PENGUIN BOOKS

Published by the Penguin Group
Penguin Books Ltd, 27 Wrights Lane, London w8 5tz, England
Penguin Books USA Inc., 375 Hudson Street, New York, New York 10014, USA
Penguin Books Australia Ltd, Ringwood, Victoria, Australia
Penguin Books Canada Ltd, 10 Alcorn Avenue, Toronto, Ontario, Canada m4v 3b2
Penguin Books (NZ) Ltd, 182–190 Wairau Road, Auckland 10, New Zealand

Penguin Books Ltd, Registered Offices: Harmondsworth, Middlesex, England

First published by Cambridge University Press 1939
Revised edition published by Penguin Books 1959
Reprinted with revisions 1967
Published with revisions and an Introduction by Viking 1988
Published in Pelican Books 1989
Reprinted in Penguin Books 1993
1 3 5 7 9 10 8 6 4 2

Copyright 1939 by Kenneth Clark
Introduction and revisions copyright © Martin Kemp, 1988
All rights reserved

Filmset in Monophoto Sabon

Made and printed in Great Britain by
Butler & Tanner Ltd, Frome and London

# CONTENTS

# LIST OF PLATES

Plates added to Clark's original list are marked *.

The dates given for undocumented works are deduced from Clark's text, the original list of plates and chronology.

All works are by Leonardo unless specifically indicated.

## PLATES FOR THE INTRODUCTION

# PHOTOGRAPHIC ACKNOWLEDGEMENTS

Windsor Castle, Royal Library, by Gracious Permission of Her Majesty the Queen: 12, 17, 20, 28, 41, 47, 49, 50, 51, 52, 53, 55, 57, 58, 59, 65, 66, 68, 69, 70, 71, 72, 73, 74, 76, 77, 78, 81, 84, 85, 89, 92, 93, 97, 100, 101, 102, 103, 104, 105, 106, 107, 108, 109, 110, 111, 112, 113, 114, 115, 116, 121; Alinari: 7, 8, 9, 24, 27, 122; Alte Pinakothek, Munich: 13; Ambrosiana, Milan: 29, 38, 40, 42, 79, 120; Soprintendenza Beni Artistici e Storici, Florence: 6, 22; Soprintendenza Beni Artistici e Storici, Milan: 54, IV, V; Biblioteca Nacional, Madrid: I, II; Osvaldo Böhm: 56, 80; British Museum, London: 3, 15, 63; Ets Bulloz: 34, 36, 43, 44, 45, 91, 94, 98; Courtauld Institute, Conway Library, London: 2; Christ Church, Oxford: 10; Documentation photographique de la Réunion Des Musées Nationaux: 16, 18, 19, 32, 39, 61, 67, 95, 96, 99, 117; Fitzwilliam Museum, Cambridge: 23; Photographie Giraudon: 21, 82; Hermitage Museum, Leningrad: 14, 31; Professor Martin Kemp: 1; Jacek Ksiazek: 37; The Metropolitan Museum of Art, New York: 33 (Rogers Fund, 1917 (17.142.1)), 46 (Rogers Fund, 1917 (14.142.2 verso)); National Gallery, London: 62, 86, 87; National Gallery of Art, Washington D.C.: 11 (Ailsa Mellon Bruce Fund, 1967); National Galleries of Scotland: 64; Offentliche Kunstsammlung, Basel: 118; Royal Library, Turin: 35; Sante Maria del Monte, Varese: 119; Foto Saporetti, Milan: 60; Scala: 4, 5, 25, 26, 48, 88; Skulpturengalerie, Staatliche Museen Preussischer Kulturbesitz, Berlin (West): 90; Szépmüvészeti Múzeum, Budapest: 83; Vatican Museum: 30; Wilton House Trust, Wilts.: 75.

AN INTRODUCTION BY MARTIN KEMP

# CLARK'S LEONARDO

T HE daunting body of literature on Leonardo contains its fair share of lunacy and more than its fair measure of scholarly nit-picking. However, it also includes a significant quantity of writing that presents exciting insights into the master's works and is worth reading in its own right. I doubt whether the writing on other major artists, Michelangelo for instance, can lay claim to comparable peaks of literary excellence. The names of four authors cited prominently in Clark's text – Goethe, Pater, Valéry and Freud – testify to the quality of earlier minds drawn to Leonardo's seductive genius. In Vasari's *Lives of the Artists*, the great sixteenth-century compendium which is the first masterpiece of historical writing on the visual arts, Leonardo receives what is probably the most compellingly personal portrait of all, although Michelangelo's life provides the ostensible climax of the series. Clark's monograph is in every respect a creatively worthy member of the tradition of Leonardo biography that runs from Vasari.

Kenneth Clark's *Leonardo da Vinci: An Account of his Development as an Artist* was first published in 1939 and stands at the mature climax of his remarkably precocious career as a writer on the visual arts. This is not to say that his later writing or extensive activities as a broadcaster should be regarded as a decline, but I think it is true to say that his aesthetic sensibility, literary gifts and powers of scholarship were never again to be seen together in such a delicate and satisfying equilibrium. Looking at the story of Clark's life during his formative years, we can see these various elements entering his life and being absorbed within his developing intellect.[1]

1. The biographical details in the following account are drawn from: Kenneth Clark, *Another Part of the Wood: A Self Portrait* (London and New York, 1974), and *The Other Half* (London and New York, 1977); M. Secrest, *Kenneth Clark: A Biography* (London, 1984).

The substantial wealth of the Scottish family into which Clark was born on 13 July 1903 was founded on Paisley cotton. His father bought the large house and estate of Sudbourne in Suffolk as the main family residence, and the young Clark came to regard Scotland as somewhere to visit rather than as his native land. His father, Kenneth Mackenzie Clark, collected paintings with some enthusiasm, though his Victorian tastes excited neither the interest of the young boy nor the retrospective admiration of the art historian in later years. Clark's autobiography places great emphasis on the autonomous and 'innate' nature of his own aesthetic responses. He recalls at the age of seven visiting a huge exhibition of everything Japanese in the company of his nurse. Resisting the more obviously showy aspects of the exhibition, he was captivated by the Japanese paintings to such a degree that he was able to recognize some of them fifty-five years later on a visit to Japan.[2] Even allowing for a degree of retrospective romanticism in the autobiography – 'I was walking on air,' he recalls – this and other incidents suggest that what he called his sense of 'pure aesthetic sensation' had begun to manifest itself at a remarkably early age.

Throughout his career the conviction that aesthetic response is an identifiable and distinct property of the human mind remained central to his practice of art criticism. In Clark's own case this response embraced music, literature and the theatre no less keenly than the visual arts. The authors to whom he was most immediately drawn were those in whom he sensed this inner response at the highest level. Amongst writers on art, Walter Pater remained the supreme exemplar. Pater's famous words on the 'Mona Lisa' – 'a beauty wrought out from within upon the flesh, the deposit, little cell by little cell, of strange thoughts and fantastic reveries and exquisite passions' – became the passage most often quoted in his writings, appearing as early as 1929 and as late as 1973.[3] In literary and aesthetic terms, the challenge of Pater's 1869 essay on Leonardo plays a prominent role in Clark's monograph.

The aesthetic precociousness that seems to have earned him some measure of distrust from his schoolboy contemporaries at Winchester, where he nurtured an early ambition to become a painter, found an environment in which to flourish at Oxford, where he went to study history in 1922. The most important result of his insinuating himself into artistic circles in Oxford was that he was permitted by C. R. ('Charlie') Bell, the idiosyncratic Keeper of the Department of Fine Art at the Ashmolean Museum, to gain sustained access to the outstanding collection of Old Master drawings. With Robinson's

2. Clark, *Another Part of the Wood*, pp. 35–6.

3. W. Pater, 'Leonardo da Vinci', *The Renaissance* (1893), ed. D. Hill (Berkeley, Los Angeles and London, 1980), p. 98 (originally published in the *Fortnightly Review*, November 1869). See Kenneth Clark, 'A Note on Leonardo da Vinci', *Life and Letters*, vol. II, 9 (February 1929), p. 132; 'Mona Lisa' in the *Burlington Magazine*, vol. CXV (1973), p. 148, and below, p. 173.

venerable catalogue in his hand, the undergraduate Clark trained his eye directly on the intense study of original drawings by Raphael and Michelangelo. Bell's support was crucial in more than this respect: it was he who proposed that Clark should write a book on the Gothic revival after graduation, and effected the introduction to Bernard Berenson in Italy that did so much to promote Clark's meteoric rise.

Visiting the strange ménage surrounding the great American connoisseur at the Tuscan villa of I Tatti in 1925, Clark was astonished, on the basis of a brief conversation, to be offered the task of assisting Berenson on a revised edition of the corpus of *Florentine Drawings*. This was to involve him in the painstaking collation of lists and the huge collection of photographs, many of which were in far from ideal condition. Each drawing, either in the original or in reproduction, was to be subject to minute judgements of attribution on the basis of almost imperceptible nuances of style and the visual 'feel' of each work in relation to comparable examples. Although Clark never became a Berensonian connoisseur in the fullest sense, he continued to respect connoisseurship as a discipline closely related to the aesthetic response at the centre of his beliefs. As he was to write in 1974, 'A serious judgement of authenticity involves one's whole faculties.'[4] However, by the time the revised volume appeared, Clark had seriously tired of the exercises of connoisseurship and listing as the sole rationale for his existence.

Concurrently he was also working intermittently on Bell's project for a book on Victorian Gothic architecture. Bell's intention had not so much been to rehabilitate the architects involved, but to explain in relation to the cultural and religious background of the Victorian age why British architecture should have succumbed to Gothic revivalism – a 'national misfortune, like the weather'.[5] To explain the buildings, Clark recognized that 'these monsters, these unsightly wrecks stranded upon the mud flat of Victorian taste', required a very different kind of history from that of the attributional connoisseur:

Under the influence of beauty, many people have an irresistible, but ill-omened, impulse to write.... This kind of writing is important, but it is not the only way in which the history of art can be approached. Instead of making a great work of art his central theme and trying to explain it by means of the social and political circumstances of the time, the historian may reverse the process, and examine works of art to learn something of the epochs which made them, something of men's formal, imaginative demands which vary so unaccountably from age to age.[6]

This ambition, closer to German *kulturwissenschaft* than to traditional

4. Clark, *Another Part of the Wood*, p. 125.     5. Clark, *Another Part of the Wood*, p. 90.
6. Kenneth Clark, *The Gothic Revival: An Essay in the History of Taste* (London, 1928), p. viii.

British art criticism, was realized in his discussions of such topics as the literary ambience, romanticism, archaeology and ecclesiology. It also occasioned a growing unease that amongst 'these unsightly wrecks' were buildings by architects of real intellectual and visual merit. Although *The Gothic Revival*, when it was published in 1928, did not unambiguously advocate a full-scale rehabilitation of Victorian architecture, it undoubtedly played an important role in leading British taste away from the dismissive attitudes that then prevailed.

His research into the Victorian period also furthered his enduring love affair with Ruskin's criticism, not only with the Ruskin who writes so movingly of Turner, but also with Ruskin as a poet of natural vision in the broader sense. Clark's continued affinity with Ruskin depended not least upon Ruskin's unwillingness to be shackled with a cut-and-dried system of aesthetics based on rigid metaphysical principles.[7]

The other major legacy of Oxford was Clark's contact with Roger Fry, whose *Last Lectures* he was to publish in 1939. Fry was not only the great modernist partisan of post-impressionist masters, but also a penetrating student of historical art. In his lectures he was capable of bringing a Poussin to life beside a Cézanne, and an African mask beside a Michelangelo. What most impressed Clark was the formal rigour of Fry's analyses, which seemed to reveal the anatomical structure of compositions in a precise way that had lain beyond earlier criticism. He felt that Fry's intense formalism provided an intellectual tool by which 'we can take up the history and criticism of art where it was left, shall we say, by Pater'.[8]

Fry, with whom he became friendly, also established the possibility for Clark of uniting the autonomy of aesthetic experience with historical analysis. As he wrote in his introduction to Fry's lectures,

the critic who wishes to maintain his aesthetic integrity must add a self-regarding austerity to his other qualities. He must be something of a scholar: for although the language of forms may be universal it is capable of great modifications in idiom and emphasis, and the detachment of mere ignorance is deaf to any inflection which cannot be immediately understood.[9]

In the ominous circumstances of 1939, Clark felt it more necessary than ever to 'show that Roger Fry's doctrine of detachment can survive in a world of violence'.

Where Clark came to part aesthetic company with Fry was over the doctrine

---

7. See also *Ruskin Today*, chosen and annotated by Kenneth Clark (London, 1964).

8. Below, p. 40, and R. Fry, *Last Lectures*, introduced by Kenneth Clark (Cambridge, 1939), p. xv.

9. Fry, *Last Lectures*, introduction p. x.

of 'significant form', by which Fry intended to signal that the ultimate worth of a work of art rested wholly in its formal properties as distinct from content. Although Fry's espousal of this view was less constant and more subtle than this bare characterization suggests, his devaluing of the more literary and psychological aspects of 'meaning' in a work of art seemed increasingly unacceptable to Clark. An example of Clark's change of opinion is provided by his analysis of the transformation of Leonardo's 'Angel of the Annunciation' (Pl. 8) into his 'St John the Baptist' (Pl. 117):

It is less easy to understand how this image [the 'Angel'] could be converted, with a single change of gesture, into a St John, and I must confess that some years ago, when art was supposed to consist in the arrangement of forms, I believed Leonardo made this alteration for purely formal motives; that he bent the arm across the figure in order to achieve a denser and more continuous volume. It is true that the St John looks much more solid than the Angel, but we can be sure that Leonardo would not have varied the pose solely for that reason. Between the two figures there is more than a formal connection.[10]

Clark then proceeds to explore the gestural and psychological relationship between the images on the basis of religious iconography and personal expression.

An important factor in his abandoning the formalist and stylistic approaches was his earliest contact with the Warburgian method. In 1929 he attended a lecture by Aby Warburg at the Biblioteca Herziana in Rome. Clark wrote that the lecture 'changed my life'.[11] Through an analysis of the symbolic language of artists such as Botticelli, Warburg sought to use art, literature, philosophy, theology and so on – cultural history in the broadest sense – to penetrate the soul of a period in all its rational and irrational complexities. Following his exposure to Warburg, Clark's 'interest in "connoisseurship" became no more than a kind of habit, and my mind was occupied in trying to answer the kind of questions that had occupied Warburg'. He points to the chapter on 'Pathos' in his 1956 book, *The Nude*, as 'entirely Warburgian'. I suspect that this epithet would surprise the present inhabitors of the Warburg Institute in its latter-day London home. In as much as Clark aspired to write cultural history through the study of images and to penetrate the period mind, he may be regarded as a Warburgian in a general way, but it is doubtful whether he really came to terms with the philosophical and psychological intricacies of Warburg's approach, and he certainly never became an avid student of symbolic language, an iconologist, in the manner of Warburg's successors such as Panofsky and Wind. Clark's approach, as in his account

10. Below, p. 250.    11. Clark, *Another Part of the Wood*, p. 157.

of the 'Virgin on the Rocks' in this monograph, remained instinctively distrustful of elaborate symbolical interpretations of works of art.[12]

His relationship to the other major approach that seemed to him to promise insight into the inner meaning of art, Freudian psychology, was similarly qualified:

Whether or not we believe the more elaborate doctrines of psychoanalysis, we are all aware that symbols come to the mind unsought, from some depths of conscious memory, and that even the greatest intellect draws part of its strength from a dark centre of animal vitality. We can no longer offer a simple explanation for every motive.[13]

He was both attracted by the potentialities of Freud's approach to Leonardo and repelled by the all too summary nature of Freud's conclusions. We may sense his relief when he was able in later editions to add a footnote reference to an article by Meyer Shapiro which undermined much of the textual base for Freud's interpretation.[14] However, as late as his 1973 lecture on the 'Mona Lisa', he was still tempted to flirt with psychological explanation:

Only in the last ten years have we been made aware publicly that the theories of sexual psychologists were not fantasies. Leonardo, who could depict the fiery ascetic of the desert with a smile and gesture of feminine allurement, was quite capable of transferring the attributes of one sex to another, and of expressing some of his obsession with Salai's smile in the smile of the 'Mona Lisa'.[15]

Salai was the wastrel servant whom Clark sees as pandering (psychologically at least) to Leonardo's homosexual instincts.

In his approach to the major masters who helped shape his approach – Pater, Ruskin, Berenson, Fry, Warburg and Freud – Clark was instinctively undogmatic. He distrusted adherence to any creed that draws lines around the infinite flexibility of aesthetic response. At heart he was profoundly untheoretical and unphilosophical (in the professional sense of the latter term). He confessed that he was 'as perplexed by metaphysics as a Trobriand islander'.[16] To the Continental mind, there is probably something deeply unsatisfactory in the writings of someone who believes in no system sufficiently profoundly to operate it at its ultimate power. Clark was a Freudian who distrusted psychoanalysis. He was a Warburgian who had little patience with the detailed analysis of symbols. He aspired to analyse formal properties

12. Below, p. 93.    13. Below, p. 41.    14. Below, p. 42 note.

15. Clark, 'Mona Lisa' in *Burlington Magazine* (1973), p. 149.

16. Clark, *Another Part of the Wood*, p. 29.

with the precision of Fry without believing in 'significant form'. He was a Berensonian connoisseur who would not be constrained by the limits of connoisseurship. There is something very English in the sheer reasonableness with which he adopts as much as is useful from other intellectual systems without following them to their logical extremes. At its worst this approach can result in eclectic shallowness, and it cannot be denied that Clark tends to skate round the direct consequences of the ideas he is annexing. However, what ultimately redeems his work is the way in which he can press the ideas into critical service, within the context of a superbly designed literary setting, to articulate his personal insight into the actual works of art. We can sense his pulse quickening as the spell of a painting or drawing begins to take effect. He has the great critic's ability to share his moments of illumination. This strength comes not from the power of an explanatory system but from a responsiveness that he has been able to structure with the aid of more dogmatic and analytical minds.

It was while the various Oxford and immediately post-Oxford influences were gathering into a coherent shape in his mind that he turned specifically to the study of Leonardo, following the completion of *The Gothic Revival*.

Instead of studying the kind of modest minor artist who is thought appropriate to a beginner, I plunged in at the deep end. I concentrated on Leonardo da Vinci. This may now sound both commonplace and ambitious. But in 1928 there were very few books on Leonardo worth reading. Stylistically there was much uncertainty; the Uffizi 'Annunciation' [Pl. 7] was thought to be by Verrocchio, and the 'Ginevra de' Benci' [Pl. 11] was not accepted as Leonardo. More important, nobody had made a serious attempt to relate the vast corpus of Leonardo's writings to his drawings and paintings.[17]

This certainly overstates the bleak picture in Leonardo scholarship at that time, but it is true that much pioneering work remained to be accomplished.

The first fruit of his endeavours was a fluent essay in Desmond MacCarthy's *Life and Letters* (London, 1929), in which the young author rubs shoulders with so distinguished a contributor as Arnold Bennett. The essay makes a valiant attempt to evoke the character of Leonardo's written and drawn legacy in response to Séailles's pioneering monograph (Paris, 1892) and what he felt to be 'the metaphysical embroideries' imposed on Séailles's account by Valéry's *Discours sur le Méthode de Leonard de Vinci* (1895).[18] In

17. Clark, *Another Part of the Wood*, p. 145.

18. Gabriel Séailles, *Léonard de Vinci, l'artist et le savant* (Paris, 1892); P. Valéry, 'Introduction à la méthode de Léonard de Vinci', in *Nouvelle Revue* (15 August 1985); and *Nouvelle Revue Française* (Paris, 1919) (trans. T. McGreevy, as *Introduction to the Method of Leonardo da Vinci* (London, 1929); and Clark, *Another Part of the Wood*, p. 145.

particular he objected to Valéry's characterization of an underlying unity of 'method' in Leonardo's thought, a unity based on an inner 'sense of harmony and purpose' in contemplating the apparently disconnected facts of nature. Clark was convinced that no such 'method' existed:

No one who has read the greater part of the notebooks can restrain his wonder at the manysidedness, the grasp and vigour of their author's mind. But I do believe that they are unconstructive, and that even if they had been published soon after Leonardo's death they would not greatly have affected the course of human thought. As a thinker Leonardo's energy is immense, but it is frustrated energy. Two hundred years earlier he might have surpassed Roger Bacon, two hundred years later he might have equalled Leibnitz. But in certain ages every controlled and vivid shape or sound contributes to that work of art or system of ideas by which the age will be remembered. Without this mute mysterious co-operation no great work can be consummated: and Leonardo da Vinci, living in the early Italian Renaissance, is best remembered by his paintings and drawings.[19]

Although Clark was later to qualify this assertion of the formlessness and unconstructive character of Leonardo's writings, and although the logic of the passage is not altogether clear, it is part of his noble attempt to construct a non-mythical Leonardo. In this endeavour, he rightly considered that an appreciation of the intellectual context is all-important:

I believe that the actual facts he records were more a matter of common knowledge among learned men of his day than is usually allowed. Scholars are gradually discovering his moral maxims in the early translations of the classics; in optics he made no advance on the Arabs nor on Roger Bacon, their pupil; in anatomy he seems to have learnt from Marc Antonio, rather than the reverse.[20]

Clark does not seem to have had much evidence for these convictions, though he may well have read Solmi's fundamental work on the sources of Leonardo's opinions. He did not take them up in his later monograph. However, they have proved to have considerable validity in the work of later researchers.

The best passages of criticism in the 1929 essay are those in which he is developing Pater's intuitions about Leonardo's response to the vital powers of nature:

Leonardo loved just that writhing organic life which it is the artist's first impulse to subdue, loved diversity more than unity, or, with a slight extension of those old philosophical terms, loved accident rather than substance. We can feel from his drawings alone, that Leonardo was a scientist rather than a mathematician; and,

19. Clark, *Life and Letters* (1929), pp. 128–9.    20. Clark, *Life and Letters* (1929), pp. 126–7.

indeed, there is a curious connection between his forms and the special objects of his researches – anatomy and the movement of water. Swirling lines of water, intricate machinery below the skin, seem, late in life, to influence the movement of everything he draws, and when we remember how deeply set in our spirit is the sense of form, it is tempting to believe that Leonardo chose these two subjects of research not only for their scientific, but also for their rhythmical appeal to him.[21]

At about this time the new Librarian at Windsor Castle, Owen Morshead, was hoping to find someone to catalogue the unrivalled collection of Leonardo drawings in the Royal Collection. The young aesthete who had cut his teeth under Bell at the Ashmolean and was known to be a protégé of the formidable Berenson was perhaps a less surprising choice for this task than Clark suggests in his autobiography. In any event it was a choice that was triumphantly vindicated. He 'worked for about three years on the Leonardo catalogue, happy, excited, confident that I was gaining new ground'.[22] There was certainly much new ground to be gained, though earlier scholars had demonstrated what the right tools could begin to achieve in the right hands. German art historians, such as Paul Müller-Walde and Anny Popp, and the Italian, Girolamo Calvi, helped to add scholarly rigour to Clark's Berensonian connoisseurship. Popp's 1928 monograph on Leonardo's drawings was particularly important in that she had made a serious and effective attempt to accomplish what was Clark's most pressing task, namely the establishing of a working chronology for the intellectual and stylistic development of Leonardo's graphic work. The *Catalogue* appeared in 1935, setting the British standard for such publications and establishing the basis for all future research on the subject. The attributions and datings made by Clark on the basis of evidence that is slim in comparison to the volume of material available today have stood up to sustained examination incredibly well. He was fully justified almost forty years later in claiming that his 'dating of the drawings is usually correct and was a step forward in Leonardo studies'. More modestly, and a little harshly, he also judged that 'The catalogue remains my only claim to be considered a scholar.'[23]

In the intervening period between the commencing and publishing of the *Catalogue*, Clark's career had taken two notable turns. In 1931 he had been appointed Keeper at the Ashmolean in succession to his old mentor, Charlie Bell, who had been ignominiously squeezed out by the authorities. Then in 1933, before his thirtieth birthday, he received the astonishing offer to become Director of the National Gallery in London. He was an instant celebrity, and the years up to the beginning of the Second World War were marked for him by what he later called 'the Great Clark Boom'. He entered vigorously into London society and was in great demand as a speaker. Happily for us, his speaking engagements included a series of lectures on Leonardo da Vinci, culminating in the Ryerson Lectures at Yale University in the autumn of 1936. It was the six Ryerson Lectures, expanded to nine, that came to be published by Cambridge University Press in 1939 as the present monograph.

The framework of his book is provided by the chronological understanding of Leonardo's artistic development as established during his work on the Windsor *Catalogue*. The scholarly detail is handled with an easy grace that belies its detailed precision, and it is only when he had to refer to sets of drawings that could not be illustrated in the earlier editions that the reader may begin to struggle – a problem that the present edition is designed to overcome. This framework also supports two chapters on Leonardo's written legacy, in keeping with Clark's belief that the student of Leonardo's art should come to terms with the contents of the manuscripts. He frankly acknowledged that this was a desideratum he could only incompletely satisfy:

The student of Leonardo is engaged in a vast jigsaw puzzle and, in spite of the labours of devoted scholars such as Müller-Walde, Calvi, and Solmi, much remains to be discovered. In particular, very little effort has been made to gauge how far Leonardo's knowledge increased and scientific method improved as his life went on. Some idea of Leonardo as a mind developing by contact with other minds is necessary if we are to form a true picture of him, and compare his scientific activity with his development as an artist. But to form this idea would require immense erudition, for not only would the student need to be familiar with all Leonardo's writings in their chrono-logical order, but he would have to know enough about the state of learning in the Renaissance to judge Leonardo's progress in relation to that of his contemporaries. Lacking this equipment, I shall not attempt a critical study of the notebooks, but simply indicate their character.[24]

'Simply' indicating their character hardly gives a clue as to what Clark actually achieved. Although he certainly lacked a systematic knowledge of the manuscripts in the manner he describes, the penetration he achieves often transcends the self-imposed limitations. It is a penetration that is at heart founded upon his intuitions in front of the paintings and drawings. To give one example, from his discussion of the 'Mona Lisa' (Pl. 67):

To Leonardo a landscape, like a human being, was part of a vast machine, to be understood part by part and, if possible, in the whole. Rocks were not simply decorative silhouettes. They were part of the earth's bones, with an anatomy of their own, caused by some remote seismic upheaval. Clouds were not random curls of the

24. Below, p. 109.

brush, drawn by some celestial artist, but were the congregation of tiny drops formed from the evaporation of the sea, and soon would pour back their rain into the rivers.[25]

This passage not only shows Clark's ability to understand the style of mind behind the writings, but also to sense vital motivating forces in Leonardo's scientific work. Not a few of Clark's hints have been richly confirmed by later research.

The tone of voice in which Clark expounds his insights is very different from that in the standard art–historical monograph of the present day. He shares the nineteenth-century daring of Pater in his willingness to cross-cut between Leonardo's works and great masterpieces of world art from other ages, particularly in the realms of music and literature. Mozart and *King Lear* are introduced with a self-confident familiarity that few would dare in such a context today. He also believed in the interpretative power of literary description, in a manner with which we are now relatively unfamiliar. Goethe provided an important model. Outlining the remarkable characterizations of the disciples in the 'Last Supper', Clark advises us that 'all these penetrations, these dramatic inventions, have been analysed once and for all by one of the few men who, by the scale of his genius, was in a position to judge Leonardo – Goethe'.[26] Clark's own literary evocations of Leonardo's masterpieces need fear no comparison with the major masters of this now unfashionable genre.

The most uneasy aspect of his characterization of Leonardo is his failure to appreciate how the geometrical temper of Leonardo's science is intimately related to his feeling for the vitality of organic life. Clark is too much of the Ruskinian vitalist to regard the geometrical and organic as anything other than polarized forces for the creative artist – though it is worth saying that Ruskin's own stance towards geometry was more complex than is normally admitted. Clark cannot but regard the pages of late variations on geometrical themes as other than 'doodles of disillusion' in which 'his beloved mathematics are no longer employed in the search for truth, but cynically, as a mere intellectual pastime'.[27] Leonardo's collaboration with the mathematician Luca Pacioli, which led to the artist devoting so much time to these 'abstract designs', is adduced as an example of 'how much his creative gifts were dominated by his intellect'.[28] What is missing here is Leonardo's conviction that the organic complexity of living nature, right down to its minutest nuances of mobile form, is founded upon the inexhaustibly rich interplay of geometrical motifs in the context of natural law. The repeated diagrams of interlocking geometrical areas are no less vital and alive for Leonardo than the petals of a flower or tricuspid valve in the heart.

Clark shows a repeated distrust for the essential regularity that Leonardo

25. Below, p. 175.    26. Below, p. 152.    27. Below, p. 39.    28. Below, p. 157.

not only saw beneath all aspects of life but also regarded as the ultimate goal of the creative scientist–artist. This distrust explains Clark's discomfort in front of the 'Last Supper' (Pl. 54):

In the 'Last Supper' the movement is frozen. There is something rather terrifying about all these ponderous figures in action; something of a contradiction in terms in the slow labour which has gone into the perfection of every gesture. And beyond this is a deeper cause. The whole force of gesture, as an expression of emotion, lies in its spontaneity: and the gestures in the 'Last Supper' are not spontaneous.[29]

Leonardo would have answered that the language of gesture can only be understood and recreated by an artist on the basis of an understanding of the anatomical mechanisms that respond to the inner causes of sensation, emotion and will. Such a recreation is to be achieved through deliberation not chance.

However, even where we may be tempted to argue with Clark, his opinions are expressed with such style and cogency that they command our respect. His book can be read by a modern Leonardo specialist with no sense of the discordant grating of obsolete facts and opinions. It can be wholeheartedly recommended to anyone who wants a personally compelling introduction to Leonardo's genius, and it remains a model for a short, unified study of a creative personality in any field of endeavour.

Its qualities were richly recognized at the time of its publication. The new Director of the National Gallery was able to endorse his arrival with a literary triumph. Eric Newton told the readers of the *Sunday Times* on 23 July 1939 that Clark's *Leonardo* 'set a new standard for art criticism in this country'. Amidst the paeans of praise none pleased and disarmed Clark more than the effusive reaction of Berenson, with whom relations had been subject to strain as the protégé had increasingly gone his own way. Looking back, it is difficult to think of any earlier British monograph that could be set beside it for a comparable balance of scholarship, critical acumen and grace. Herbert Horne's great 1908 book on Botticelli is one of its few worthy ancestors, albeit on a more monumental and specialist scale.[30] It is a testimony to the staying power of Clark's treatment of Leonardo that editions and reprintings have become more frequent over the years, following the revised edition published by Penguin Books in 1959. In his later introductory note Clark even more clearly identifies the need for a co-ordinated treatment of Leonardo's art and science and felt tempted to write a new book altogether. However, a defensive tone is not necessary, either then or in presenting the book now, in that he showed himself to be fully aware of where he could not legitimately

29. Below, p. 153.

30. Herbert Horne, *Alessandro Filipepi commonly called Sandro Botticelli, painter of Florence* (London, 1908).

go, and was yet able intuitively to point new ways into the uncharted territory to a degree that still seems remarkable.

Clark was to return to Leonardo not infrequently in later years. There were to be a number of commissioned essays and papers, most notably those on 'Leonardo and the Antique', 'Mona Lisa' and his *Lettura Vinciana* delivered in Vinci in 1977.[31] These provide useful revisions and amplifications to ideas expressed in the monograph, but I think it is true to say that they do not convey the sense of fresh excitement so apparent in his earlier work. Leonardo also crossed his path in his grand traverses of visual art and culture throughout the ages, most notably in *Landscape into Art* (1949) and *The Nude* (1956). The section on the Deluge drawings (Pls. 111–15) in the former book shows that fresh insights were still emerging:

Leonardo's scientific knowledge of nature, and his even more extraordinary intuitions as to the hidden potentialities of matter, have enabled him to pass into a different world from the old medieval Apocalypse with its confused oriental symbolism; and to arrive at a vision of destruction in which symbol and reality seem to be at one.[32]

In what is now approaching a half-century since the original publication of Clark's *Leonardo*, the body of primary and secondary source material available to the student has increased enormously, apparently according to some exponential law decreeing that each new contribution is bound to be followed by at least two others. It would be out of keeping with the spirit of Clark's original enterprise if I were to attempt a comprehensive review of the new developments in the full range of scholarly literature. The bibliographical additions at the end of the book have been made in keeping with Clark's wish to limit himself to a fair conspectus for the general reader – though Clark's 'general reader' was presumed to possess linguistic and critical attributes that we would be unwise to take for granted. In giving the present reader some idea of what has happened since the original publication, I shall concentrate during the remaining part of this introduction on those developments that have the clearest implications for Clark's own text.

The new material to be taken into account is of two main kinds: firstly primary sources, in the form of newly discovered products of Leonardo's

31. Kenneth Clark: 'Leonardo and the Antique' in *Leonardo's Legacy*, ed. C. O'Malley (Berkeley and Los Angeles, 1969), pp. 1–34; 'Mona Lisa' in *Burlington Magazine* (1973), pp. 144–50; 'Leonardo e le curve della vita', *XVII Lettura Vinciana* (Vinci, 1977; Florence, 1979). See also *Leonardo da Vinci im Selbstzeugnissen und Bilddokumenten* (Reinbeck bei Hamburg, 1972); 'Una donna fatale' in *Bolaffiarte*, V (Turin, 1974), pp. 32–9; 'La sant' Anna' in *Leonardo, La Pittura* (Florence, 1977), pp. 69–74; and his introductions to *An Exhibition of Drawings by Leonardo da Vinci from the Royal Collection*, The Queen's Gallery, Buckingham Palace, 1969–70, and C. Pedretti, *Leonardo da Vinci on Painting: A Lost Book (Libro A)* (Berkeley and Los Angeles, 1964; London, 1965).

32. Kenneth Clark, *Landscape into Art* (1949) (Harmondsworth, 1956), p. 60.

own hand and documentation of his career, and secondly interpretative writing that puts his work in a fresh perspective. Pride of place amongst the primary sources must go to the two volumes of Leonardo's own writings re-discovered in the Biblioteca Nacional at Madrid in 1965, to which Clark was able to make only a passing reference in later printings of his book.[33] From our present point of view their most important element is the group of seventeen folios in Codex Madrid II that deal with Leonardo's renewed activity on the design and casting of the equestrian monument to Francesco Sforza. Two of the folios are dated 1491 and 1493. Leonardo deals with the technical procedures for casting and transporting the huge bronze horse, providing diagrams that confirm the walking pose for the horse (Pl. 52) and some exciting drawings of casting mechanisms. The other section of Madrid II consists of 140 folios of miscellaneous material from about 1503–05, including a vivid account of a storm interrupting his work on the 'Battle of Anghiari' on 6 June 1505, some interesting plans and memoranda relating to his work as a military engineer in the autumn of 1504 at Piombino where he was assisting the local lord on behalf of the Florentine government, and schemes for a canal to link Florence to the sea (Pl. I). The other new codex, Madrid I, is datable largely to the late 1490s and is devoted most particularly to mechanics, theoretical and applied. It contains some of Leonardo's most beautiful and finished drawings of machinery, including a series of studies for a volute gear (Pl. II). These demonstrate his ability to create forcefully compact designs in keeping with dynamic law – in this case to equalize the diminishing force in an unwinding spring – and are drawn with the hatching lines 'hooked' around the forms in the way that becomes characteristic of his artistic drawings during the subsequent period.

The most important of the new documents are those discovered by Grazioso Sironi in Milan, which relate to the 'Virgin of the Rocks'.[34] These refer, amongst other things, to the permission granted to Ambrogio da Predis on behalf of Leonardo to remove the panel from its setting in October 1508 in order to make a copy. This may appear to solve at a stroke the problem of the second (London) version of the painting, and arguments to this effect have indeed been advanced.[35] But we are then faced with the conclusion that the Paris version must have been unfinished as late as 1506, when the legal battles were still raging, and that the London version dates wholly from 1508 or later. Neither of these consequences can be reconciled readily with the

33. Ladislas Reti (ed.), *The Manuscripts of Leonardo da Vinci ... at the Biblioteca Nacional of Madrid*, introduction, transcription, translation and commentary by Reti (5 vols., New York, 1974).

34. G. Sironi, *Nuovi documenti riguardanti la 'Vergine della Rocce' di Leonardo da Vinci* (Milan, 1981).

35. W. Cannell, 'Leonardo da Vinci – "The Virgin of the Rocks". A Reconsideration of the Documents and a new Interpretation' in *Gazette des Beaux Arts* (1984), pp. 99–108.

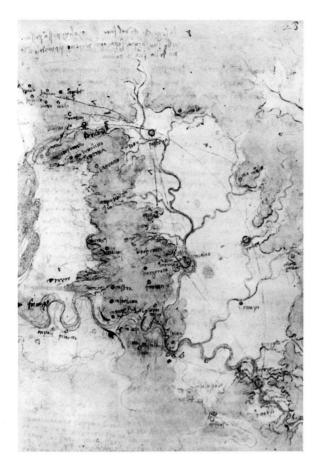

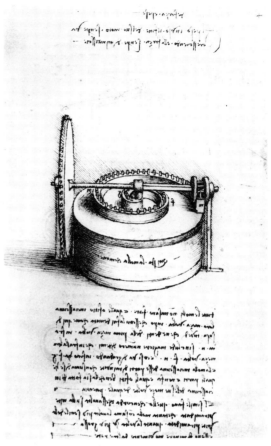

*I Scheme for a Canal to Join Florence to the Navigable Section of the Arno, c. 1503–5. Biblioteca Nacional, Madrid*

*II Study for a Volute Gear and Spring Barrel, c. 1498. Biblioteca Nacional, Madrid*

existing documentation or the visual evidence. The new documents seem to me to cause as many problems as they solve.

Modern techniques of conservation and scientific investigation are also revealing new primary evidence. The 'Last Supper' is undergoing a rigorous restoration, aimed at stripping away all the earlier overpaintings. This campaign is uncovering some strikingly brilliant details of drawing and colour (Pls. III and IV). These not only confirm Clark's intuition that the expression of the heads had been deadened by earlier restorations, but also reinforce the suspicion that the remaining surface of Leonardo's original painting consists of a series of scattered archaeological fragments that can barely produce a coherent overall effect even in the more moderately well-preserved areas. The contemporaneous technical investigations being undertaken in the Florentine Council Hall in which Leonardo painted the 'Battle of Anghiari', using ultrasonic investigation of lower layers of plaster, have not so far led to the

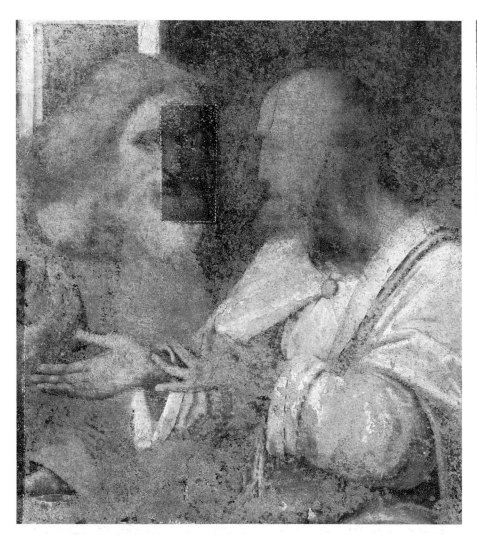

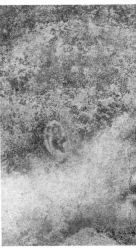

*III Detail of St Matthew from 'The Last Supper', 1497. Sta Maria delle Grazie, Milan, during the course of restoration*

*IV Detail of St Thaddeus and St Simon from 'The Last Supper', during restoration*

uncovering of unequivocal traces of Leonardo's unfinished masterpiece, although some of the preliminary results were encouraging.[36]

One of the most revealing of the new discoveries in relation to Clark's text is not a work by Leonardo himself – in my judgement – but what appears to be an early copy of his lost cartoon of the 'Virgin and Child and St Anne' (Pl. V). The drawing in a private collection in Geneva is inscribed on the reverse 'Leonardo alla Nuntiata'.[37] The composition corresponds so closely

36. H. T. Newton and J. R. Spencer, 'On the location of Leonardo's *"Battle of Anghiari"*' in *Art Bulletin*, LXIV (1982), pp. 45–52.

37. See C. Pedretti, *Leonardo* (Bologna, 1979), p. 42, and his introduction to *Leonardo dopo Milano*, catalogue of exhibition at Vinci, ed. A. Vezzosi (Florence, 1982), p. 18 and no. 21.

to the first-hand description by Pietro da Novellara in 1501 that it may be provisionally accepted as a record of the lost cartoon made when Leonardo was resident at the Annunziata. It helps reinstate the Brescianino painting in Berlin, which Clark originally accepted as a rather wooden reworking of Leonardo's composition, and tends to reinforce rather than weaken the

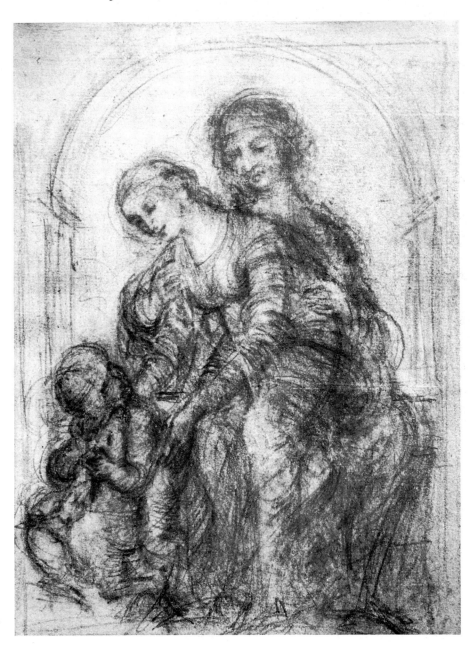

V After Leonardo (?),
'The Virgin, Child
and St Anne', Geneva,
Private Collection

chronology of the St Annes upon which he eventually settled in later editions of the book.[38]

Amongst the interpretative developments, the transcriptions and commentaries accompanying the new generation of facsimiles are playing a particularly important role. The voluminous writings of Carlo Pedretti, who has furthered our knowledge of the chronology of the manuscripts more than anyone since Calvi, and the dedicated researches of Augusto Marinoni are providing vital tools for students of Leonardo's mind. Some of their finest work has been published in connection with the breathtakingly expensive facsimiles of the newly restored *Codice Atlantico* in Milan, and the great collection of drawings at Windsor, on which Clark worked with such profit. The manuscripts owned by the Institut de France are similarly being re-published under the general guidance of André Chastel.

The major intellectual reshaping of our perspective on Leonardo has occurred in our knowledge of his scientific endeavours. This has arisen (much as Clark forecast) partly as a result of our much greater understanding of the true achievement of medieval science and partly from detailed studies of Leonardo's own science, particularly in the broader setting of his intellectual development. The most effective evocation of Leonardo's scientific personality has been written by the Russian scholar, Vasilij Zubov,[39] while more recently Kenneth Keele has studied Leonardo's anatomical work as a key to the profile of the artist's scientific thought throughout his career. The books by Zubov and Keele can both be profitably read in parallel to Clark's text. For my own part I have been attempting to bring Leonardo's art and science together as a whole, not I hope by forcing a spurious unity but by looking at reciprocal patterns.[40] On re-reading Clark's text for the present edition I have been continually taken aback by how far he anticipated the programme that later scholars have pursued.

Leonardo scholarship has never been richer than at present. With the initiative sponsored by Armand Hammer to establish a Chair of Leonardo Studies at the University of California at Los Angeles, and to publish a specialized Journal, this vigour is set fair to continue. With the world-wide exhibitions of Leonardo drawings that seem to arise in ever-growing numbers, and attracting considerable crowds of enthusiastic spectators, Leonardo is familiar to a wider public than ever before. All this activity, far from rendering Clark's monograph obsolete, has served to underline the validity of his vision

38. Below, p. 164, note 8.

39. Vasilij Zubov, *Leonardo da Vinci*, trans. D. Kraus (Cambridge, Mass., 1968); and K. Keele, *Leonardo da Vinci's Elements of the Science of Man* (London and New York, 1983).

40. Martin Kemp, *Leonardo da Vinci: The Marvellous Works of Nature and Man* (London, 1981).

of the great master. His masterly essay has a continuing role to play in our understanding of one of the towering products of European civilization.

## NOTE TO THIS EDITION

This edition arises from the conviction that Clark's *Leonardo* is a classic book and that it should continue to be available in print. The text of the revised edition of 1967 has remained substantially untouched. The footnotes integrate the references in the later editions with those notes from the 1939 book that had been excluded from the pocket version.

No attempt has been made to introduce a comprehensively updated series of references, which would constitute a pedantic commentary on Clark's text and burden it with an apparatus incompatible with its spirit. The major change is the greatly increased number of illustrations from 67 to 127, taking advantage of printing technology unavailable to Clark in 1939. The new plates have been selected on the following principles: (i) to illustrate all paintings discussed by Clark (apart from passing mentions); (ii) to illustrate a wider selection of the drawings to which Clark refers, based on A. E. Popham's *The Drawings of Leonardo da Vinci*, which was largely planned by Clark himself; (iii) to create a visual complement to the text. The list of dates has been amplified and the bibliography has been modestly expanded so that it can continue to fulfil the needs served by Clark's original selection. I am grateful to Thereza Crowe, Thacher Alexander and Richard Kay for their enthusiastic and valuable assistance with the editorial work, and Dawn Waddell for secretarial services beyond the call of duty.

# PREFACE
## TO THE FIRST PELICAN EDITION

THIS book grew out of a number of lectures I gave between 1933 and 1936, culminating in the Ryerson Lectures, at Yale. It was first published in 1939, and a second edition with a few changes appeared in 1952. My thanks are due to the Cambridge University Press for allowing me to reprint it as a Pelican. I have made a number of alterations and additions to the text in order to include the results of recent Leonardo studies, and some changes in my own opinions.

For the drawings mentioned but not illustrated I have inserted a reference to Popham's *The Drawings of Leonardo da Vinci*, London, 1946, thus (P. 123).

*September 1957*     K. C.

# INTRODUCTORY NOTE
# TO THE FIRST PELICAN EDITION

THE defects of this book are not such as can be cured by revision, and my first thought on re-reading it was to write a new one. Other commitments make this impossible, but I may take this opportunity of outlining, in a few sentences, the theme which I would develop were I able to start again from the beginning. It would depend upon changing my first paragraph, in which I draw a distinction between Leonardo's art and his thought, and say that I am concerned with the first alone. There was a valid reason for this distinction, but it was a dangerous one, because it suggests the early twentieth-century belief that art is an activity which can be studied in isolation. In the fifteenth century art aspired to be a branch of knowledge, in which a permanent record of natural appearances was valuable both for its own sake and because it could furnish men's imaginations with credible images of God, his Mother, and his Saints. Leonardo was concerned, as an artist, to increase his knowledge of the physical world by observation, comparison, and analysis. It is true that at a certain point he preferred to perpetuate this knowledge through notes and diagrams rather than through drawings and paintings, but the two forms of record are really inseparable and react on one another at every stage of his life.

Leonardo began as an observer of surfaces. He was content to be so because he accepted, without question, the Florentine idea of harmony expressed through numbers. Although a professed adversary of Neo-Platonism, he did not doubt this unchallenged assumption, and wrote, for example, in Manuscript K, that 'proportion is not only to be found in number and measure, but also in sounds, weights, times and places, and in every power that exists'. This belief is the perfect basis for a clear, formal style. Natural objects do not need to be analysed or recreated with a suggestion of their vital complexity, but reduced to their simplest and most measurable elements, and arranged in harmonious relationship with one another. But Euclidean order could not satisfy Leonardo for long, for it conflicted with his sense of life. He was more in sympathy with that other aim which had occupied Florentine artists in the preceding fifty years, the rendering of movement through style; and like them, he felt that movement, to be perpetuated in art, must be of a special kind. It must be the visible expression of grace.

Although Renaissance writers left no formal definition of that word, they would all have agreed that it implied a series of smooth transitions. It was to be found, perfectly exemplified, in flowing gestures, floating draperies, curling or rippling hair. An abrupt transition was brutal; the graceful was continuous. Leonardo inherited this tradition of movement and grace in the parts, and extended it to the whole. There is no more complete and complex demonstration of continuous flow than the 'Virgin and St Anne' in the Louvre. But his striving for continuity had far more profound results than Hogarth's Line of Beauty; for it was not simply a *maniera*, but part of his search for the true facts of vision. His diagrams of light striking a sphere are attempts at continuous modelling, which were to be carried a stage further in the 'Mona Lisa', and furthest of all in the Louvre 'St John'.

The connection between continuity and the scientific rendering of appearances fixes a point at which the demands of grace and truth are one.

The whole movement of Leonardo's mind was from mechanism to organism. In anatomy, for instance, he starts with structure, the skeleton and the skull, and proceeds to the study of generation and the action of the heart. The most revealing example is that of geology. He begins, in the 'Virgin of the Rocks', to give the fantastic rocks of Hellenistic and medieval tradition the character of observed truth. Next he takes a scientific interest in landscape as a whole and sees rock forms as part of the earth's structure. Finally he turns his attention to geology, and observes that marine fossils can be found in the rock and rubble of mountains. And what is his conclusion? That the earth, like man and plants and light, is in a state of continual change. What blood is to the body, water is to the earth. *L'acqua é il vetturale della natura.* This explains the immense, and, to the student of Leonardo, discouraging amount of space occupied in his notebooks by descriptions and diagrams of the movement of water. They are studies, and symbols, of that continuous energy which Leonardo's observations had led him to place at the centre of his cosmic system.

On p. 238 I recognize the fundamental connection between flowing hair (grace) and flowing water (continuous energy). But I do not sufficiently emphasize what a serious matter for Leonardo was this discovery of universal flux. For if everything was continually in movement it could not be controlled by that mathematical system in which Leonardo had placed his faith. The passage quoted on p. 111 leaves us in no doubt of the real fervour of his belief in mathematics in the 1490s, and its gradual annihilation must have been a shattering blow to him. No wonder he became more and more disheartened by the mass of his recorded observations, which, not only by their bulk, but by the nature of their evidence, had passed tragically out of his control. This state of mind is symbolized in the Deluge drawings, where flux and continuous energy are represented as being the destroyers of human contrivance. And complementary to the Deluges are the hundreds of geometrical diagrams drawn in his last years, which are the doodles of disillusion. His beloved mathematics are no longer employed in the search for truth, but cynically, as a mere intellectual pastime.

Continuous change, which threatened the intellectual foundations of Leonardo's thought, developed one of his deepest instincts: his sense of mystery. The pointing finger and the smile – the one indicating a power outside our field of vision, the other reflecting an inner process which is equally beyond our comprehension – had a symbolic importance to him even in his early work. And as his sense of mystery was intensified and confirmed by his researches, the use of these symbols became more conscious. The 'Mona Lisa' has been irreverently described as 'the cat that's eaten the canary': which expresses well enough the smile of one who has attained complete possession of what she loved, and is enjoying the process of absorption. And Leonardo has discovered that this mysterious, continuous process has the same rhythm as that in which rain pours from the clouds, wears away the earth, flows to the sea, and is sucked up into the clouds again. In the Louvre 'St John' these two symbols of mystery are united and concentrated, and this gives the image its obsessive power. Attributes of grace, the smile and the turning movement, become extremely sinister, because they are now indistinguishable from attributes of continuous energy; and these, being beyond human reason, are felt as hostile to human security. Yet just as Leonardo, in his intellectual pursuit of natural forces, hung on with a kind of inspired tenacity, so in the 'St John' we feel him pressing closer round the form, penetrating further and further into the mystery, till at last he seems to become a part of it, so that, like his contemporaries, we no longer think of him as a scientist, a seeker for measurable truths, but as a magician, a man who, from his close familiarity with the processes of nature, has learnt a disturbing secret of creation.

# CHAPTER ONE

# 1452–1482

THIS book is concerned with the development of Leonardo da Vinci as an artist. His scientific and theoretical writings can be studied intelligently only by those who have a specialized knowledge of medieval and Renaissance thought. His art, and the personality it reveals, is of universal interest, and like all great art should be re-interpreted for each generation.

There are several reasons why such a new interpretation is worth attempting. In the last century the popular idea of Leonardo's work was still vague. Many of the pictures on which it was based, and practically all the drawings, were far from being authentic and gave a false notion of his character. It thus became the first duty of criticism to clear away the parasitic growths which obscured the true shape of his genius; and while this process continued, it absorbed the best energies of all considerable students of Italian art, and left no time for criticism in a more humane sense. But after fifty years of research and stylistic analysis, we have at last reached some sort of general agreement as to which pictures and drawings are really by Leonardo. Great problems of attribution remain to be solved, but we can no longer hope to settle them by comparison of morphological details. We must look at pictures as creations not simply of the human hand, but of the human spirit. And so we can take up the history and criticism of art where it was left, shall we say, by Pater, with the difference that Pater in his beautiful essay on Leonardo writes, in large part, about work which Leonardo did not execute. He is not concerned with Leonardo, but with the Leonardesque, and his essay suffers from some of the unreality which affects any study of an abstraction. Had he known the full range of Leonardo's own work, how much deeper and more living it would have become!

We have another advantage over earlier generations in our wider range of aesthetic comparison. We are no longer bound to assess Leonardo's work by classical standards of correctness, nor to admire only those drawings which resemble the style taught in academies. A freer approach to the problems of creation, born of our acquaintance with primitive and oriental art, has revealed the expressive qualities of work which earlier critics regarded as merely eccentric; and we see that Leonardo's personal, liberated drawings bring us closer to the sources of his genius than the wrecks of his great, formal achievements in painting. Finally, we may claim that our knowledge of psychology is fuller than it was. Whether or not we believe in the more elaborate doctrines of psychoanalysis, we are all aware that symbols come to the mind unsought, from some depths of unconscious memory and that even the greatest intellect draws part of its strength from a dark centre of animal vitality. We can no longer offer a simple explanation for every motif. In particular is this true of the character and work of Leonardo. The grand generalizations, the words of praise and blame, the categories of excellence in which older criticism abounds, cannot be applied to him without absurdity. He is a standing refutation of the comfortable belief that all great men are simple. No more complex and mysterious character ever existed, and any attempt at simplification would run contrary to the whole action of his mind.[1] He had such a strong sense of organic life, of growth and decay, of the infinitely small and infinitely big, in short of the nature of the physical world, that he rarely attempted an abstract proposition which was not mathematical; and we must observe the same caution in our attempts to study him.

But although we may try to avoid conjecture and theory in the greater part of Leonardo's life, in the first thirty years they are inevitable. The available facts are so meagre that if we are too scientific, too closely bound by documents and stylistic criticism, we shall lose some of the truth. Almost from his youth Leonardo was a legendary figure, and some of the characteristics which we recognize as truest and most valuable in our picture of him are known only from legend and in particular from Vasari's biography.

Leonardo was born at Anchiano, a village near the little town of Vinci, 15 April 1452. His father, Ser Piero, was to become a successful notary; his mother was a peasant named Caterina. As far as we know he was brought up in the countryside where he was born, and Pater, with his usual insight, has seen how life on a Tuscan farm, 'watching the lizards and glow worms and other strange small creatures which haunt an Italian vineyard', could colour the boy's imagination and give him his enduring preoccupation with organic life. Vasari expresses this truth in the familiar story of how Leonardo as a boy painted a dragon on the shield of one of his father's peasants, 'and

---

1. Cf. his note on abbreviators quoted on p. 111.

for this purpose carried into a room of his own lizards great and small, crickets, serpents, butterflies, grass-hoppers, bats and such like animals, out of which, variously put together, he formed a great ugly creature'. The shield has disappeared – may never have existed; but we do not need its material presence to know the truth of Vasari's description, for in his enumeration of twisting creatures we recognize the forms which reappear in Leonardo's latest drawings.

One other legend of Leonardo's youth must be remembered: his beauty. We have no contemporary description of him as a young man and no identifiable portrait, but in Vasari and all the early authors the accounts of his beauty are so emphatic that they must be based on a living tradition. He was beautiful, strong, graceful in all his actions, and so charming in conversation that he drew all men's spirits to him: of this his later life gives full confirmation. Vasari's account of his love and mastery of horses is also confirmed by numerous drawings; and the story of how he would buy birds in the market-place, take them in his hand and let them go, giving them their lost liberty, is part of a love of nature, visible in all his work.[2] To these early biographers he was himself a masterpiece of nature and seemed to be initiated into her processes. Even the almost magical powers with which he was credited in old age, they interpreted as part of his physical perfection. Naïve and incomplete as this interpretation is, it contains one small part of the truth worth adding to a complex whole. Another fragment, of an almost contrary kind, is to be found in one of Leonardo's own notebooks, and is practically the only record of his youth which they contain. It is a memory, or a symbolic dream, which still retains the disturbing quality of an emotional experience deeply secreted in the unconscious mind. 'In the earliest memory of my childhood it seemed to me that as I lay in my cradle a kite came down to me and opened my mouth with its tail, and struck me many times with its tail between my lips. This,' he adds, 'seems to be my fate.'[3] We are still too ignorant of psychology to interpret such a memory with any finality, but it is not surprising that Freud has taken this passage as the starting point for a psychological study of Leonardo. His conclusions have been rejected with horror by the majority of Leonardo scholars, and no doubt the workings of a powerful and complex mind cannot be deduced from a single sentence nor explained by a rather one-sided system of psychology. Freud's study, though

2. *Leonardo da Vinci: la 'Vita' di Giorgio Vasari*, a cura di *Giovanni Poggi* (Firenze, 1919). This is confirmed by Andrea Corsali, *Lettera allo Illmo. Sig. Duca Juliano de Medici, Venuta dell india del mese di Octobre Nel MDXVI*, f. 4 recto, in which he speaks of a certain tribe 'so gentle that they do not feed on anything which has blood, nor will they allow anyone to hurt any living thing, like our Leonardo da Vinci'.

3. For a reasonable and scholarly explanation of this passage, which deprives it of most (not quite all) of its interest to the psychoanalyst, cf. Meyer Schapiro in *Journal of the History of Ideas*, vol. XVII, no. 2 (April 1956), pp. 147–78.

it contains some passages of fine intuition, is perhaps as over-simplified as that of Vasari. Yet it helps our conception of Leonardo's character by insisting that he was abnormal. We must remember this undercurrent when examining the surface of his early work. Later we shall not easily forget it.

We know that by 1469 Leonardo had come, with his father, to live in Florence, and in 1472 he was inscribed on the roll of the guild of St Luke as a painter – *Leonardo di ser Piero da Vinci dipintore*. He was then twenty years old and if he followed the usual course of apprenticeship he must have been learning the art of painting for at least four years. Tradition and the evidence of style tell us that his first master was Verrocchio; and we learn from documents that he was still in Verrocchio's workshop in 1476; so that it is important for us to know something about an artist with whom Leonardo spent six or seven years.

Verrocchio has always been regarded as the typical craftsman of the Florentine Renaissance, ready to undertake any work which demanded skill in the handling of materials, from the setting of a precious stone to the casting of the sphere of gilded copper which still surmounts the Duomo.[4] But no single formula can cover Verrocchio in both his painting and his sculpture. Verrocchio's pictures, as they have come down to us, form a small coherent group. They are largely and firmly drawn, and in each one the figures dominate the landscape with a certain grandeur. But they do not stir the imagination. Their forms are metallic, their colours unsubtle and bright. The world they create for us is the prosaic world of a practical man; whereas in Verrocchio's sculpture there is a suggestion of the incalculable forces and fantasies which we associate with Leonardo. For this reason the relation between Leonardo and Verrocchio the sculptor is close yet problematic, and to understand the formative influences on Leonardo, we must begin by looking at the principal pieces of sculpture executed by Verrocchio while Leonardo was in his workshop.[5] Of datable works we have first the group of the 'Incredulity of St Thomas' at Or San Michele. It was commissioned in 1463 and we know that Verrocchio was at work on the model between 1467 and 1470. The Lavabo in the Sacristy of San Lorenzo must date from before 1469, the sarcophagus tomb of Piero and Giovanni de' Medici is dated 1472 (Pl. 1). Of undated pieces we can be sure that the bronze 'David' in the Bargello and the terracotta relief of the Resurrection from Careggi belong to the years of Leonardo's apprenticeship. To a later period, but one in which

---

4. This must have been one of the principal works in hand when Leonardo entered Verrocchio's workshop. The ball was hoisted into place, to the singing of Te Deum, on 27 May 1471.

5. Verrocchio was not the only artist to influence Leonardo through his sculpture. He also took something from the rival workshop, that of Antonio Pollaiuolo, whose energetic linear style is reflected in Leonardo's first pen drawings; and he seems to have looked with particular attention at the work of Desiderio da Settignano.

Leonardo was still in Verrocchio's shop, belong the silver relief of 1477 in the Opera del Duomo, and most probably the lost bronze reliefs, which Lorenzo de' Medici sent to Mathias Corvinus. Now a characteristic which these works have most markedly in common is a love of twisting movement, either in the whole composition or in details. The St Thomas group is the

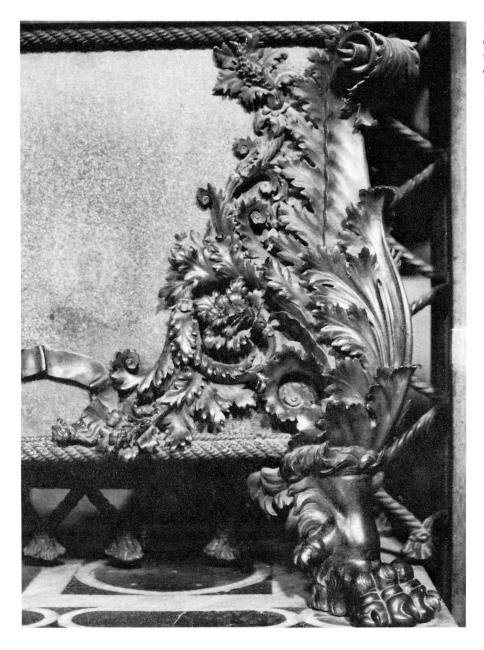

*1. Verrocchio, detail of 'Tomb of Piero and Giovanni de' Medici', c. 1469–72. San Lorenzo, Florence*

first instance in the Renaissance of that complicated flow of movement through a composition, achieved by contrasted axes of the figures, which Leonardo made the chief motif of all his constructions, and which, through him, became the foundation of the mannerist style. Even the bronze David has an alert twist of the body, and in the Careggi relief the movements and attitudes of the figures are extraordinarily like Leonardo's early drawings. As for twisting movement in the details, Vasari describes how Verrocchio loved to draw knots and elaborately plaited hair and we have ample confirmation of this in the bronze flowers which writhe and flow with the exuberance of nature round the porphyry sarcophagus of the Medici; or in the drawings of actual hair in the British Museum, plaited in almost exactly the same style that Leonardo was to use, more than thirty years later, in his cartoon of Leda. We must suppose that Leonardo's love of curves was instinctive, born of his earliest unconscious memories, but that his master showed him the forms in which his innate sense of rhythm could most easily find expression.

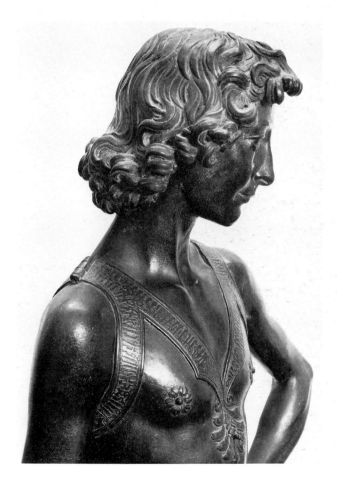

*2. Verrocchio, profile of 'David', c. 1473. Museo Nazionale del Bargello, Florence*

Secondly, Verrocchio's sculpture shows the same facial types that we find in Leonardo's early drawings. Seen in profile, the David (Pl.2) is very like one of Leonardo's elegant young men with wavy hair. He even has the hardly perceptible smile that was to become a part of the Leonardesque ideal, and we may find this smile on other works of Verrocchio, the St Thomas or the heads that decorate the basin in S. Lorenzo. It was Verrocchio, too, who first used this type of pretty boy in contrast with ferocious nutcracker old men. The motif survives in the silver relief of the 'Beheading of St John the Baptist', where the old warrior is strikingly Leonardesque; but no doubt its classical expression was to be found in the famous pair of bronze reliefs of Scipio Africanus and Darius, whose original forms can be deduced from replicas in different mediums – marble, stucco, glazed terracotta. It is possible that Leonardo himself made free versions of these reliefs. A marble in the Louvre and a stucco in the Victoria and Albert Museum have enough Leonardesque character of modelling and design dimly to reflect his Scipio; and his Darius is known from the silver point in the British Museum, one of the most finished and elaborate of his early drawings (Pl. 3). A more enduring influence of these reliefs – the whole notion of contrasting youthful and aged, effeminate and virile heads – I shall treat more fully when I come to speak of Leonardo's caricatures.

At this point the question begins to form in our minds, do not these similarities suggest that Leonardo was responsible for much of Verrocchio's sculpture? Leonardo refers to his practice as a sculptor in his letter to Ludovico Sforza (p. 84), and the list of his works on p. 86 includes a relief of the Passion. There is nothing inherently improbable in the suggestion; but unfortunately there is no conclusive evidence such as might be supplied by a document or a drawing. With painting the position is much clearer.

Those pictures which seem to have been executed by Verrocchio himself must date from before 1472. After that date he seemed to abandon painting altogether. It is perhaps no coincidence that our earliest evidence of Leonardo as a painter dates from this year, and it is in the next six years that we must place the paintings that most critics are now agreed to call his earliest works: the 'Annunciation' in the Uffizi, the 'Virgin with the Flowers' in the Munich Gallery, the portrait formerly in Liechtenstein,[6] and the 'Benois Madonna' in the Hermitage. These pictures all have qualities in common which connect them with the first indisputable painting of Leonardo, the Paris 'Virgin of the Rocks', and which are in contrast to the paintings of Verrocchio. Instead of Verrocchio's clear local colours, they are conceived in low tones of olive green and grey; instead of his bold, firm modelling, the heads and hands are drawn with a curious delicacy and an eye for minute gradations

6. See p. 57.

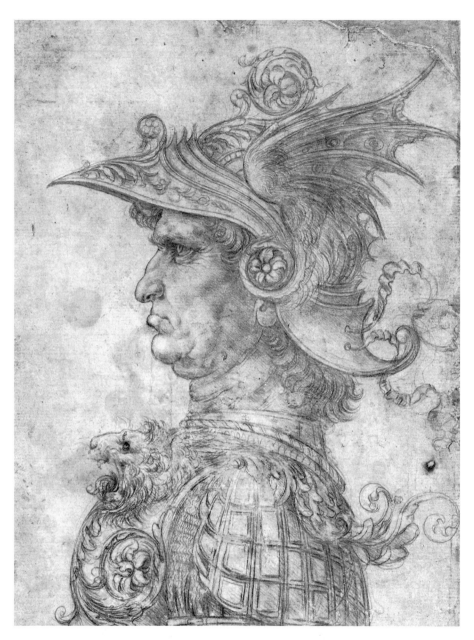

3. 'An Antique
Warrior', ? Darius, c.
1475. British Museum,
London

of surface. None of Leonardo's contemporaries imagined this twilit world,
so different from the bright enamelled daylight of the *quattrocento*. These
pictures, then, owe little to Verrocchio. Yet we can be sure that they were
executed in his shop, not only because Leonardo was working with him at
the time, but because they contain certain of his studio properties. In fact,

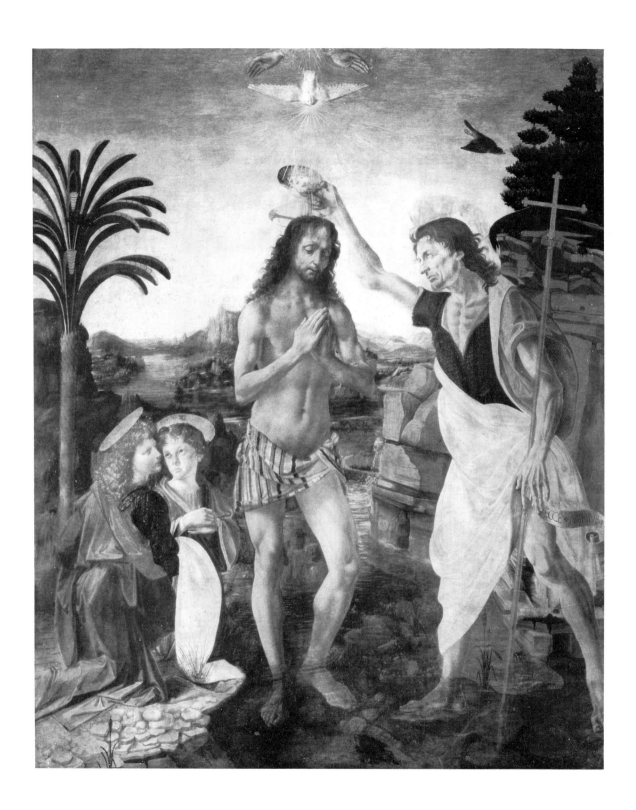

*4. Verrocchio, 'Baptism of Christ', c. 1472. Uffizi, Florence*

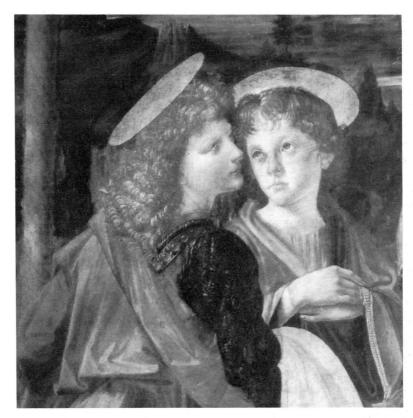

*5. Detail from Verrocchio's 'Baptism', c. 1472. Uffizi, Florence*

we can deduce from the documents for the Pistoía altar-piece that they were commissioned and sold as works of Verrocchio, or rather of 'Verrocchio and Co.'. Leonardo in his master's workshop held a position not unlike that of a head cutter in a small but distinguished firm of tailors, and it was natural that the proprietor, though himself a capable *homme du métier*, should leave to his gifted assistant that part of the work in which he himself had least interest. Here again we can find a core of truth in Vasari's story of how Leonardo painted the angel in Verrocchio's 'Baptism' (Pl. 4), 'which,' he says, 'was the reason why Andrea would never again touch colours, being most indignant that a boy should know more of the art than he did'.[7] Possibly Verrocchio, when he saw such striking evidence of his pupil's skill, did give up painting, not so much from motives of jealousy or shame, as from expediency. It was enough to have one good painter in the firm: in future he could confine himself to his favourite arts of sculpture and goldsmithy.

We must now examine Leonardo's early painting in detail. Vasari's statement that he painted an angel in Verrocchio's 'Baptism' (Pl. 5), although

7. This is, of course a typical legend of master and pupil, repeated by Vasari apropos of Cimabue and Giotto, Francia and Raphael. It may, however, be true of Verrocchio and Leonardo.

discredited in a recent period of scepticism, is confirmed by documentary and stylistic evidence. It appears in a meagre guide to Florence, Albertini's *Memoriale*, which, since it was written in 1510, when Leonardo was still in Italy, must be looked on as a reliable source. Above all, we have, in the angel's head, unmistakable evidence of Leonardo's early style, all the more clearly seen in contrast to the angel of Verrocchio. With the prophetic power sometimes found in the earliest work of genius, Leonardo has foreshadowed a change that was to come over Italian art in his lifetime. Verrocchio's angel is of the same family as all the angels of the *quattrocento*, since the time of Luca della Robbia's singing boys. He has the same broad bony face, the same short nose, the same wavy hair. The treatment is perfectly naturalistic. He seems to look with astonishment at his companion, as at a visitant from another world; and, in fact, Leonardo's angel belongs to a world of the imagination which Verrocchio's never penetrated. In every line of the nose, cheek, and chin this head reveals an ideal of perfection. To some extent this ideal, like all our dreams of physical perfection, was inspired by the antique, fragments of which Leonardo must have seen in Florence at the time. But the cascade of hair, rippling over the angel's shoulder, is his own invention, where, as in a miraculous bud, is one side of Leonardo's art, the 'beauty touched with strangeness' of Pater. Yet his head, which foreshadows so much of his mature vision, is obviously the work of a young painter, more intent on the delicate outlining of detail than on mass and structure. It must date from between about 1470 and 1472. The angel's draperies are also by Leonardo and show a curious system of folds, rather stiff and angular but most delicately rendered. Here, too, we have confirmation in Vasari, who says that when Leonardo was a student 'he often made figures in clay which he covered with a soft worn linen dipped in clay, and then set himself to draw them with great patience on a particular kind of fine Rheims cloth or prepared linen; and he executed some of them in black and white with the point of a brush to a marvel, as some of those which we have in our book of drawings still bear witness.'[8] A number of these drawings still exist, and from their hard, stiff folds we can see that Vasari's account of their origin is correct. The angel's draperies were certainly painted from such drawings – two of them may even have been amongst the studies used – and the peculiar character of Leonardo's early draperies can be understood.

Far from accusing Vasari of invention, I believe that he did not go far enough. Leonardo's part in the 'Baptism' did not end with the angel; he was also responsible for the landscape, and here again has drawn from his imagination a foretaste of his future style. Verrocchio, unlike his rival,

8. Five are in the collection of Mme la Comtesse de Béhague; three in the Louvre, one of which appears to be the later; three in the Uffizi; one in the British Museum.

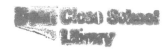
Antonio Pollaiuolo, had no personal or original conception of landscape. He followed the current fashion, introduced through Flemish pictures and illuminated manuscripts, of round trees dotted about on a plain, with a horizon of rounded hills. Everything is tidily arranged and sharply defined. He could not have painted the background of the 'Baptism' with its wide, romantic stretch of hills, lakes, shining mists and pools, anticipating the backgrounds of the 'Mona Lisa' and the Louvre 'St Anne'. Some of the distant hills have been damaged by overpainting, but the nearer part is intact and recalls Leonardo's famous drawing of a landscape in the Uffizi inscribed *didi Sta Maria della neve addi 5 d'aghossto 1473* (Pl. 6). As often in Renaissance

*6. The 'Val d'Arno', 1473. Uffizi, Florence*

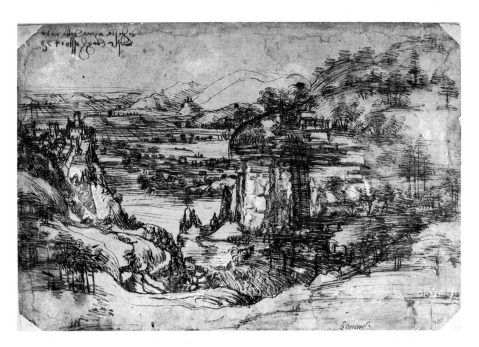

art, the drawing is more naturalistic than the picture, but both have the same motif of shining rocks and trees framing a distant plane. We are aware of landscape as something full of movement, light moving over the hills, wind stirring the leaves of trees, water flowing and falling in cascades; all of which is rendered in brilliant broken touches, with scurries and flutters of the pen, or flicks of golden paint from the brush. The drawing is in fact one of the most important documents for our study of Leonardo's early work. It shows him already master of an original and developed technique in which effects of light are achieved with a directness quite at variance with the formal style of the period. There is a kind of genial recklessness about the touch which does not suggest the painstaking goldsmith's apprentice.

Next in date to the 'Baptism' comes the 'Annunciation' now in the Uffizi (Pls. 7, 8 and 9). It is the sort of large composite picture which artists keep in their studios for many years, and work at intermittently; and it lacks the unity of a work carried out under a single impulse. Perhaps for this reason scholars were long unwilling to accept it as being from the hand of Leonardo, but it is perfectly in character with his other early works both in the general twilit tone, and in the drawing of the details. Moreover, there exists a drawing for the angel's sleeve which is unquestionably his (Pl. 10). The draperies in the 'Annunciation', with their thin straight folds, are so like those of the angel's robe in the 'Baptism' that the picture must have been begun at the same time,[9] and it is interesting to notice that the over-prominent lectern

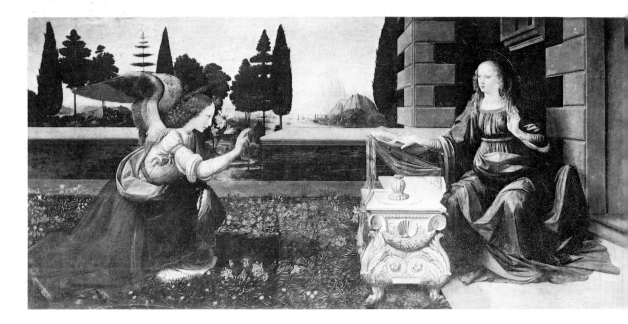

seems to belong to the period, *c.* 1472, in which Verrocchio's workshop was occupied with the similar sarcophagus of the Medici in San Lorenzo. The composition is so awkward that scholars have accused the painter of errors in perspective, but the perspective of the architecture is correct – painstakingly and amateurishly correct. The vanishing point is exactly in the middle of the picture horizontally and two-thirds the way up vertically. But this insistence on the linear perspective of the architecture, irrespective of the position of the figures or the composition as a whole, is the sign of a very young painter. He has learnt the trick of perspective without understanding its true intention,

7. 'Annunciation', 1472–3. Uffizi, Florence

9. Or at least done from the same series of studies on linen, two of which, in the Comtesse de Béhague's collection, are remarkably close to the drapery of the Virgin's robe.

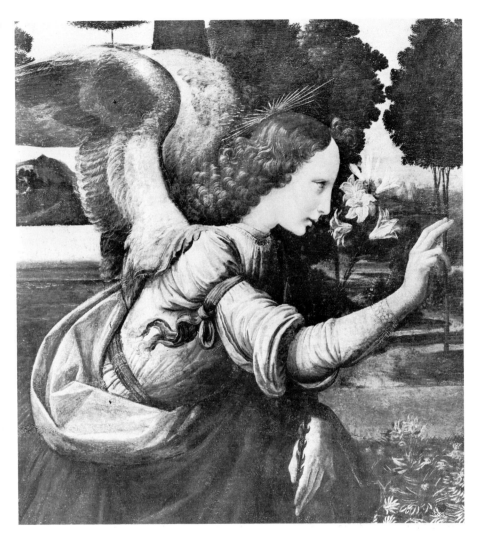

*8. The Angel from the 'Annunciation', 1472–3. Uffizi, Florence*

that is to say, the placing of objects in the picture space in a clear and harmonious relation to one another; and Leonardo has, in fact, made what appears to be a mistake of spatial relationships in making the Virgin place her farther hand on the near side of her lectern which, as we can see from its base, is a few feet nearer the spectator than she is.

The general effect of the Uffizi 'Annunciation' is obscured by its condition. The whole surface is extremely dirty and the draperies are discoloured by old retouches and congealed varnish. But even allowing for this, the execution must have been rather uneven and in places relatively coarse; and the red of the angel's robe can never have borne much relation to the pink of the Virgin's skirt. Incidentally, we must notice that the angel's wing has been lengthened

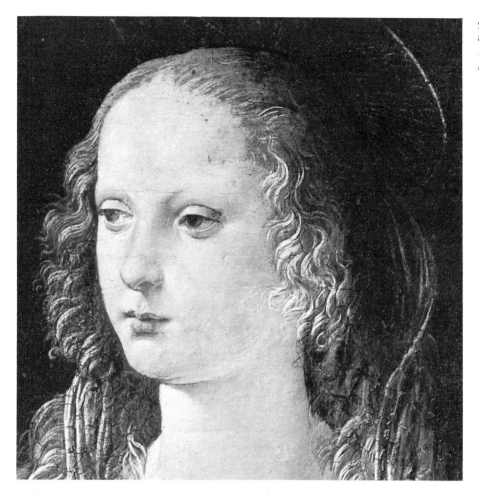

*9. The Virgin from
the 'Annunciation',
1472–3. Uffizi,
Florence*

to canonical proportions by a very crude overpainting and hangs like a brown
smear above the enchanting landscape to the left. The original short wings
are directly painted from the wings of a bird, and fit the angel's shoulders
with convincing naturalism. The angel's head (Pl. 8) is nearer to the traditional
*quattrocento* type than anything else in Leonardo's work, and at first sight
has some of the tameness of a Ghirlandaio. Steadier contemplation will
disclose a subtlety of outline and modelling, especially round the nose and
eye, and a greater technical confidence than in the angel in the 'Baptism'. The
Madonna's head (Pl. 9), on the other hand, is very like the earlier angel. The
features are not felt as part of the structure of the face, but are drawn on it,
and if we compare it with the 'Mona Lisa' we may begin to realize the
immense labour which Leonardo devoted to studying the science of his art.

    In spite of certain faults, the 'Annunciation' remains a lovely and original
picture, in which shortcomings of composition are outweighed by beauties

of detail and of mood. No other work of Leonardo does so much to support Vasari's account of his early sympathy with nature. Other painters of his century had painted nature decoratively or accurately, but none, unless it were the blessed Angelico, had interpreted her moods, and used them to set the emotional key of a picture. In the 'Annunciation' the black trees silhouetted against the grey evening sky are one of those effects which first, in our childhood, made us feel the poetry and, as it were, the closeness of nature. It is an effect which, from its easy appeal, has been often abused, but Leonardo has deprived it of all sentimentality. The distant view of a river with high hills beyond is more in the Flemish fashion than any other of Leonardo's backgrounds, but the lesser landscape to the left of the angel, dimly perceptible through the dirt and varnish, has the personal vision of the Uffizi drawing. Even more similar to his mature work are the flowers in the foreground. The artists of the *quattrocento* had spread their flowers like verdure tapestry, or drawn them in isolation, like botanical specimens, but Leonardo has given to his flowers and grasses something of the turbulence that he felt to be the

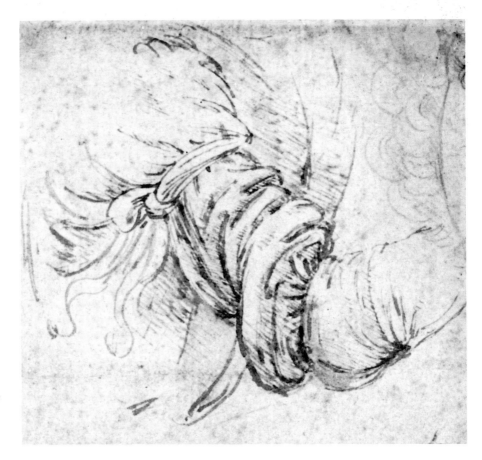

10. *Study of the Angel's Sleeve for the 'Annunciation', c. 1472–3. Christ Church, Oxford*

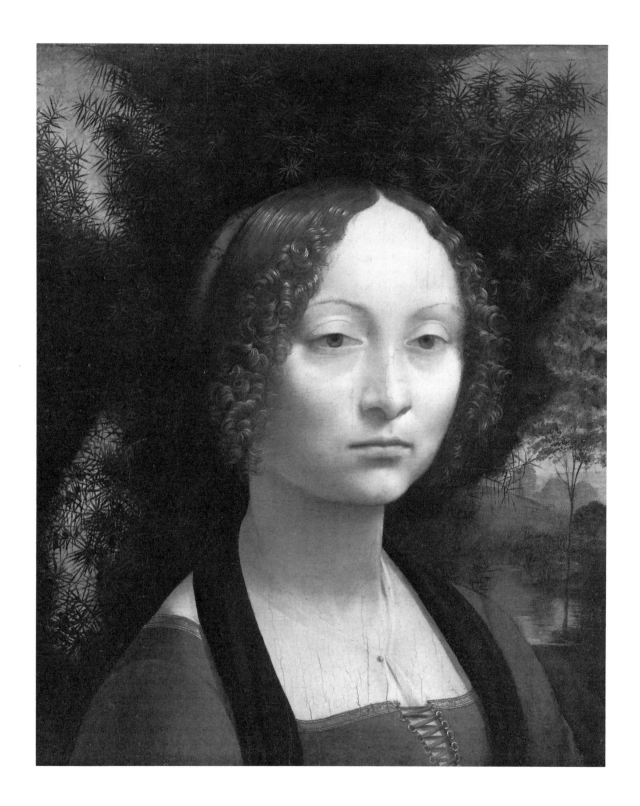

11. 'Ginevra de'
Benci', 1474. National
Gallery, Washington

essence of nature. They twist and surge like little waves over the space
between the angel and the Madonna, giving vitality to what would otherwise
have been a dead area in the composition.

Soon after the 'Annunciation' Leonardo must have painted the portrait of
a lady now in the National Gallery, Washington (Pl. 11). It is based on the
same sequence of tones as the angel's head – the pale flesh, the dark mass of
foliage, the luminous grey sky; but the head is more firmly modelled than the
Virgin Annunciate, and must be slightly later. The Washington portrait is of
an exquisite melancholy beauty, far outside the range of Verrocchio and
beyond the power of Credi; and personally I have little doubt that it is
the portrait of Ginevra de' Benci, mentioned in Vasari and the Anonimo
Gaddiano,[10] although Vasari says that this was painted during Leonardo's
second Florentine period. It seems to represent a lady called Ginevra, for not
only does a bush of juniper[11] form the background of her head, but on the
reverse of the panel is a sprig of juniper encircled by a wreath of laurel and
palm. Most Florentine portraits of women were painted to celebrate their
marriages. Ginevra de' Benci was married in January 1474, and this is a
possible date for the picture on grounds of style.

We can guess by its unusual shape that the picture has been cut at the
bottom, and this fact is confirmed by the truncated wreath at the back. By
completing the curve of the wreath and allowing for decorative ribbons, etc.,
we can calculate that the amount cut off must have been at least nine
centimetres, which would give it the classical proportion of 3 to 4. This would
also make it large enough to contain the lady's hands, and Bode, who was
the first scholar to give the picture full attention, suggested that these hands
were known to us in a famous and beautiful silverpoint drawing at Windsor
(Pl. 12). The hands at Windsor, with their long-jointed fingers, are like enough
to those of the Virgin in the Uffizi 'Annunciation', and the style of the drawing
is just possible for 1474, although firmer and more masterly than anything
else of that date which has survived. Assuming that the drawing was for the
'Ginevra', we see that the fingers of her right hand would have been touching
the lower laces of her bodice; and in the picture these laces are in fact
repainted. Unfortunately, we can tell from the back that the bottom of the
picture has been damaged and a new piece has been added, so that an X-ray
would not reveal the vanished fingers.

In spite of mutilation the 'Ginevra de' Benci' is the best preserved of all
Leonardo's early pictures, and shows most clearly his intentions at this period.
Areas of light and dark are strongly contrasted, but within the light oval of
the face there is very little shadow, and the modelling is suggested by delicate

10. Also known as the Anonimo *Magliabecchiano*, ed. Frey (Berlin, 1892), p. 111. Henceforth I refer to
this source as the Anonimo.

11. In Italian *ginepro*; in Romance dialects *genevra*.

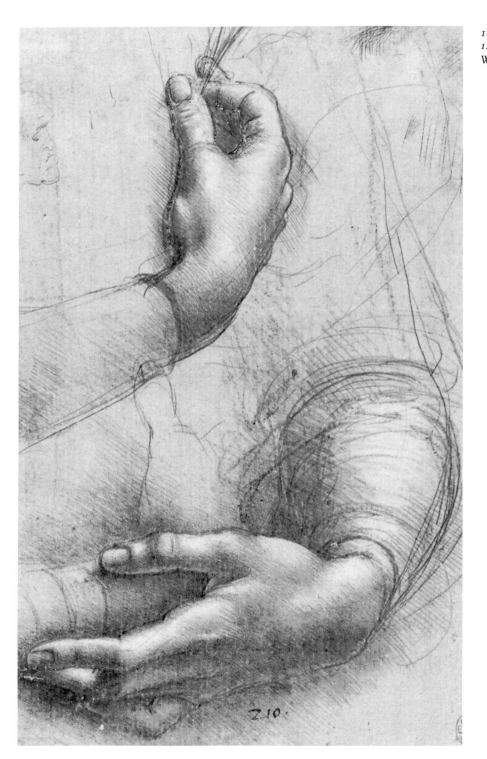

12. *Study of Hands,
1474? Royal Library,
Windsor* (RL 12558)

gradations of tone, especially in the reflected lights. We see a similar treatment of form in Desiderio's low reliefs, controlled by the same sensibility to minute variations of surface. There are passages, such as the modelling of the eyelids, which Leonardo never surpassed in delicacy, and here for once he seems to have had none of that distaste for the medium which we can deduce from his later paintings, no less than from contemporary descriptions of his practice. Most ingenious is the way in which all the light areas except the face are given broken irregular contours by the juniper leaves, or the shimmering water, so that the outline of the lady's cheek and brow dominate the design. There is a similar contrast in texture between the beautiful curves of her ringlets and the stiff, spiky character of the juniper. But all these technical devices are subordinate to the feeling of individual character with which Leonardo has been able to charge his portrait, so that this pale young woman has become one of the memorable personalities of the Renaissance.

Assuming that the 'Ginevra' was painted in 1474, how did Leonardo spend the next four years? There are no documents bearing on his work till 1478, no drawings and only one picture which seems to belong to the period. At twenty-five years of age, he cannot have been obscurely devilling for Verrocchio, although we know that he lived with Verrocchio till 1476; and he had not yet begun the scientific studies which, in his later life, account for intervals in the sequence of his paintings. Presumably Leonardo, like other young men with great gifts, spent a large part of his youth in what is known as doing nothing – dressing up, talking, taming horses, learning the lute, learning the flute, enjoying the <i>hors d'œuvres</i> of life, till his genius should find its true direction.

There is one picture which can be dated in this period with some show of evidence, the Virgin with the vase of flowers in the Munich Gallery. It is connected in many ways with the studio of Verrocchio. Credi did a drawing and picture of the same model in the same costume, and an almost identical pose was used in a composite production of Verrocchio's shop, the altarpiece in Pistoia Cathedral.[12] Perhaps the fact that the 'Munich Madonna' (Pl. 13) was little more than a workshop commission accounts for the absence of most of those qualities which we value in Leonardo's other work. The picture is hard to judge in its present condition. The Virgin's head has been entirely repainted in a medium containing too large a quantity of oil, resulting in a craquelure so unlike that of any Italian technique that Morelli believed the whole picture to be a Flemish copy. The same medium was used to rework the shadows, especially round the baby's head, of which a different

12. This connection with Credi suggests a date as late as 1478. On the other hand, the way of painting and the study for the Virgin's head referred to below point to a period not later than the 'Annunciation'. The years 1474 to 1478 are the most inexplicable in Leonardo's career, and short of the discovery of some new documents I see no hope of their being elucidated.

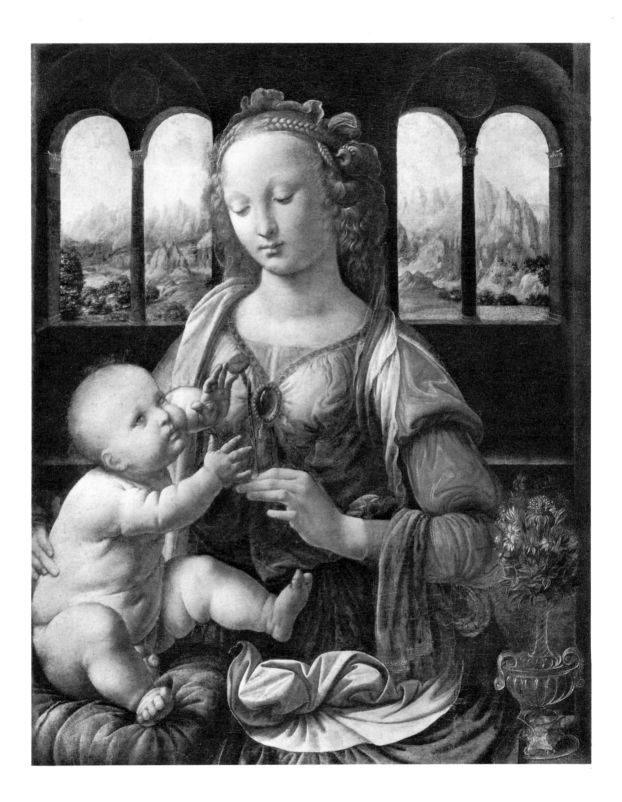

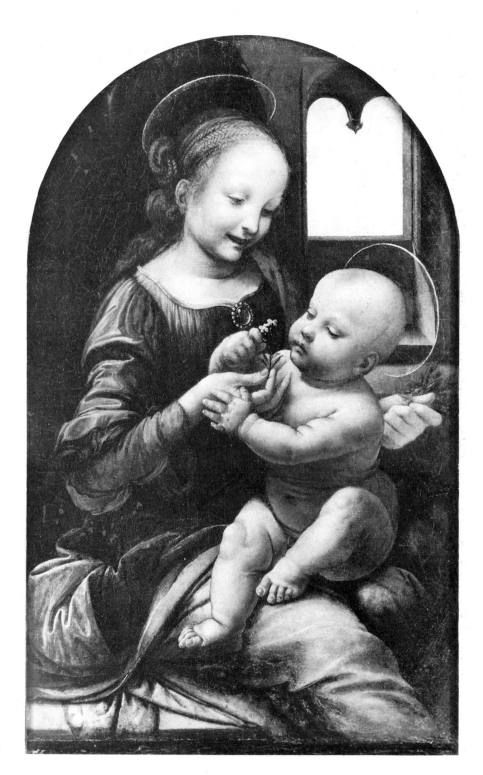

13. 'Madonna and Child', c. 1476. Alte Pinakothek, Munich

14. The 'Benois Madonna', 1478–80. Hermitage, Leningrad

outline is faintly perceptible. There are many other damages, and it may well be asked on what grounds the picture can be ascribed to Leonardo. The answer is that all the surviving parts are wholly characteristic. The Virgin's plaited hair, and her left hand, large parts of her drapery, and the flowers in the vase at her side, are all painted in exactly the same style as the Uffizi 'Annunciation', and they combine to give the picture as a whole a quality of form and colour which is unlike anything else of the period. For further confirmation there is the panorama of mountains seen through the arched windows of the background of the 'Annunciation'. Already Leonardo has felt it necessary to turn the horizontal line of the background into a series of verticals by rows of precipitous mountains. Like the flowers in the 'Annunciation' these gothic pinnacles are a negation of repose, a refusal to allow that anything in nature should be devoid of movement. It is instructive to compare this charmless picture with the exquisite little 'Virgin and Child' from the Dreyfus Collection, now in the National Gallery, Washington, which must be a very early work by Lorenzo di Credi. Both were painted from the same studio model and perhaps at the same time. The 'Dreyfus Madonna' is executed with a delicacy and minuteness of touch which resists enlargement up to ten times its original size. It is the work of a born prize-winner. Where the 'Munich Madonna' has the unpleasant vitality of immature genius, the 'Dreyfus Madonna' has the amiable complacency of the craftsman.

In January 1478 we have the first record of Leonardo being given an important independent commission, the altar-piece in the Chapel of St Bernard in the Signoria, Florence. A first payment was made, but for some unknown reason the work was never delivered, and in 1483 the commission was given to Ghirlandaio. The Anonimo Gadiano says that it was finally executed by Filippino Lippi, who worked 'on the design of Leonardo',[13] but Filippino's altar-piece in the Uffizi, dated 1485, shows no connection with Leonardo either in spirit or design.[14] To the same year belongs a drawing of two heads with a fragmentary inscription which mentions the town of Pistoia and states that in the autumn of 1478 Leonardo had begun two pictures of the Madonna – ... *bre 1478 inchominciai le 2 Vergine Marie*. One of these must almost certainly be the so-called 'Benois Madonna', now in the Hermitage (Pl. 14). The 'Benois Madonna', the latest of the four pictures painted in the 1470s, is the one which is most generally accepted by the critics. Indeed, it is the unquestionable authenticity of this picture which has driven all but the most idealistic critics to accept the other three. The 'Benois Madonna' does not owe this position so much to its intrinsic merits as to the fact that there exist several drawings for the composition which are unde-

13. *Il Codice Magliabecchiano*, ed. Carl Frey (Berlin, 1892), p. 116.
14. No. 1568, dated 1485.

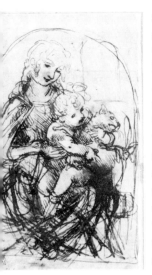

*15. Study for the 'Madonna with the Cat', 1478–80. British Museum, London*

niably by Leonardo. Here, for the first time, we are able to study his art with a method which is always illuminating, namely by comparing his drawings with his finished pictures. And immediately we find evidence of a conflict between spontaneity and perfection. With the drawings for the 'Benois Madonna' we may also consider a rather more numerous series of drawings for a Virgin and Child, now lost, in which the Child is playing with a cat or tame weasel (Pl. 15), and by treating these Madonna studies as a single group we can take a wider basis for our generalizations.[15] These studies are so fresh and natural that they are now amongst the most popular of all Leonardo's drawings. They show, as nothing else in his work, a direct and happy approach to life; and they show his matchless quickness of vision, which allowed him to convey every movement or gesture with the certainty and unconscious grace of a great dancer performing a familiar step. In one sense the word 'certainty' does not apply to these early drawings. Technically they are still experimental. The line is recklessly free; sometimes they are scrawled over and covered with blots and washes of sepia so that they resemble drawings of the seventeenth century – Rembrandt or Guercino. But the general effect is one of a graceful speed and of a hunter's certainty of eye. The largest and most beautiful of this series is a study in the Louvre of the Virgin holding out a plate of fruit to the Infant Christ, in a pose close to that of the 'Benois Madonna' (Pl. 16). It is drawn with a few rapid and summary strokes, as though Leonardo's whole aim had been to note down action; and yet he has achieved a perfect composition. The rhythmic relation of the two heads is as spontaneous and as inevitable as the relation between two bars of Mozart.

In the 'Benois Madonna' this unity of effect is lost. What has come between the sketch and the picture? To answer this question we must glance for a moment at the two traditions which divided Florentine art of the fifteenth century. One of these is the tradition of linear grace and fancy, the tradition of Lorenzo Monaco, Fra Filippo, and Botticelli; the other is the tradition of scientific naturalism founded by Masaccio and kept alive in Leonardo's own day by his master Verrocchio. Inevitably these traditions overlapped. Botticelli had a phase of naturalism; Pollaiuolo belongs as much to one side as the other. Leonardo, as we see from his drawings, belonged by nature to the first group. But by training he was of the second, and his powerful intellect led him to sympathize with the scientific approach. Thus between the sketch and the picture he was forced to attempt a complete change of mood and to adapt his fleeting visions to the severe standards of academic Florentine art. We have plenty of evidence how this adaptation was effected. First come the

15. It is possible that the 'Madonna with the Cat' studies may be a year or two later, about 1480, but this does not affect the question.

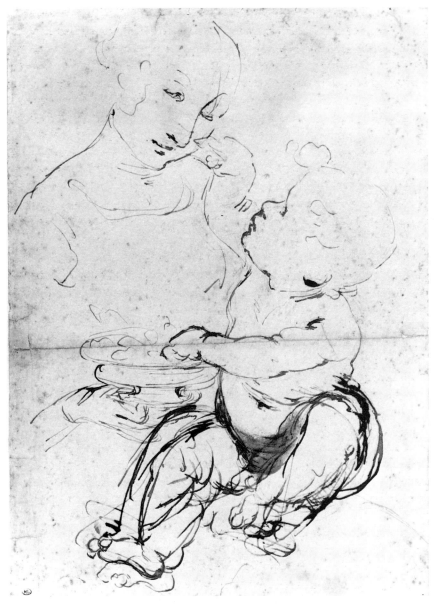

*16. Study for the
'Benois Madonna',
1478–80. Louvre, Paris*

studies of action, just described, the motifs which are later to be used in the picture. Then come what I may call the diagrams. These are usually quite small drawings, done from memory, and are syntheses of the most satisfactory motifs. One of the diagrams for the 'Benois Madonna' has survived (P. 16) and is typical in its severity; typical, also, in that Leonardo has followed it closely. So far I imagine that his powers were perfectly uninhibited, and had he been content to rely on suggestion rather than complete statement, like Rembrandt, or to accept the formulae of his time, like Raphael, he might have been a prolific painter. But he would neither improvise nor conform. He determined to work out every detail according to his own standard of perfection, a standard which included scientific accuracy, pictorial logic, and finish. To achieve this ideal, the period between the sketch or diagram and the finished picture was one of intense intellectual effort, in which every detail was studied and assimilated to a satisfactory form.

This stage, too, we know from drawings, highly finished studies of detail, which often tell us more about Leonardo's final intentions than the actual picture; because by the time he began to paint, constant labours and anxieties had so deprived him of all appetite for his subject that his pictures were either left unfinished, or, as with the 'Benois Madonna', were carried through without that vitality, that spontaneous rendering of action, which was the original motive of his whole conception.

But it is a mistake to look in the 'Benois Madonna' for the charm and freshness of the *quattrocento*. Rather, we must think of it as a changeling from the high Renaissance, an immature sample of that intellectual, classical style which Leonardo was to evolve while painting the 'Last Supper'. How near he came to this style as early as 1480 we can see by comparing the drapery of the Madonna's right leg and thigh with the studies of drapery made for the Louvre 'Virgin and St Anne' about thirty years later (Pl. 96). The system of folds is almost exactly the same, and there can be no doubt that Leonardo, in the most mature and complex of all his works, used as a point of departure this design of his youth. The composition of the 'Benois Madonna', which has an air of perfect naturalness and simplicity, is remarkably original, since it is based on a scheme of diagonal recession unusual in painting before Leonardo. Even the absence of ornament, the contempt for mere decoration which is one of its least attractive qualities, is a presage of the austere and elevated style which was to become fashionable some forty years later.

For all these reasons the 'Benois Madonna' is a great advance on the Madonna with the vase of flowers at Munich; but it suffers from many of the same defects. The condition is equally bad in a less obvious way. Under the discoloured varnish it is covered with small stippled touches which deprive it of all transparency of handling. The Virgin's teeth, for example, are so entirely obscured by dirt that one distinguished critic, judging from a photograph, wrote of her as toothless. As the eye gradually penetrates these obstructive layers, her whole head takes on some of the vitality of the original drawings, and it is possible that the deadness which I have just referred to is partly due to condition. But parts of the composition can never have been happy: the baby was always monstrous and the drapery of the sleeve laboured. Finally, the one redeeming feature of the Munich picture, the landscape seen through a window, is absent from the background of the 'Benois Madonna'. The window itself, lacking a central transom, is ugly enough, and without a landscape it is really painful. Perhaps a landscape once existed and has been overpainted, with the result that a large patch of light sky puts the Virgin's

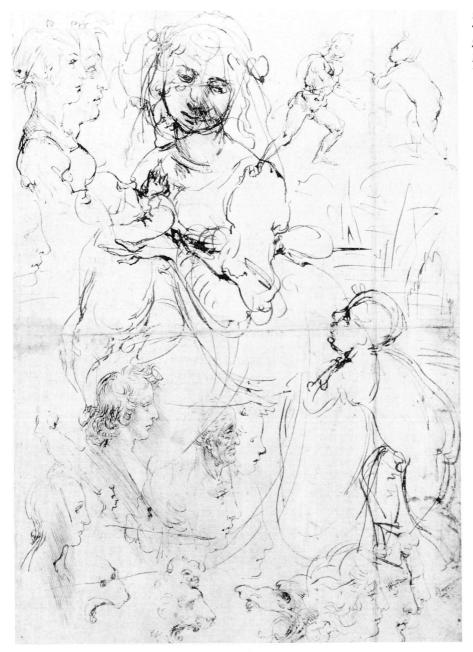

*17. Study for the 'Madonna, Child and St John', c. 1476. Royal Library, Windsor (RL 12776r)*

face out of tone and destroys the unity of focus – the very mistake which Leonardo so skilfully avoided in the portrait of Ginevra de' Benci.[16]

It is possible to reconstruct at least two more pictures of the Virgin and Child dating from this period. One of these, the Virgin almost in profile, known from the 'Madonna Litta' in the Hermitage, which is either a copy or a ruined original, is discussed in my next chapter. The other is known to us from a drawing on the famous sheet at Windsor which also contains some of the earliest of those characteristic profiles, the pretty boy and the toothless Roman warrior, which were always to be the first scribbles to flow from Leonardo's pen. The Virgin is represented half kneeling on her left knee, holding the Child on her right, with the infant St John standing close beside her (Pl. 17). The drawing is summary, but we know that it represents something like Leonardo's final version of the subject, as the group of the Virgin and Child is reproduced almost exactly in a picture by Andrea da Salerno at Naples. This proves that Leonardo carried the idea much further than a sketch, perhaps to a painting, certainly to a cartoon. And what an immensely influential composition it was! Mr Berenson has shown that it is probably the earliest representation of the Virgin and Child to include the infant St John, and even if earlier instances could be found, it is certain that the use Leonardo has made of this iconographic motif is in the highest degree original. He has discovered the secret of that pyramidal composition which became an academic dogma of the high Renaissance; for the infant St John, standing beside the seated Virgin, gives just that weight and balance to the base of the pyramid which the Virgin and Child alone would otherwise have lacked. Having invented this motif and used it once, Leonardo abandoned it, with all its permutations and combinations, to be worked out by Raphael. The 'Belle Jardinière', 'Madonna with the Goldfinch', 'Madonna of the Meadows', and the 'Esterhazy Madonna' are variations on a theme by Leonardo: which, as any musician knows, does not make them less beautiful or personal.

One picture of this period remains to be discussed, the small 'Annunciation' in the Louvre (Pl. 18). It is a work of unusual perfection. Unlike the 'Annunciation' in the Uffizi, it is composed with complete mastery of spatial intervals. The handling is precise but sensitive, and some passages, such as the angel's wing, are evidence of a steady, penetrating eye. We can praise it more unreservedly than almost any of Leonardo's works of this period, and having done so, it may seem paradoxical to doubt its authenticity. It is now certain, however, that the Louvre picture is part of the predella of an altar-piece in the Cathedral of Pistoia, documented as a Verrocchio and executed by

16. Some years ago (i.e. before 1939) I asked the curator of the Hermitage to have the picture X-rayed, to see if the traces of the original landscape still existed, but owing to lack of apparatus he was unable to do so.

Lorenzo di Credi; and there is in Detroit a small panel representing San Donato of Arezzo and a tax-collector which has no great charm, but is manifestly part of the same predella. The Louvre 'Annunciation' is thus in the position of a beautiful orphan who is suddenly discovered to have a number of undesirable relations. True, it was not uncommon for a predella to be executed by a different artist, and at a different time, from the main part of an altar-piece; and Leonardo might have been attracted by the task while the empty frame was waiting, as it did for ten years, in Verrocchio's workshop. But a careful analysis of style supports the documentary evidence. The flowers lack Leonardo's sense of growth, the hands and draperies are exactly similar to those in the 'Dreyfus Madonna'; and a conclusion that it is one more example of Credi's precocious talent seems to be irresistible.[17]

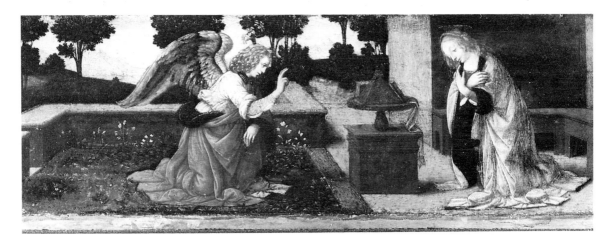

18. *Lorenzo di Credi (?), 'Annunciation', Predella of the Pistoia Altar-piece, c. 1478– 85. Louvre, Paris*

Looking back on the paintings done by Leonardo in Verrocchio's studio, we see that they form an intelligible series, recognizably by the same hand as the 'Virgin of the Rocks'. But it is not surprising that an earlier generation of critics was unable to accept them as his. They differ in many ways from his later painting, and are particularly unlike the exaggerated pupil's work on which the conception of Leonardo's style was formerly based. Of the scientific approach to picture-making, which expressed itself in the use of chiaroscuro and contraposto, they are almost entirely innocent; and they have little of that sense of mystery, that disturbing quality of expression which comes first to mind at the mention of Leonardo's name. Moreover, we must admit that the early pictures are less good than we should expect them to be. Only one of them, the Liechtenstein portrait, is wholly successful as a

17. An added complication is the disputed date of Credi's birth. I accept as correct his mother's assurance that he was born in 1459–60.

work of art. The others must be enjoyed in detail or 'read backwards' in the light of his later work.

But it would be unfair to judge the young Leonardo on his surviving paintings alone. Throughout life he was an untiring draughtsman and a larger number of his drawings have survived than of any other Renaissance painter. It is these which allow us to follow the continuous process of his growth as an artist, and it is in the drawings of this early period that we see his promise in relation to his maturity. Nothing in his later work surpasses in spontaneity his pen and ink sketches of the Mother and Child (Pl. 15), nor in a kind of austere delicacy the silverpoint study for the head of the Madonna Litta (Pl. 32). At twenty-five Leonardo had the rapid perception and the rhythmic discipline of hand of a Watteau or a Degas. But how little this tells us about the painter of the 'Last Supper'! In these early drawings he floats so swiftly on the stream of his talent that he is hardly aware of its depths – those unfathomable depths into which he was afterwards to peer so intently. It was not by improving or refining upon these gifts that he evolved the massive and mysterious structure of his art, but by employing them with an intellectual power of which his early work gives us hardly any indication. But before this process had begun to fade the *quattrocento* freshness of his vision, he was to attempt one great composition in which his genius for swift notation was for the first time controlled by his speculative intelligence: the 'Adoration of the Magi' from San Donato a Scopeto.

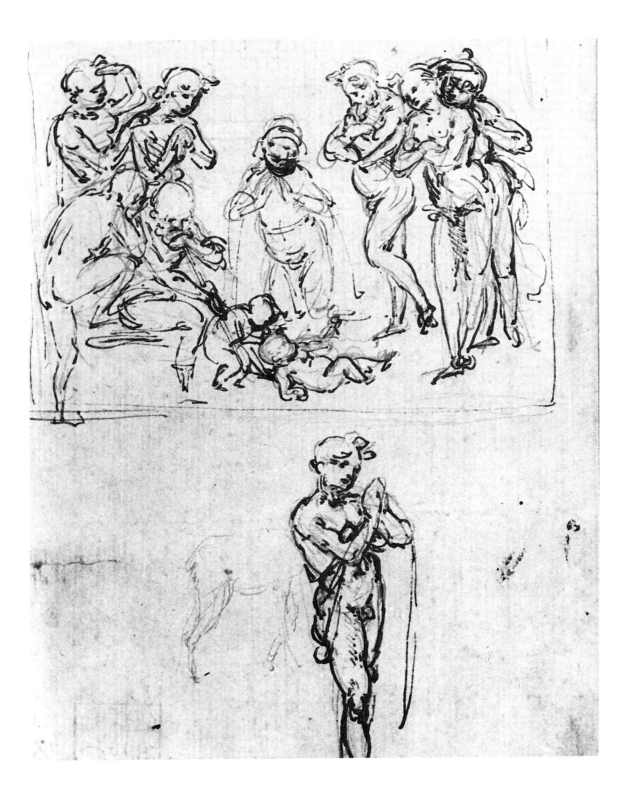

# CHAPTER TWO

## 1481‑1490

*19. Study for the
'Adoration of the
Shepherds', 1478–80.
Musée Bonnat,
Bayonne*

BY grouping together Leonardo's early pictures of the Virgin and Child, I have been forced out of strict chronology. I must now return to a period in the late 1470s to find the roots of Leonardo's first great composition, the 'Adoration of the Kings', now in the Uffizi. As is the case with most great artists, Leonardo's energies were throughout life devoted to the exploration of a limited number of subjects, each one taken up, sketched, attempted, abandoned, reconsidered, and not brought to a final shape till all its expressive possibilities were exhausted. It is in following such transformations, or perhaps I should call them excavations – for with each change a deeper layer of Leonardo's spirit is brought to light – that we learn most of his art.

The sources of the Uffizi 'Adoration' are to be found in sketches for a very different composition, the most important of which are three pen and ink drawings in the Musée Bonnat (Pl. 19), the Venice Academy (P. 40), and the Hamburg Kunsthalle (P. 41). These drawings, by their short firm shading, are datable about 1478. The number of studies which can be related to them show that this was an important commission. Perhaps it was for the altarpiece in the Chapel of St Bernard in the Signoria, commissioned in 1478, but never finished. The subject of these sketches was the Nativity, and the Bonnat drawing shows the adoring shepherds forming two sides of a square in the centre of which the Virgin kneels behind the holy children. It is the type of formal composition which Leonardo would have learnt in Verrocchio's shop, and in fact it became a favourite with his fellow pupils.[1] Perugino used it with variations, for example, in the Villa Albani triptych, and Credi, in a

1. For example, in the Villa Albani triptych and the fresco of the 'Adoration' in the Cambio at Perugia.

picture at Berlin, imitated exactly the central figures. Closely connected by style with these drawings of the whole composition is a series of studies at Windsor of raw-boned horses (Pl. 20), some cropping the grass with out-stretched necks, and a sketch of the ox and the ass. All these studies suggest that the scene was conceived in a traditional spirit, rustic, homely, realistic. In some of the shepherds we recognize motifs which reappear in the Uffizi 'Adoration' – young men with similar gestures of wonder, and an old man in meditation. The Virgin with the children gives, as we shall see, a first hint of the composition of the 'Virgin of the Rocks'. Yet, as a whole, the lost 'Adoration', in contrast to the Uffizi picture, must have come from the surface of Leonardo's imagination.

Externally this contrast is expressed in a change of subject. The fable of the Adoring Shepherds is abandoned in favour of the allegory of the Adoring Kings. I doubt if this change was dictated by Leonardo's patrons, for artists at that date took great liberties with the subjects commissioned; more probably it signified a change in Leonardo himself. During his apprenticeship he had learnt the current forms of Florentine art, and his first instinct was to

*20. Study of Horses for the 'Adoration of the Shepherds', 1478–80. Royal Library, Windsor (RL 12308)*

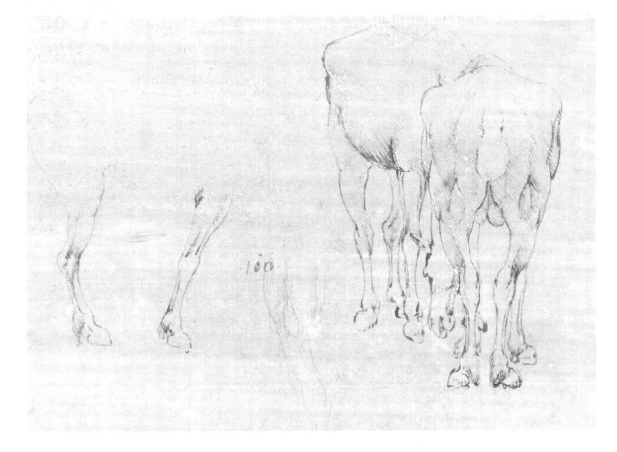

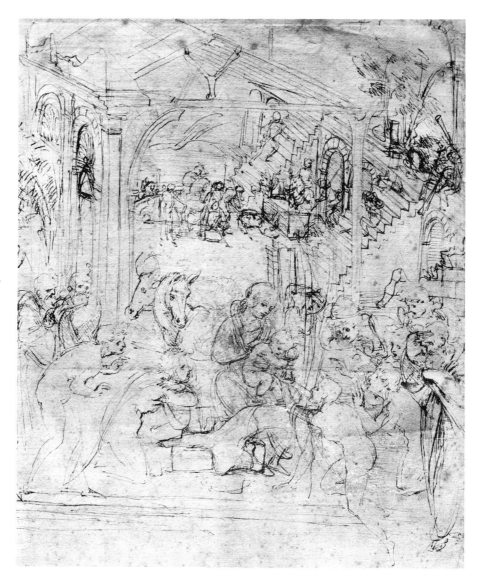

reproduce them, with uncommon delicacy and a certain overtone of poetry, but no striking deviation. But as Leonardo penetrated beneath the surface of professional skill, he discovered a strange visionary world, demanding expression in very different forms. This change was gradual and seems to have antedated the commission for the San Donato altar-piece, for we find in certain drawings connected with the earlier composition a hint of the rhythms which were to dominate the latter. Beside prosaic horses, with angular necks stretched down to feed (Pl. 20), are wild ethereal horses, with nervous heads thrown back (P. 59). They are the spies and outriders of Leonardo's

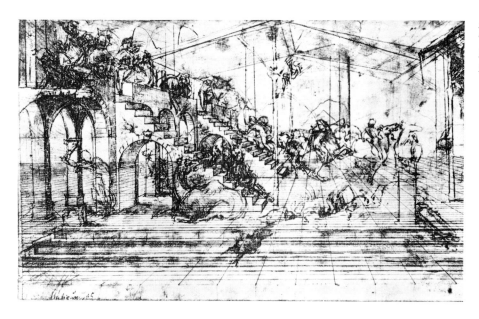

*22. Study for the 'Adoration of the Kings', 1481. Uffizi, Florence*

imagination entering the world of conventional Florentine art, soon to be followed by the mysterious company which fills the Uffizi 'Adoration'.

In studying the 'Adoration of Kings' it is usual to take as a point of departure the drawing in the Louvre formerly in the Galichon Collection, which shows one of his early attempts to arrive at the whole composition (Pl. 21). It is a relatively feeble drawing. The touch is weak, the emphasis diffused, as if Leonardo was thinking aloud. But already he has discovered one of the chief motifs of the final picture, the flow of adoration conveyed by figures kneeling and bending forward; and this is already contrasted with the detached vertical figure of the philosopher. He has also hit on the architectural motif of the background – the courtyard of a ruined palace of which only one side, with two staircases and a gallery, remains. Like the rest of the sheet, this architectural background is drawn with curious uncertainty and lack of perspective; and to correct this Leonardo made the only other study for the whole composition which has come down to us (Pl. 22). This sheet, now in the Uffizi, is one of the most revealing of all his drawings. Ostensibly it is an exercise in formal perspective of a type common in Florence since Brunelleschi. The staircase wall of the courtyard with its two flights and elaborate arcades was sufficient pretext for such a study and is rendered with great mastery. Actually it is our earliest evidence of Leonardo's scientific attainments, and from the first science is made the scaffolding for his imagination. For this carefully measured courtyard has been invaded by an extra-ordinary retinue of ghosts; wild horses rear and toss their heads, agitated figures dart up the staircase and in and out of the arcades; and a camel, appearing for the first and last time in Leonardo's work, adds its exotic bulk to the dreamlike confusion of forms.

This drawing must date from an advanced stage in the development of the composition, since Leonardo has decided to transfer the staircase to the left, a decision involving some certainty in the disposition of the foreground figures. It is an indication of the immense pains he took over all his work that in the final version this elaborate drawing was not used. The ruined staircases were retained on the same plan, but in a different perspective.

In addition to these composition studies we have a number of drawings which can be related to the Uffizi 'Adoration'. The most magical of these are silverpoint studies of horses (P. 64), in which the delicate medium is used to give a curious lunar quality of light (Pl. 23). The figure sketches are in pen

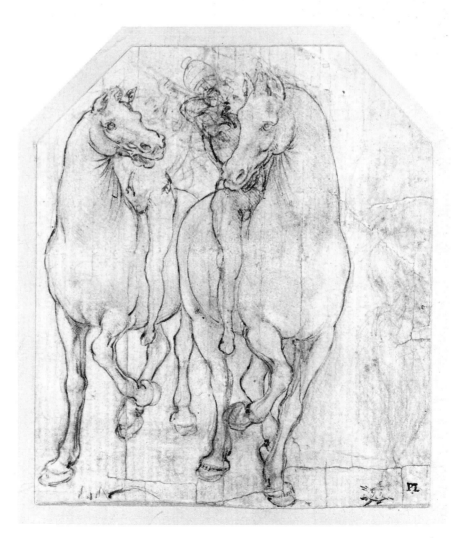

23. Study for the
'Adoration of the
Kings', 1481. Clarke
Collection,
Cambridge

and ink, drawn with the light rapid stroke of Pollaiuolo (P. 43). They are notes of action, and some are simply leaves from sketchbooks of about this date, to which he naturally turned for suitable poses, following that practice which he was afterwards to recommend in the *Trattato* (95) of collecting and composing, in the long winter evenings, the nude studies done in the preceding summer. Others were done with the 'Adoration' in mind, and show him preoccupied with two figures in particular, the youth bending forward with an expression of wonder, and the old man standing aloof in meditation (P. 48). Both appear in perfected forms in the Uffizi picture, but for most of the figures no preliminary sketch survives. Our drawings for the 'Adoration', relatively abundant, can only be a fraction of the whole.

The final composition has been made the subject of much ingenious analysis, some of it more exhaustive than the unfinished state of the picture will allow (Pl. 24). But I may point out how the simple parallelism of the earlier compositions has been entirely superseded. Instead, the main lines form a triangle backed by an arc. The right side of the triangle is a relatively straight line from the kneeling King's foot to St Joseph, and is echoed in the background by the line of the staircases. The left side rises in a series of curves, which are repeated in the arcades of the ruin, and supported by the leading gestures and glances. Round this triangle, an arc of shadowy figures flows like the Stream of Ocean of Ptolemaic geography. To stabilize this restless pattern Leonardo has placed four verticals, the two trees near the centre of the triangle, the two upright figures at its bases.

Even this bare, geometrical analysis of the composition gives a hint of its dramatic meaning. The symbolical homage of wisdom and science to a new faith is firmly expressed by the main figures; but pressing round them, like ghosts from the magical paganism of Apuleius, are those evasive creatures which writers on Leonardo are content to call angels. In the background, agitation of spirit inhabits the half-ruined construction of the intelligence. There remain the two figures at the sides, which seem to stand outside the scene, like leaders of a Greek chorus.[2] To the left is the philosopher, whose noble form we saw in evolution. Morally and materially he has the grandeur of one of Masaccio's apostles. Opposite the Masaccio is a Giorgione: for no other name will fit the deeply romantic figure of a youth in armour on the right (Pl. 25). He looks out of the picture with complete indifference, and as is usual with such detached figures a tradition has grown up that Leonardo has here portrayed himself. Whether or not this is true in a literal sense we cannot tell but the student of Leonardo may feel that in these two figures of youth and age, moral and physical beauty, active and passive intelligence, he

2. A more pronounced and probably more conscious use of this device is in the Hugo van der Goes 'Adoration of the Shepherds' in Berlin, which is clearly inspired by the scene of a miracle play.

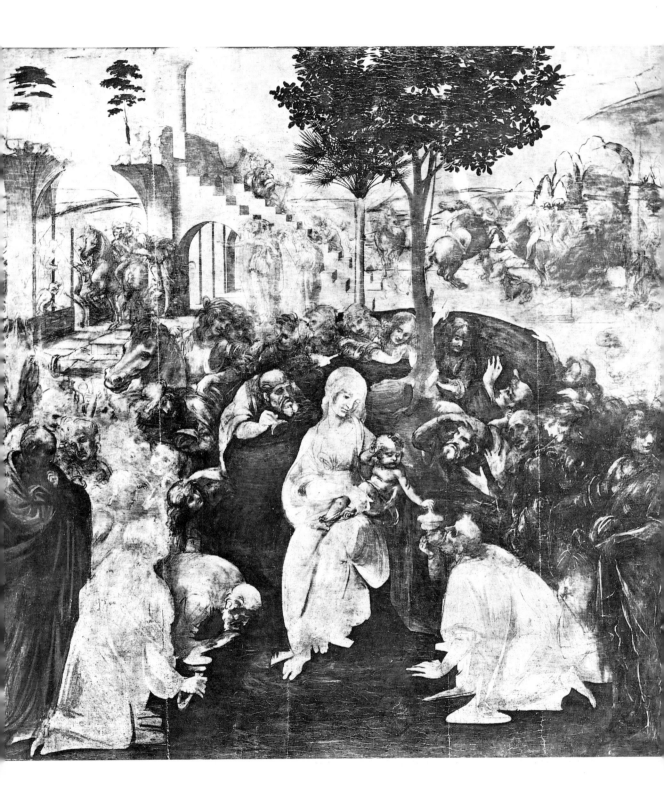

has indeed represented his own spirit, symbolizing his dual nature as he does in those familiar expressions of his unconscious mind, the contrasted profiles (see p. 121).

The 'Adoration' is an overture to all Leonardo's work, full of themes that will recur. Joseph has the emphatic grimace of St Andrew in the 'Last Supper'; the bearded King who raises his hand to his head anticipates St Peter; the beautiful profile of a young man standing one away from him is very close to St Philip, as we know him in the Windsor drawing (Pl. 59). Between them an old man with sunken eyes bears an obvious resemblance to the Vatican

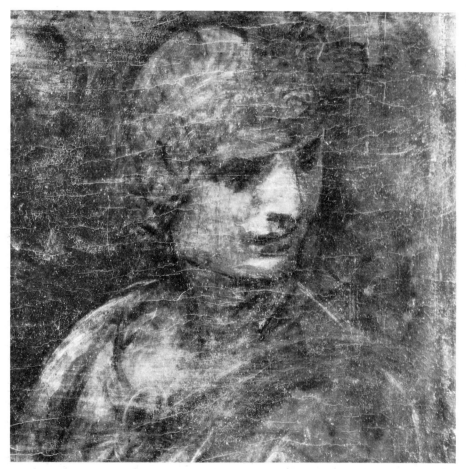

*25. Detail of standing youth in the 'Adoration of the Kings', 1481–2. Uffizi, Florence*

'St Jerome'; and amongst the angels is one who raises his hand to point upward his outstretched finger (Pl. 26), a gesture which so obsessed Leonardo that his imitators made it into a sort of trade mark. Most remarkable of all is the skirmish of horsemen in the background, which derives from an earlier project of mounted men fighting a dragon and was used again twenty-five years later as the central motif of the 'Battle of Anghiari'. This recurrence of relatively few forms, noticeable in the work of all great draughtsmen, does not of course spring from a poverty of invention, but serves, rather, to distinguish art from imitation. Out of the wealth of nature only a few shapes can be made to fit the artist's inner vision, and so become recreated images; and the development of such an artist as Leonardo is not marked by the frequent discovery of new forms but by the rendering of inherent forms more finally expressive.

*26. Detail from the 'Adoration of the Kings', 1481–2. Uffizi, Florence*

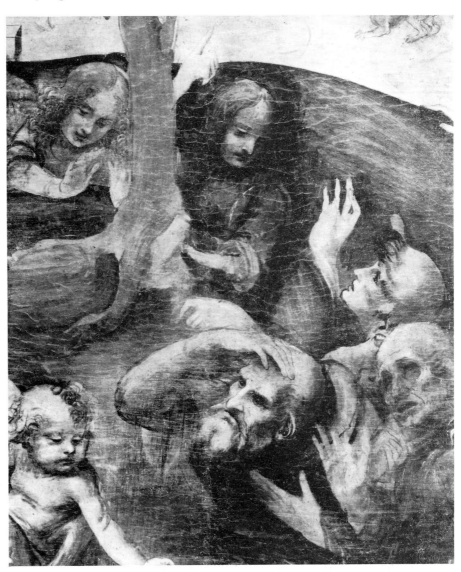

It is one of the ironies of art history that the 'Adoration', the most revolutionary and anti-classical picture of the fifteenth century, should have helped to furnish that temple of academic orthodoxy, Raphael's Stanza della Segnatura. When in 1509 Raphael embarked on his first great compositions, Leonardo's 'Adoration' was already twenty-eight years old; yet it remained the most dramatic and most highly organized composition of its kind, and Vasari tells us how Raphael stood before it speechless, wondering at the expressiveness of the heads and the grace and movement of the figures. This quality of vital grace he strove to imitate by borrowing directly poses and expressions from the 'Adoration': and as with the Madonna groups he was able to assimilate them to his own style, so that at first we are hardly conscious that the figures bending and kneeling to the left of the *Disputà* owe anything to Leonardo. But the 'School of Athens' shows us that this process of assimilation was gradual. In the great cartoon for this composition in the Ambrosiana the Leonardesque borrowings are very obvious. Two figures in particular, an elderly pythagorean and an oriental, are not only Leonardo's types, but have retained some of his peculiar intensity, which strikes a disturbing note in the general calm of the composition. Raphael has not been able to shake off what Blake would have called the outrageous demon of Leonardo. In the final fresco, by subtle modifications of emphasis, order is restored, and the disturbed shades of Leonardo are transformed into Raphael's noble, confident humanity.

By his contract with the monks of San Donato a Scopeto, dated March 1481, Leonardo undertook to finish the altar-piece in twenty-four or at most thirty months. During July and August he was paid regularly, but after 28 September there is no further payment, and we can infer that the picture had reached its present stage. The Uffizi 'Adoration' is the work of seven months: a fact which forces us to reflect on the significance of the word finish. No doubt the picture is unfinished; parts of it are lost in darkness – many of the heads and hands have no bodies; and parts are merely sketched on the ground, so that they seem to be dissolved in light (Pl. 27). The central figure of the Virgin and Child is little more than a large drawing. Moreover, the whole clarity of the composition depends on leaving the Virgin and chief magi blank against the circle of dark figures; and an academic critic might say that Leonardo has made the common mistake of young painters who attempt large compositions: he has made the greater part of it too dark. All this would be relevant if the creation of works of art were a sort of obstacle race, in which that painter won who overcame the greatest number of difficulties. But finish is only of value when it is a true medium of expression. To have carried the 'Adoration' any further without depriving it of magic would have taxed even Leonardo's genius, and would have taken him seven years instead of seven months. For one thing the composition is immensely ambitious. The

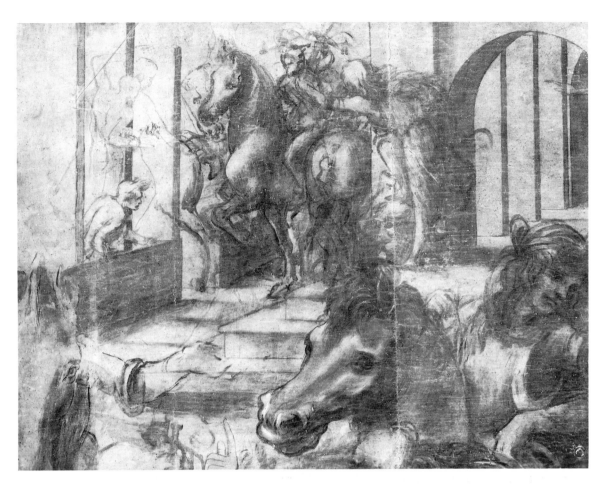

27. Detail from the 'Adoration of the Kings', 1481–2. Uffizi, Florence

precepts of classical art had warned the painter above all things to avoid representing a crowd; but the figures in the 'Adoration' are innumerable – as we begin to count them they vanish and reappear, like fish in a muddy pool.[3] To have brought every one of them to the conventional degree of finish, without destroying the unity of the whole, would have required years of labour and mature skill. Moreover, the whole subject is conceived in a spirit opposed to clear statement. It is an allegory, with an allegory's equivocations; a dream, with the dissolving protagonists of a dream. The Virgin and Child, Joseph and the chief magi, these are clear enough, and capable of further elaboration. But in that circle of adorers, peering, swaying, gesticulating, are

3. Dr Jens Thiis, whose *Florentine Years of Leonardo da Vinci* (London, 1914) contains the fullest analysis of the Uffizi 'Adoration', thinks he has counted sixty-six figures and eleven animals, more, that is to say, than in Raphael's 'School of Athens'. The model for such crowded, but controlled, compositions was Ghiberti's relief of Solomon and Sheba on the second doors of the Florentine Baptistery, which undoubtedly influenced Leonardo's 'Adoration'.

many of those half-formed thoughts which must remain inarticulate unless they are expressed by a hint or a cadence. Nowhere else in Italian art, unless perhaps in the *Tempesta* of Giorgione, are intuitions so remote and so fragile given visible shape. Could they have survived the Florentine ideal of finish?

Such thoughts must occur to a modern critic, for Tintoretto, El Greco, Degas, and Cézanne have shown him how the greatest artists can achieve a complete and coherent style with a degree of definition no greater than that of Leonardo's 'Adoration'. But to Leonardo and his contemporaries these reflections would have seemed ridiculous or incredible; and in fact a great part of his *Trattato della Pittura* is concerned with how to bring a work in the state of the 'Adoration' to the state of the 'Last Supper'. For although the finest passages in the *Trattato* are those in which Leonardo describes the springs of the painter's genius, a far larger part is concerned with the science of representation, and with that thorough knowledge of natural appearances without which the painter cannot assume his godlike role of recreating the visible world. A rendering of nature complete and learned enough to satisfy his interest in its function seemed to involve the idea of finish, and his own preternatural sharpness of eye tempted him in the same direction. Photography, reacting on the aesthetic theories of the last century, has led us to believe that he was mistaken; that all the knowledge of anatomy, botany, and geology with which he enriched his art could have been suggested rather than described, and could have found more vivid expression in a few spontaneous hints than in an accumulation of careful statements.

We may be fairly certain that the reason why the monks of San Donato stopped payment for the 'Adoration' is that Leonardo had gone to Milan. Apparently they continued to hope that he would return and finish it, because it was fifteen years before they called in Filippino to paint another picture – the 'Adoration', now also in the Uffizi – to take its place.[4] We have no evidence of the exact date when Leonardo went to Milan, but the Anonimo Gaddiano says that he went in his thirtieth year – that is in 1482 – and this is confirmed by the fact that his first documented commission there dates from 1483. Why did he go there? The Anonimo says, and Vasari repeats, that he was sent by Lorenzo the Magnificent to present the Duke Ludovico il Moro with a silver lyre in the form of a horse's head, on which he was an exquisite performer. Since we can no longer hear the music that Leonardo produced from the lyre, we are inclined to assume that it was less important than his drawings and pictures, but to his contemporaries it may have seemed the reverse. Socially a young virtuoso musician is sure of a more enthusiastic welcome than a talented painter, and it is easy to understand why Ludovico received Leonardo as a musician rather than as a painter. Nor is there

4. No. 1566, dated 1496.

anything surprising in the fact that Lorenzo de' Medici allowed him to leave
Florence, for, although an enlightened patron of literature, Lorenzo took
small interest in art, and cannot be given credit for commissioning any of the
great paintings in his day. It is, perhaps, surprising that later, when Leonardo's
real greatness was established, Lorenzo made no effort to bring him back to
Florence. And this, I think, can only be due to the lack of sympathy which
existed between Leonardo and the Medicean circle. He was essentially a
scientist and mathematician; the Mediceans were of course Platonists of an
almost religious ardour. *Non mi legga chi non e matematico.* These words
of Leonardo's are rightly placed on the first page of Richter's anthology.
*Mathematicae non sunt verae scientiae.* This is the first of Pico della Miran-
dola's famous theses, approved by the Florentine Platonists. Beside this
Platonism, and developing out of its mystic tendencies, were the doctrines of
Savonarola with which Leonardo was equally out of sympathy – which were
in fact the object of his expressed contempt.[5] By contrast, Milan was
predominantly Aristotelian, which at this date still meant encyclopedic. At
the court of Ludovico there were ingenious men in plenty, doctors, scientists,
tacticians, mathematicians, military engineers, men of fact and experience,
who could feed Leonardo's insatiable craving for information. It is understandable, therefore, that as Leonardo's scientific bias grew with his development as a painter, Lorenzo felt no inclination to recall him, nor Leonardo to
return; and unless he could be sure of employment by the Medici there were
many reasons why a young artist should be anxious to leave Florence.
Competition was very severe, and conditions of life were continually being
made difficult by war, plague, and taxation which prevented the public bodies,
who were the chief patrons, from fulfilling their contracts. In fact, most
Florentine artists preferred working for kings or popes, and left Florence as
soon as they had a chance of doing so. For Leonardo, the luxurious and
elaborate life of the Sforza court must have had a particular attraction. We
know from all accounts that he was an exquisite, careful in dress, reserved
and mysterious in manner. Such a character did not fit him for the Forum
life of Florence, with its open workshops, hard sarcastic criticism, and those
terrible practical jokes which figure so largely in contemporary lives of the
Florentine artists[6]. Moreover, Ludovico Sforza was an admirable patron.
The fact that his patronage lacked the literary element which distinguished
Medicean circles, made him more sympathetic to Leonardo, who could hardly
have been persuaded to paint the graceful allegories of Politian. The variety
of the work which, as a man of ingenuity about the court, he was called upon

5. Cf. *Trattato della Pittura* di Leonardo da Vinci, ed. Borzelli (Naples, 1914), para. 74.
6. Cf. A. Manetti's *The Life of Brunelleschi*, ed. H. Saalman, trans. C. Engass (London and Pennsylvania,
1970).

to perform – the founding of cannon, the supervision of pageants, the installation of central heating – appealed to his curiosity and his love of technical experiment. For all these reasons it is easy to understand why he never attempted to leave Milan until the fall of Ludovico Sforza compelled him to do so. Yet we may regret a prosperity which kept him so long absent from the bracing air of his native country. Even Donatello admitted that his spirit began to rust when away from the keen, critical atmosphere of Florence; and the court life of Milan may have brought out a certain effeminacy sometimes perceptible in Leonardo's art and wholly destructive of the work of his disciples.

The ostensible reason why Leonardo remained in Milan is to be found in a letter of self-recommendation to Ludovico which has come down to us in the *Codice Atlantico*.[7] It is not in Leonardo's own handwriting, but most scholars are persuaded that it is genuine. Leonardo recommends himself almost entirely as a military engineer. 'Most illustrious Lord,' he says, 'having now fully studied the work of all those who claim to be masters and artificers of instruments of war ... I will lay before your Lordship my secret inventions, and then offer to carry them into execution at your pleasure.'

He then proceeds to detail under nine headings the different instruments of war which he is prepared to construct: 'An extremely light and strong bridge. An endless variety of battering rams. A method of demolishing fortresses built on a rock. A kind of bombard, which hurls showers of small stones and the smoke of which strikes terror into the enemy. A secret winding passage constructed without noise. Covered wagons, behind which whole armies can hide and advance.' Under a tenth heading he says:

In time of peace, I believe myself able to vie successfully with any in the designing of public and private buildings, and in conducting water from one place to another. Item: I can carry out sculpture in marble, bronze, or clay, and also in painting I can do as well as any man. Again, I can undertake to work on the bronze horse, which will be a monument ... to the eternal honour of the Prince your father, and the illustrious house of Sforza.

The fact that Leonardo only speaks of himself as an artist in six lines out of thirty-four is so much at variance with the opinion of posterity as to seem like a piece of elaborate irony. We may be sure that it was not so intended. In the Renaissance war was the most vitally important of all the arts, and demanded the services of the most skilful artists. Giotto had designed the fortifications of Florence early in the fourteenth century. Michelangelo was to re-design them during the siege of 1529. Of such warlike arts the casting

7. For an account of the *Codice Atlantico*, see p. 109.

of cannon needed skill and experience in the handling of material found only in the most accomplished craftsmen. It was natural that Verrocchio should have been so employed by Lorenzo de' Medici; and natural that his pupil, with an especial love of ingenious design, should have begun early to draw guns and ballistas. About twenty-five sheets of such drawings in the *Codice Atlantico* seem to have been done in Florence: in a slightly later style there are over forty, and since they represent all the military devices mentioned in his letter to Ludovico we can see that Leonardo's offer of help was serious (Pl. 28).

During five years Leonardo's war machines improved. Those done in Florence are in the dry, diagrammatic style of other fifteenth-century engineering drawings, such as those by Francesco di Giorgio, and display the same rather primitive notion of cause and effect (Pl. 29). Later the drawings become much more ambitious and so elaborate that it seems doubtful if they could ever have been constructed. In particular a series of gigantic catapults and crossbows (P. 302) seem to be beyond the technical skill of the period. It would be interesting to know if Leonardo's war machines added to the efficacy of the Milanese forces; but that is no part of my present subject.

*28. Study for Guns and Machines of War, c. 1485. Royal Library, Windsor (RL 12652r)*

*29. Study for a device for repelling scaling ladders, c. 1475–80. Ambrosiana, Milan*

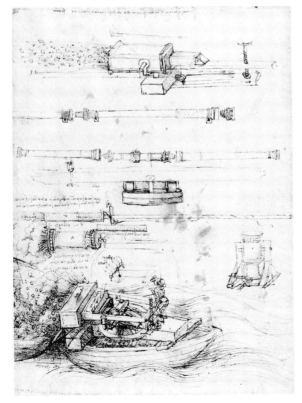

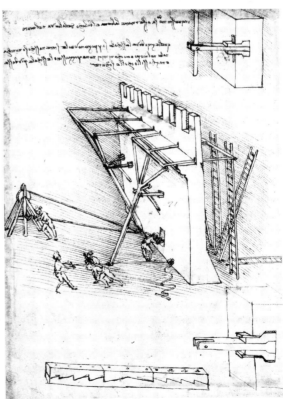

Of Leonardo's activities as an artist during his first years in Milan, we have interesting evidence in a list of his pictures, drawings, and sculpture, written in his own hand, and certainly dating from this period, which is to be found on a sheet in the *Codice Atlantico*. From the number of markedly Florentine subjects it contains, it may even be the list of the work taken with him from Florence to Milan: though it includes *una testa del duca* – presumably Ludovico. This list is so important for the study of Leonardo's painting that I shall make no excuse for analysing it at some length.[8]

First the list shows a predominant interest in the human figure. Among the sketches are measurements of a finger, many nudes, many studies of arms, legs, feet, and poses; among the subjects are those beloved of the Florentine anatomical painters such as Castagno and Pollaiuolo – eight St Sebastians, and certain St Jeromes. Of the eight St Sebastians there remains only a hint in two slight drawings.[9] Of the St Jeromes there exists the unfinished monochrome in the Vatican, which on grounds of style alone should be placed in this period. Both in pose and treatment it is close to the Uffizi 'Adoration' and, like the 'Adoration', it may have been unfinished when Leonardo left Florence. If so, the entry on the list may refer to studies for this picture.

The Vatican 'St Jerome' is one of the few works by Leonardo whose authenticity has never been questioned (Pl. 30). But the original makes less impression than it should. This is probably due to the fact that it has been badly damaged. The two halves of the panel are said to have been discovered

---

8. head, full face, of a young man with a fine head of hair
   many flowers, drawn from nature
   a head, full face, with curly hair
   certain figures of St Jerome
   the measurements of a figure
   drawings of furnaces
   a head of the Duke
   many drawings of knots
   four drawings for the painting of the holy angel
   a small composition of Girolamo da Fegline
   a head of Christ done with a pen
   eight Sebastians
   many compositions of angles (or angels!)
   a chalcedony
   a head in profile with fine hair
   some barrels (or jars) in perspective
   some machines for ships
   some machines for water
   a portrait head of Atalanta raising her face
   the head of Geronimo da Fegline
   the head of Gian Francesco Boso
   many throats of old women
   many heads of old men
   many complete nude figures
   many arms, legs, feet, and poses
   a madonna finished
   another almost, which is in profile
   the head of Our Lady ascending into heaven
   the head of an old man with a very long neck
   a head of a gipsy
   a head with a hat on
   a scene of the Passion made in relief
   a head of a girl with knotted hair
   a head with hair elaborately coiled

9. A silverpoint in the Bonnat Collection and a pen and ink drawing at Hamburg (P. 213b). Both seem to be of about the date on the list. A picture of St Sebastian by Marco d'Oggiono in the Ehemals Staatliche Museen, Berlin, evidently derives from a Leonardo drawing similar to the Hamburg sketch.

by Cardinal Fesch in two different places, and one was being used as a table-top. As a result the nervous drawing has been overlaid with retouchings, and some of Leonardo's magic has evaporated; but we are still able to appreciate the composition as a whole, dominated by the grandiose gesture of the Saint. Both as an embodiment of passion and as what Roger Fry would have called a plastic sequence, this figure is a great invention. It stands midway between

*30. 'St Jerome', c. 1483. Vatican Gallery*

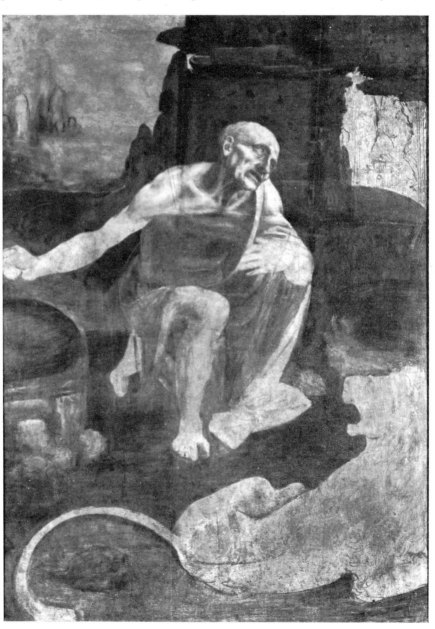

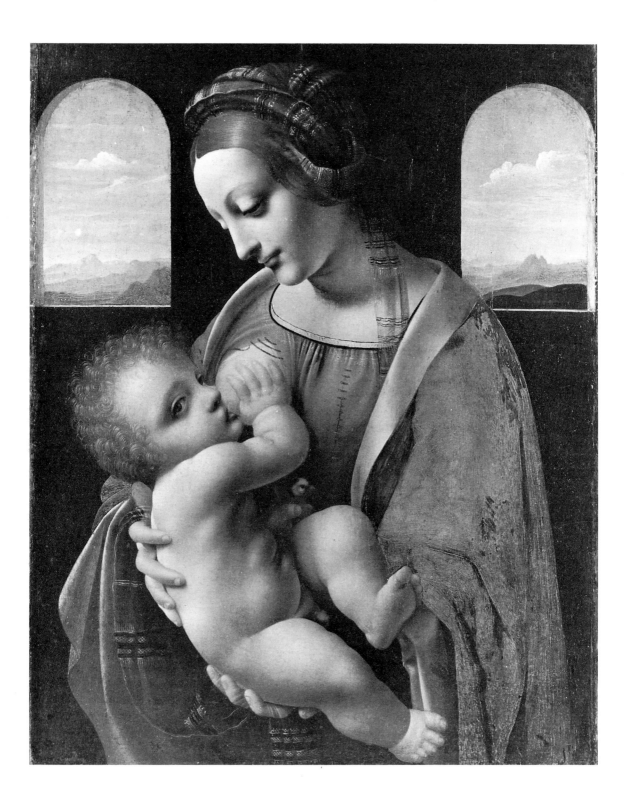

31. Leonardo(?), 'Madonna Litta', c. 1480–1. Hermitage, Leningrad

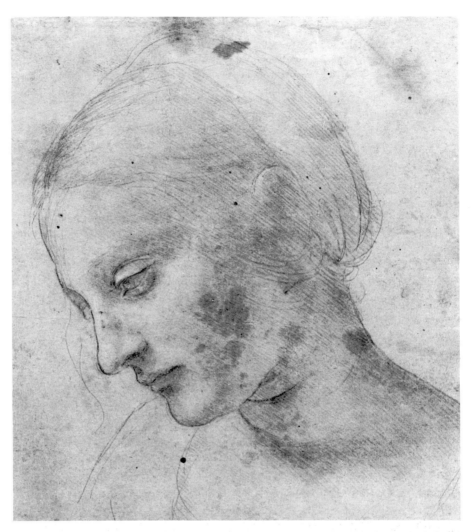

32. Study for the 'Madonna Litta', c. 1480. Louvre, Paris

Signorelli and Michelangelo, recalling the former in the sharply defined planes of the torso, the latter in the rhythmic continuity of the pose. The concentration on a single theme is unusual for Leonardo. More characteristic are the accessories of the composition, the snarling lion, the landscape, and the dark cave foreshadowing the 'Virgin of the Rocks'.

Finally, we reach the two consecutive items, *una nosstra donna finjta; un altra quasi che n proffilo*, 'our lady finished; another almost, who is in profile'. Of the first picture we know nothing, but the second I have always believed to be the 'Madonna Litta' in the Hermitage (Pl. 31).[10] It is the only one of Leonardo's Virgins which could be called 'in profile', and we know from

10. See K. Clark, 'The Madonna in Profile' in the *Burlington Magazine*, XII, 1933, pp. 136–40.

drawings that the design must date from about 1480. Unfortunately, the 'Madonna Litta' has been totally repainted at least twice, once when it was finished by a Milanese artist about 1495, and once in the nineteenth century, when it was transferred from panel to canvas. It now looks like an oleograph. But even in this ruined condition it has qualities which are not found in shop work. The Virgin's head is still close to Leonardo's exquisite drawing in the Louvre (Pl. 32), and the Child's body is based on one of the studies of babies at Windsor (P. 21). The Child's head, on the other hand, is quite unlike Leonardo, and cannot even have been designed by him. And of this we have proof in a drawing for the head which is certainly not by Leonardo,[11] but is perhaps an early work of Boltraffio. We can therefore give some meaning to the expression *quasi finita*. The pose, the Virgin's head, and part of the Child's body were finished; the Child's head, details of costume and landscape were left at a stage which we can deduce from the Uffizi 'Adoration'.

I have left till now the masterpiece of Leonardo's early period, the 'Virgin of the Rocks' in the Louvre (Pl. 33). My reason for doing so is that hitherto the majority of scholars have assumed that this was the picture commissioned by the Confraternity of the Immaculate Conception on 24 April 1483; and in the first edition of this book I did not question this assumption. I am now convinced that I was mistaken.[12] The picture commissioned in 1483 is the version of the 'Virgin of the Rocks' now in the National Gallery, London (Pl. 86). We know that this was bought from the Confraternity, and had the picture been painted twice for the Confraternity, this fact would certainly have been referred to in the various legal documents in which Leonardo and the brothers Preda made claims against them for increased payment. The last of the documents, the settlement of 1506, implies that the picture originally commissioned was still unfinished and gives Leonardo two years in which to complete it. Now the Louvre 'Virgin of the Rocks' is perfectly finished in Leonardo's early style, whereas the 'Virgin of the Rocks' in the National Gallery is in Leonardo's later style, and parts of it are still no more than underpainting. It is therefore impossible to maintain, as I did in my earlier edition, that the later version was substituted for the earlier after 1506. Although there are no documents referring to the Louvre picture, we may assume that it was painted in Florence, and we may guess that Leonardo brought it with him to Milan as a specimen of his skill.

Even when I believed that it was the picture of the commission, I recognized that the Louvre 'Virgin of the Rocks' belongs essentially to Leonardo's first

*33. The 'Virgin of the Rocks', 1482–3. Louvre, Paris*

---

11. Lugt Collection, Paris. It is by the same hand as the Child in the Poldi Pezzoli 'Madonna', usually ascribed to Boltraffio.

12. I owe this change to Mr Martin Davies, whose thorough and inflexible examination of the documents is contained in a publication of the London 'Virgin of the Rocks', published by the National Gallery (1947). (Ed. note: Davies himself later revised his 1947 opinion, and reverted to a substitution theory.)

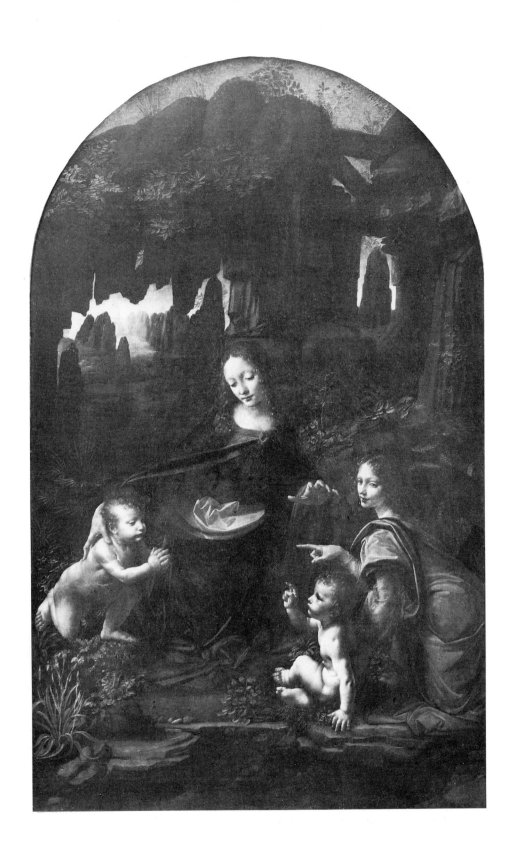

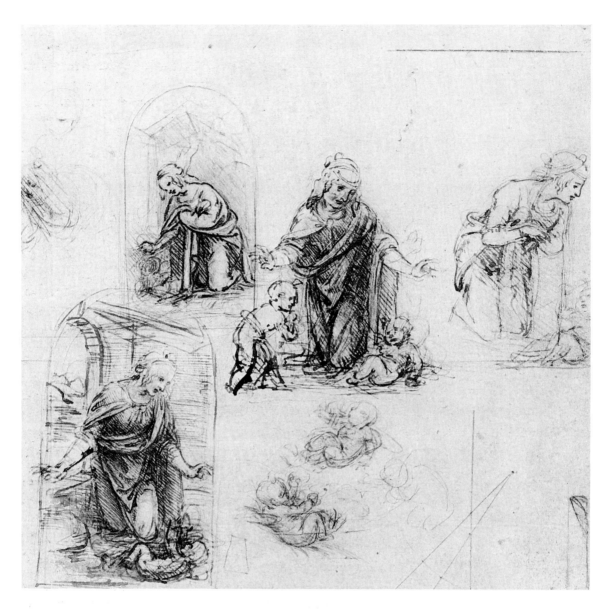

34. *Studies for the
'Virgin and Holy
Children', 1492–3.
Metropolitan
Museum of Art, New
York*

Florentine period. By its twilit tones and delicate naturalism it is connected with the sequence which began with the Uffizi 'Annunciation'. In conception, too, it sums up a series of projects and experiments which go back to the period of the early 'Adoration'. The motif of the Virgin kneeling before the holy children can be traced back to the drawings in the Bonnat Collection and the Venice Academy. But in them she is surrounded by adoring shepherds, and above her head is a ring of flying angels. A few years later Leonardo returned to the subject of the kneeling Virgin and children, this time without shepherds and angels. A drawing in the Metropolitan Museum shows him searching for a motif which would give unity to the group, and finding it in the protective gesture of the Virgin, who spreads her arms above the children like the Madonna della Misericordia of traditional iconography (Pl. 34). This sheet is often considered as preparatory to the 'Virgin of the Rocks', but before arriving at the final composition, Leonardo took one of the groups – that in the bottom left-hand corner – and made it into a separate picture known in several replicas, the best of which, in the Ashmolean Museum, Oxford, must give a clear idea of Leonardo's original. The Virgin kneels with hands outstretched over the two children who are playing around her; the infant John grasps his lamb, while the infant Jesus peeps at him from behind the sleeve of his mother's mantle. It is an *allegro grazioso* preluding the *adagio* of the 'Virgin of the Rocks'; for the later picture is conceived in a mood of great solemnity. The children no longer play as equals. St John kneels in adoration, shielded by the Virgin's cloak, for he typifies the human race in need of protection. Apart from him, and in front of the Virgin, sits the infant Christ, supported by divine inspiration in the form of an angel. His pre-eminence is marked by the two hands which are poised above his head like nimbs, giving him the isolation of a vertical in the pyramid of the whole composition. He blesses mankind. The angel who, by his glance, invites us to take a part in these mysteries, is himself the most mysterious figure. Why does he point so emphatically at the St John? Towards whom are his eyes directed? We only know that in the more formal London version, where hand and outward gaze are omitted, the picture loses some of its magic. Like deep notes in the accompaniment of a serious theme the rocks of the background sustain the composition, and give it the resonance of a cathedral. Aesthetically their meaning is clear. Have they a further significance? Was Leonardo thinking of some legend of the apocryphal gospels in which the Holy Family during the flight into Egypt seek refuge in a cave and are visited by the youthful Baptist? Behind most of the curious subjects in Renaissance art lie myths and symbols long since forgotten; but in the enthusiasm of discovery their importance can be overrated. Viewed more closely in the creative process, pictorial symbolism can be a pretext rather than an end in itself, and so the rocks, whatever their apocryphal justification, may have originated in the memory of a childhood expedition to the caves of Monte Ceceri.[13]

The 'Virgin of the Rocks' is Leonardo's last *quattrocento* picture and still shows the graces of that enchanted interval. Mastery of execution has not overlaid the freshness of the types. The balance between natural and ideal beauty is perfectly held: indeed the process of idealization has given an added life, as can be seen by comparing the angel's head with the silverpoint study for it at Turin (Pl. 35). The drawing – one of the most beautiful, I dare say, in the world – aims at the fullest plastic statement. The painting is sweeter, lighter, more unearthly. This is still idealization in the gothic sense. The same is true of the Madonna's head, but here our standard of comparison must be the later version (Pl. 86), which, although perhaps not entirely executed by Leonardo, was certainly designed by him. In comparing the two heads, the delicate imaginative beauty of the first, the waxen chiaroscuro of the second, we cannot help feeling how far Leonardo's theories of painting led him away from our affections. A comparison of the two St Johns yields the same result. Only in the later angel's head do we feel that Leonardo, by sacrificing freshness to regularity, gained a new quality of classical completeness, though, to our eye, the gain is not worth the sacrifice.

Complementary to this gothic idealization is the exquisite naturalism of the details (Pl. 36). Hands and feet and hair are observed with a curiosity hardly to be found elsewhere in painting. Leonardo has mastered their structure, but his real delight is in their surfaces, in the delicate skin stretched taut or relaxed into tucks and dimples, with a play of line and light beyond ordinary observation. Similarly, flowers and grasses are depicted with a gothic understanding of their individual character. They recall the finest carved capitals of the thirteenth century. The Flemish painters, who loved to scatter flowers over their foregrounds, never gave this feeling of growth and inner life, and Leonardo's pupils, who imitated his profusion of plants, could not make them coherent parts of the whole design.

Although the imagery and, to some extent, the details of the 'Virgin of the Rocks' are still perceptible, we must always remember how much of Leonardo's intention is obscured. We can form no real conception of the colour, the values, or the general tone of the original, buried as it is under layer upon layer of thick yellow varnish.[14] In the darks some mixture of bitumen has made the surface cake and crack like mud, and there are innumerable patches

13. Rocks of this kind occur in the 'Nativity' by Fra Filippo Lippi in the Ehemals Staatliche Museen, Berlin, which also includes the youthful Baptist, and in other pictures of the fifteenth century. They seem to have been the accepted iconographical symbol for a wilderness.

14. The picture has been transferred from panel to canvas and therefore cannot be cleaned without exposing much damage. The disfigurements are less obvious in photographs, partly because the camera penetrates varnish, and partly, it must be remembered, because the photographs from which it is known have generally been retouched.

35. *Study for the Angel's Head in the 'Virgin of the Rocks', 1483. Royal Library, Turin*

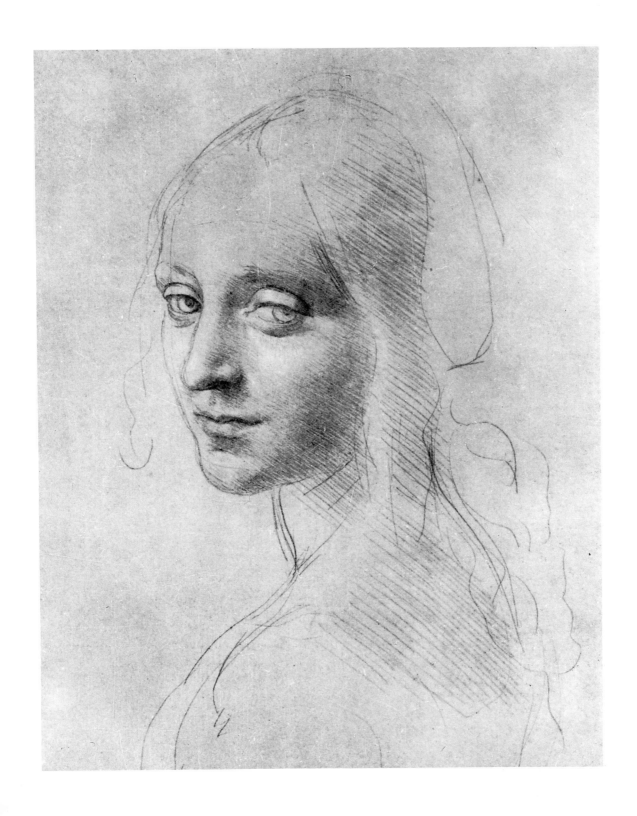

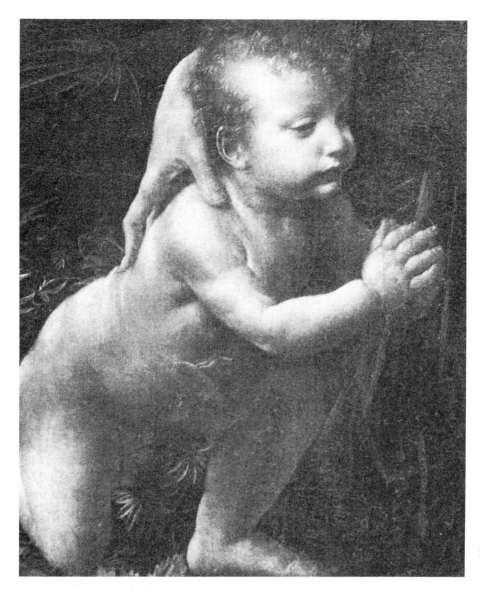

*36. St John from the
'Virgin of the Rocks',
1482–3. Louvre, Paris*

of old repaint all over the picture. All this must be borne in mind before we say that at this date Leonardo was a dark painter and an uninteresting colourist. Even from its present condition we can see that the 'Virgin of the Rocks' was once remarkably luminous, with a subtle feeling for reflected light; and it is this luminosity which distinguishes Leonardo from his Milanese followers.

Such, then, was the picture which Leonardo took to Milan as a proof that he had mastered or surpassed the traditional skill of Fra Filippo Lippi,

Verrocchio, and other Florentine masters of devotional painting. Soon after he arrived he was introduced to the Confraternity of the Immaculate Conception, who were looking for a painter to fill the central part of an elaborate carved frame left on their hands by the sculptor del Maino. He may have owed the introduction to two local painters, the brothers Evangelista and Ambrogio Preda (now generally known as da Predis), since their names appear with his in the commission, and Ambrogio continued to take a leading part in the subsequent disputes. They were unskilful artists, and Leonardo can have been associated with them only because of their workshop connections. As things turned out they also proved to be unbusinesslike.

The subject of the picture which they asked him to paint is stated in the contract: 'Our Lady and her Son with the angels, done in oil with the utmost care; and with these two prophets'. In fact, Leonardo chose to make another version of his 'Virgin of the Rocks' (Pl. 86). Since, in subsequent documents, the Confraternity never mention this change of subject, it is possible that Leonardo showed them his Florentine masterpiece and persuaded them to accept a replica of it. He may have thought the sum offered too small to justify the labour of a fresh composition, and perhaps hoped that his patrons would be satisfied with a copy largely executed by Ambrogio da Predis. But the Confraternity were determined to have a work from his own hand, and for this reason the central panel was left unfinished for twenty-three years. During that time Predis and Leonardo made two appeals for additional payment: one by Predis alone dated 1503, and one by the partners jointly. They pointed to the small sums paid to them in comparison with that expended on the frame and estimated their work at 1,200 lire, of which 400 was to go towards Leonardo's picture, instead of the 100 originally promised him. Their appeals were evidently dismissed, and in fact they seem to have been slightly disingenuous: for example they do not allude to the fact that Leonardo's picture was unfinished. Yet it may have been no more than a grisaille sketch, for when the final settlement was reached in 1506 he was given two years in which to complete it. The frame, whose costly splendours were the cause of Predis's petition, has long since disappeared, and of his part nothing survives except the left-hand angel which came, with Leonardo's central panel, to the National Gallery. It is in an old-fashioned Lombard technique, unmodified by Leonardo's influence save in the drawing of the draperies. The right-hand angel, also in the National Gallery, is by a different hand, perhaps by the pupil who assisted Leonardo with the central panel, and must have been painted considerably later.

Apart from the 'Virgin of the Rocks', Leonardo's time seems to have been entirely taken up with work for the court. We know from various contemporary references that he practically held the post of court limner, and painted portraits of two of Ludovico's mistresses, Cecilia Gallerani and

Lucrezia Crivelli. Several portraits dating from this period have survived with ancient ascriptions to Leonardo, but their authenticity has always been open to doubt, chiefly on account of a prosaic quality which the amateur is reluctant to associate with him. Leonardo's drawings show that he could be prosaic, or rather objective, if occasion demanded, and these portraits need a liberal and patient examination.

Most modern critics believe that the picture at Cracow, of a 'Lady with an Ermine', represents Cecilia Gallerani, and is Leonardo's original (Pl. 37). This picture was celebrated in a sonnet by the court poet Bellincioni (who died in 1492), in which he describes the sitter as seeming to listen and not to speak. It is also referred to in a letter from Cecilia Gallerani to Isabella d'Este written on 29 April 1498. Isabella had asked her to send her portrait by Leonardo; but Cecilia Gallerani replies that she would rather not do so as it no longer resembles her, not through any shortcoming in the master but because it was done when she was still immature and her appearance had since changed completely. Cecilia became Ludovico's mistress in 1481, and to judge from her letter to Isabella d'Este the portrait must have been painted soon afterwards. All this evidence fits in very well with the picture at Cracow. Knowing how Renaissance women contrived to look middle-aged before they were twenty, we may say that the sitter can have been no more than a girl. Her attentive expression is exactly that described by Bellincioni, and the beast which she holds on her arm is doubly symbolical of her identity: first, because the ermine was frequently used as Ludovico's emblem, and secondly, because its Greek name γαλέη or γαλη had a punning reference to her own name. Finally, the Cracow picture must date from the first years after Leonardo's arrival in Milan. Those parts which are well preserved are still in the clear colours of the Florentine *quattrocento* tradition. Parts of the picture are in bad condition. The whole background is new and the left side of the figure has been repainted. But certain parts are intact – the ermine, the lady's face, and her hand, all but the tips of the two lower fingers. These parts alone are sufficient evidence that the picture is by Leonardo. The face has lost a little subtlety through the repainted background sharpening the original outline, but the drawings of the eyes and nose still have the beautiful simplification which we find in the early silverpoint drawings. Although the outline of the shoulder has been hardened, we can still recognize Leonardo's sense of form, which we find again, twenty years later, in a red chalk drawing for the 'Madonna with the Yarn Winder' (Pl. 65). The hand shows an understanding of anatomical structure and a power of particularization none of Leonardo's pupils possessed. But most convincing of all is the beast. The modelling of its head is a miracle; we can feel the structure of the skull, the quality of skin, the lie of the fur. No one but Leonardo could have conveyed its stoatish character, sleek, predatory, alert, yet with a kind of heraldic dignity. The

*37. 'Portrait of Cecilia Gallerani', c. 1483–8, Czartoryski Gallery, Cracow*

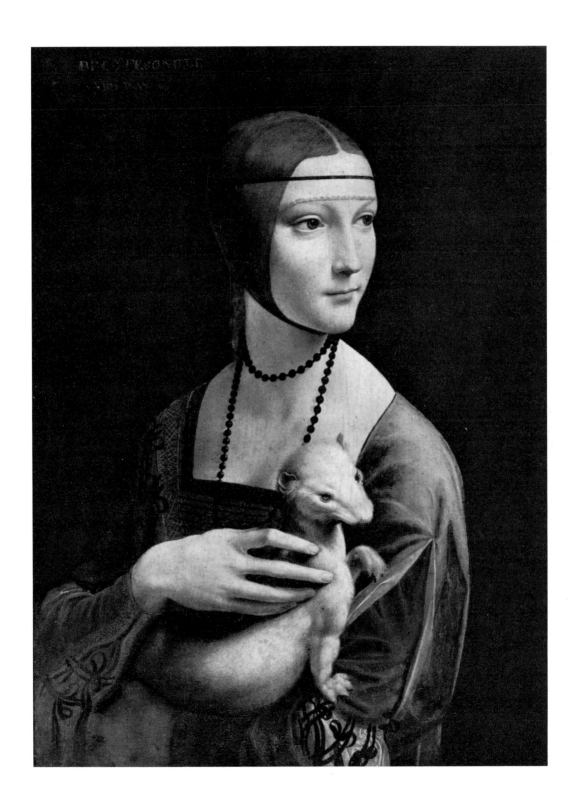

serpentine pose of the ermine gives, in epigrammatic form, the motif of the whole composition and it is this movement, quite apart from the details, which distinguishes it from the other portraits of this date attributed to Leonardo, such as the 'Belle Ferronnière' in the Louvre.

One other portrait of this date seems to me to be by Leonardo's own hand alone and unaided: the 'Portrait of a Musician' in the Ambrosiana (Pl. 38). The modelling of the head (the body is unfinished) is very similar to that of the angel in the 'Virgin of the Rocks', and even closer to the preparatory

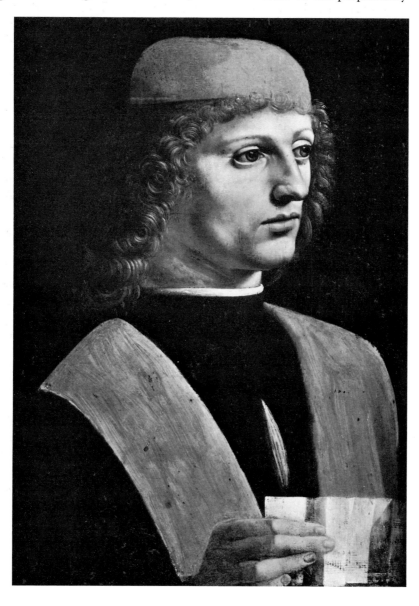

*38. 'Portrait of a Musician', c. 1485, Ambrosiana, Milan*

drawing for the angel at Turin, which was done direct from nature. It must date from about 1485–90. Comparison with other Leonardesque portraits of men, such as that in the Brera inscribed *Vita si scias uti longa est*, is perhaps misleading, since they reflect his later manner in a cold chiaroscuro; but even allowing for a difference of date, their waxen pallor must be due to pupils, the subtle luminous modelling of the 'Musician' to Leonardo himself. The delicate observation of light, as it passes across the convex forms, should be considered with drawings of the same date, studies of horses for the Sforza monument, or skulls in the Anatomical MS. B. They remind us how far Leonardo's naturalism had developed before he chose to abandon it. This portrait has the further distinction that it is perhaps the best preserved of Leonardo's paintings. We are thus able to learn something of his actual use of pigment, elsewhere obscured by dirty varnish, and we see that it was less smooth and 'licked' than that of his followers.[15]

We now come to two famous portraits which are generally considered the work of pupils. They belong to a period, about 1490, when we have the first records of two pupils with whose individual work we are acquainted, Giovanni Antonio Boltraffio and Marco d'Oggiono. Boltraffio was the most respectable of all Leonardo's immediate pupils and, although his documented work dates from a later period, his style is consistent enough for us to attribute to him two beautiful pictures of the Virgin and Child which must belong to the 1490s, one in Budapest, the other in the Poldi Pezzoli Museum, Milan. I believe that he was also responsible for some very fine heads in silverpoint, which are amongst the most popular works of the Milanese School; and in fact his silverpoint drawings are more than once mentioned in Leonardo's notes. It is reasonable to suppose that Leonardo, occupied in multifarious commissions for the Sforzas, allowed this promising youth to complete work from his designs, and that under his guidance the pupil achieved a delicacy absent from his later, independent work.

Some such hypothesis has been used to explain the authorship of the portrait in the Louvre, known as 'La Belle Ferronnière' (Pl. 39). This title, the nickname of one of Henry II's mistresses, is due solely to a confusion in an early inventory, and the sitter's identity has never been established. The portrait has been frequently claimed as the portrait of Lucrezia Crivelli, who in 1495 succeeded Cecilia Gallerani as the mistress of Ludovico il Moro. Leonardo undoubtedly painted a portrait of this lady which is recorded in three epigrams, and if the Louvre picture represents her (for which there is not the least evidence) it must be by his own hand. This has long been doubted. Mr Berenson expressed the feeling of all students of Leonardo towards this picture when he noted in the 1907 edition of his *North Italian*

---

15. It is worth noting that Antonello da Messina was court painter in Milan in 1475, and Leonardo must have studied his portraits carefully.

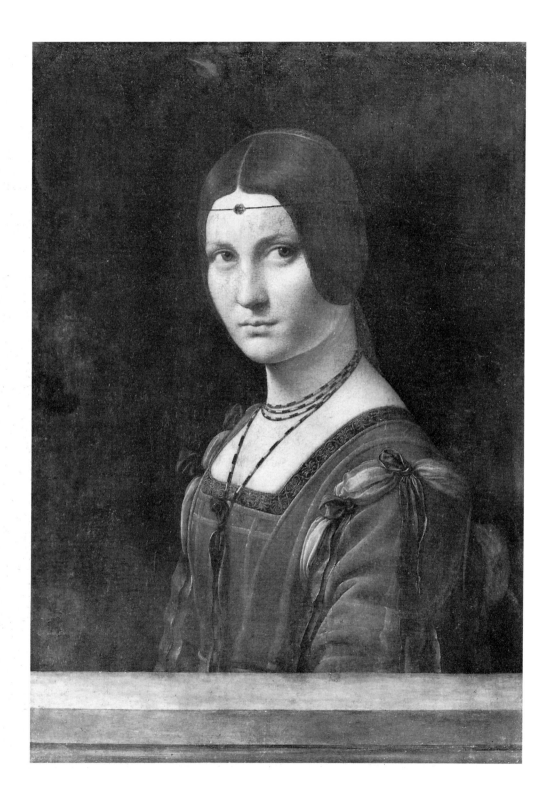

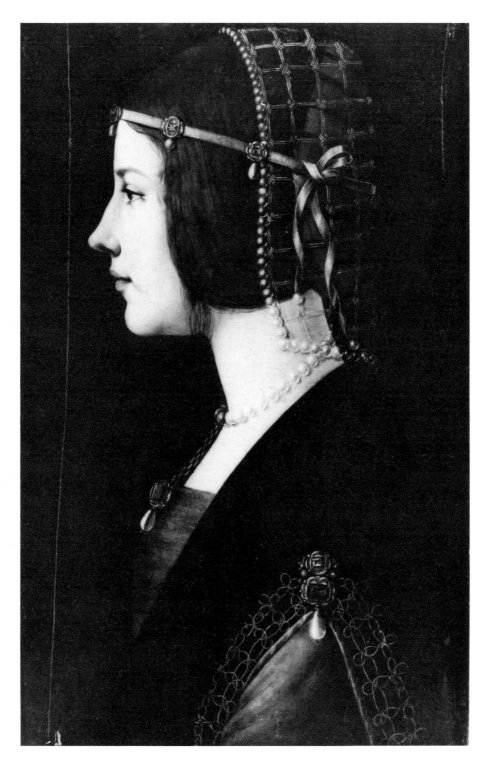

39. 'Portrait of a
Lady' ('La Belle
Ferronnière'), c. 1495.
Louvre, Paris

40. Ambrogio da
Predis?, 'Portrait of a
Lady in Profile', c.
1495–1500.
Ambrosiana, Milan

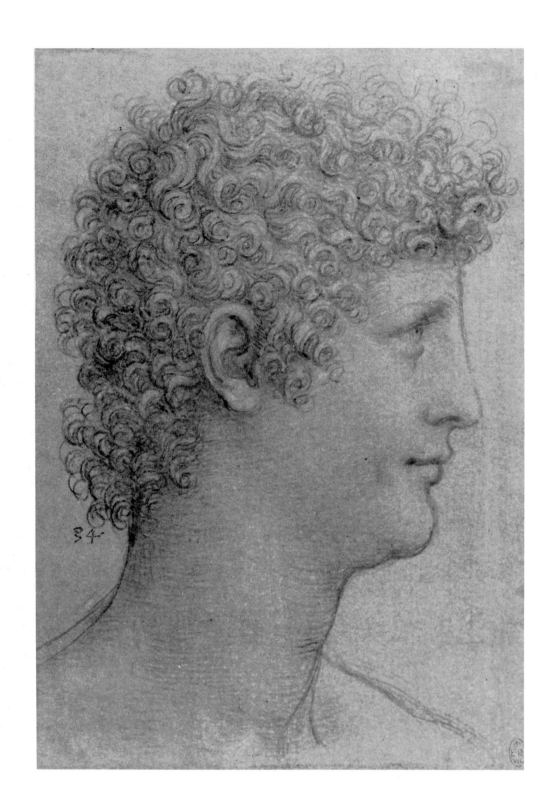

41. *Presumed 'Portrait of Salai', c. 1504. Royal Library, Windsor (RL 12554)*

*Painters* 'one would regret to have to accept this as Leonardo's own work'.[16] Could Leonardo have been content with such a commonplace pose? Not only is the relationship of head and shoulders uninteresting, but the head itself is turned to the light in such a way as to deprive it of half its plastic possibilities. Compared to the Turin drawing of an angel's head, it looks almost as tame as a Costa. An obvious defect is the insensitive drawing of the snood and necklaces, which do nothing to indicate the modelling; but it must be remembered that there was a strong tradition in Milanese portraiture by which dress and jewellery were treated with an almost heraldic stiffness, and certain details of the Belle Ferronnière's costume, notably the ribbons on her shoulder, are remarkably close to Leonardo. The face, too, has great beauty of modelling, easily appreciated when the numerous copies of the Louvre picture are compared with the original, and photographic enlargements of her features show the extraordinary knowledge of structure with which they were drawn. No one who prefers truth to finality should be dogmatic about the 'Belle Ferronnière', but I am now inclined to think that the picture is by Leonardo, and shows how in these years he was willing to subdue his genius to the needs of the court.

The other portrait in question is the well-known profile of a lady in the Ambrosiana (Pl. 40). This is certainly not by Leonardo, and has been long attributed to Ambrogio da Predis, chiefly for the reason that the sitter is in profile. It is of a very much higher quality than the only certain works by Predis; yet the underlying character, stiff, cold, and thin, is connected with him through a series of other profiles which, at their worst, resemble his authentic work. If the lady in the Ambrosiana is by Predis, it must have been painted under the immediate inspiration of Leonardo, who may even have touched some of the details of the head-dress, pearls, and ribbons, painted with unusual skill. We thus have the curious situation that although the documents of the time imply that Predis's relation to Leonardo was that of a senior partner or even contractor, the evidence of style suggests that he was Leonardo's pupil. The dual relationship is not impossible. Predis had an established position before Leonardo came to Milan, and may have continued to be more acceptable to conservative patrons; but as Leonardo's superior accomplishments increased his favour at court, Predis may have decided to learn from him what he could. In this inspiring atmosphere he succeeded in painting the portrait of Bartolommeo Archinto in the National Gallery, London, which bears a monogram A M P R E and the date 1494, which, with the profile in the Ambrosiana, is his finest achievement. We must suppose that when Leonardo was no longer there to help him Predis's skill declined, so that in 1502 he could produce the feeble portrait of the Emperor Maximilian

16. In the 1932 edition, however, it appears as a Leonardo.

in the Vienna gallery which, out of pride in his sitter's greatness, he elected to sign.

Although some such hypothesis can be made to account for Ambrogio da Predis, the Milanese School during the years of Leonardo's residence remains completely mysterious. We should come nearer to understanding it if we could name the author of a famous picture in the Brera, the so-called Pala Sforzesca of 1495, in which Ludovico Sforza, his wife and children are presented to the Virgin and Child; for there we see the first repercussions of Leonardo's style on the old Lombard manner. But this picture, and practically all the portraits and drawings associated with it, are nameless. On the other hand there are records in Leonardo's notebooks of pupils whose names we cannot associate with a single picture. Only one of these pupils need be mentioned here, not because his work survived or ever had any merit, but because he played an important part in Leonardo's life. This was Giacomo Salai. Vasari tells us that 'while in Milan he took for his servant Salai, a Milanese, who was most comely in grace and beauty, having fair locks abundant and curly, in which Leonardo much delighted', and Leonardo himself has recorded in MS. C the precise date of this event.

Giacomo came to live with me on St Mary Magdalene's day [22 July] 1490, aged ten years. The second day I had two shirts cut out for him, a pair of hose, and a jerkin, and when I put aside some money to pay for these things he stole the money (4 lire) out of the purse; and I could never make him confess although I was quite certain of it. The day after I went to sup with Giacomo Andrea, and the said Giacomo supped for two and did mischief for four, for he broke three cruets and spilled the wine.

And then in the margin, *ladro, bugiardo, ostinato, ghiotto* – thief, liar, obstinate, glutton. There follow many other accounts of Salai's mis-demeanours: how he stole silverpoints from Boltraffio and Marco d'Oggiono, stole money from Messer Galleazzo's servants, sold a piece of Leonardo's leather to a cobbler and spent the money on sweets flavoured with anis. As he began, so he continued, stealing, stuffing, lying, so that Leonardo had difficulty in keeping him out of prison. From Leonardo's drawings we can see the effect of those activities on Salai's face. The pretty boy with curling ringlets grows fatter and coarser and more complacent (Pl. 41). In spite of all this, however, Leonardo never gave him up; on the contrary, he arranged a dowry for his sister, and mentioned him in his will.

These facts, and the character of the drawings of Salai, inevitably suggest that his relation with his master was of the kind honoured in classical times, and partly tolerated in the Renaissance, in spite of the censure of the Church. There is, in fact, concrete evidence that Leonardo's contemporaries believed him to be a homosexual. In 1476 complaints were twice laid before the magistracy in Florence that he and several young artists had been guilty of misdemeanours with a certain Jacopo Saltarelli, and, although the accusation does not seem to have been proved, it cannot be passed over as being no more than a malicious rumour.[17] To my mind the proof of Leonardo's homosexuality need not depend upon a rather sordid document. It is implicit in a large section of his work, and accounts for his androgynous types and a kind of lassitude of form which any sensitive observer can see and interpret for himself. It also accounts for facts which are otherwise hard to explain, his foppishness in dress combined with his remoteness and secrecy, and the almost total absence, in his voluminous writings, of any mention of a woman. Perhaps we may say that it explains the element of frustration which even those who are most conscious of his greatness are bound to admit. I would not press too far into a matter which is more the domain of the psychologist than the art critic, but I cannot omit it from an honest survey of Leonardo as an artist because it colours his outlook in a way that the same characteristic in other great men does not always do. We cannot look at Leonardo's work and seriously maintain that he had the normal man's feelings for women. And those who wish, in the interest of morality, to reduce Leonardo, that inexhaustible source of creative power, to a neutral or sexless agency, have a strange idea of doing service to his reputation.

17. The documents are accessible in Herbert Horne's *The Life of Leonardo da Vinci by Giorgio Vasari* (London, 1903), p. 12.

# CHAPTER THREE
# THE NOTEBOOKS

To the early years of Leonardo's residence in Milan belong the first of those notebooks and manuscripts which, for the remainder of his life, give us a full record of his activities, both practical and scientific. It is a curious fact that these records only begin when Leonardo was thirty, an age when the average busy man ceases to take notes; yet the few scraps surviving from the earlier period of his life do not suggest that he was then in the habit of recording his interests, or indeed, that his interests were very wide. They consist of some drawings of machinery and engines of war done in a simple diagrammatic style, with a primitive notion of dynamics, and show that in spite of his boasting letter to Ludovico, Leonardo's knowledge of military engineering was not in advance of his time. But as official artificer to the Sforza court he was expected to undertake a number of duties demanding technical skill – architecture, engineering, the conduct of masques and pageants. In order to increase and display his mastery of such work he began to keep notes of machinery and ingenious devices of all sorts, either seen or invented. Before Leonardo's time other Renaissance artists had set out the result of their inquiries into machinery, architecture, and fortification in the form of treatises: such, for example, is a manuscript in the Laurentian Library (cod. Ashb. 361) by Francesco di Giorgio, which actually belonged to Leonardo and is annotated in his handwriting. It contains plans of churches, drawings of weapons and machinery – everything, in fact, which we find in the early manuscripts of Leonardo, and although the style of drawing is more primitive the technical knowledge displayed is hardly inferior. Inspired by some such compilation as this, Leonardo began to arrange his notes with a view to a systematic treatise, and the result was the so-called MS. B in the Library of the Institut de France.

Before analysing these early notebooks as evidence of Leonardo's interests at this date, it may be convenient to give some account of his manuscripts as a whole. He seems to have kept nearly everything he wrote, and at the end of his life he bequeathed these writings to his disciple Francesco Melzi.[1] A great part has survived and forms a mass of material for the understanding of Leonardo's thought. The most important collection is the great scrapbook of notes and drawings in the Ambrosiana Library, known as the *Codice Atlantico*. It contains about four thousand sheets of various dates and sizes, dealing with every subject, all covered with Leonardo's minute writing, and was put together by the same hand as the collection of drawings now at Windsor Castle, probably by the sculptor, Leoni, who bought Leonardo's papers from Melzi's heirs. The compiler has made a half-hearted attempt at arrangement, but has done little more than classify certain drawings of machinery, and for all practical purposes the sheets are in no order. It is our greatest source of knowledge about Leonardo's movements, friends, pupils, reading, and mental habits.

Then come thirteen manuscripts in the Library of the Institut de France, which are referred to by the letters A to K inscribed on their covers. They are all of different dates and sizes, and most of them were used for a period of one or two years. Some are half-arranged treatises; others are quite small and may properly be called notebooks. The Library of the Institut also contains one of these pocketbooks dealing with the flight of birds, and three more of the same size are in the Victoria and Albert Museum, Forster Collection. There are other Leonardo manuscripts in the collection of Armand Hammer, in the Trivulzio Collection, and at Turin, and there is a very important manuscript in the British Museum which belonged to the Earl of Arundel, the original possessor of the drawings now at Windsor. Two-thirds of this manuscript dealing with dynamics were written consecutively at one date; a third is a collection of odd sheets like the *Codice Atlantico*.

This mass of material is the most exacting subject of study because of its complete lack of continuity. At any point, on any sheet, embedded in the most trivial discussion, there may be some important evidence of Leonardo's movements or opinions. The student of Leonardo is engaged in a vast jigsaw puzzle and, in spite of the labours of devoted scholars such as Müller-Walde, Calvi, and Solmi, much remains to be discovered. In particular, very little effort has been made to gauge how far Leonardo's knowledge increased and scientific method improved as his life went on. Some idea of Leonardo as a mind developing by contact with other minds is necessary if we are to form a true picture of him, and compare his scientific activity with his development as an artist. But to form this idea would require immense erudition, for not

1. See p. 230.

only would the student need to be familiar with all Leonardo's writings in their chronological order, but he would have to know enough about the state of learning in the Renaissance to judge Leonardo's progress in relation to that of his contemporaries. Lacking this equipment, I shall not attempt a critical study of the notebooks, but simply indicate their character.

I have said that Leonardo's earliest notebooks are chiefly concerned with technical matters, and that a number of entries are no more than a record of ingenious devices. But almost from the first, Leonardo's penetrating grasp of construction, combined with his restless curiosity, gave his notes on technical matters a more general value. He was not content to record how a thing worked; he wished to find out why. It is this curiosity which transformed a technician into a scientist. We can watch the process at work in the manuscripts. First, there are questions about the construction of certain machines, then, under the influence of Archimedes, questions about the first principles of dynamics; finally, questions which had never been asked before about winds, clouds, the age of the earth, generation, the human heart. Mere curiosity has become profound scientific research, independent of the technical interest which had preceded it. In this gradual change of attitude towards the objects of his curiosity Leonardo preserved an unusual capacity for self-education. He had received the ordinary training of a poor boy in Florence, practically confined to reading, writing, and that characteristically Florentine instrument of education, the abacus; and at an early age he was apprenticed to Verrocchio. Nothing in his education can have prepared him to wrestle with the crabbed and tortuous encyclopedias in which the scientific knowledge of antiquity was embalmed. Yet the notebooks give evidence of very wide reading. They are full of reminders to borrow or consult books, and research has shown how many passages, which used to be taken as original discoveries, are copied word for word from other authors. The turning-point in this process of self-education – we may almost say in Leonardo's life – was the period about the year 1494 in which he taught himself Latin. We have evidence of this process in two manuscripts, H and the Trivulzian, into which he has copied out almost the whole of a contemporary Latin Grammar by Niccolò Perotti, and a large part of a Latin Vocabulary by Luigi Pulci. At that date few of the scientific writings of the ancients were accessible in the vulgar tongue. In particular the works of Archimedes, which, as Séailles rightly pointed out, were the greatest single influence of Leonardo's thought, seem to have existed only in Latin translations. We can imagine how this new key to the mysteries of nature made Leonardo, as contemporaries describe, *impacientissimo del penello*, out of all patience with his brush.

Love of learning alone does not account for the contents, still less the form of Leonardo's notebooks. His passion for finding things out was accompanied by a far less profitable passion for writing them down. His notebooks are like the result of a Chinese examination in which, as we are told, the examinee is placed in a room alone and asked to write down all he knows; and in part they are little more than commonplace books – selections from his reading, often of the most unexpected kind. He seems to have enjoyed exposition. He wished his demonstrations to be perfectly clear and unmistakable, and repeats his proofs from every angle so that all contradiction is impossible. He also repeats the same demonstration several times in different parts of the manuscripts, rather than risk an unsupported statement. This thoroughness is an essential characteristic of his mind, and he defends it in a passage which may well make the author of a brief study of Leonardo pause in embarrassment.

Abbreviations do harm to knowledge and to love, seeing that the love of anything is the offspring of this knowledge, the love being the more fervent in proportion as the knowledge is more certain.... Of what use, then, is he who abridges the details of those matters of which he professes to give thorough information, while he leaves behind the chief part of the things of which the whole is composed? It is true that impatience, the mother of stupidity, praises brevity, as if such persons had not life long enough to serve them to acquire a complete knowledge of one single subject, such as the human body; and then they want to comprehend the mind of God in which the universe is included, weighing it minutely and mincing it into infinite parts, as if they had to dissect it![2]

A result of this characteristic was his dislike of general principles. Rather than risk a formula he would repeat a proof many times for each particular instance, and it was only mistrust of generalizations which prevented him from anticipating many of the discoveries of later scientists, amongst them the circulation of the blood. The only form of abstraction which he allowed himself – and it is safe to say that he did not recognize it as such – was mathematics. 'The man who blames the supreme certainty of mathematics feeds on confusion and can never silence the contradictions of sophistical sciences which lead to interminable conflict.' 'There is no certainty in sciences when mathematics cannot be applied.' These and similar pronouncements are to be found throughout the manuscripts, and show that to Leonardo mathematics were not simply a convenient means of measuring his researches. They were an article of belief. It is significant that the *certainty* of mathematics is more than once contrasted with the *uncertainty* of theological discussions.[3] Living on the eve of the Reformation, Leonardo seems to have anticipated the

2. Windsor, Royal Library, 19,084. Jean Paul Richter, *The Literary Works of Leonardo da Vinci* (London, 1919) para. 1210, from Anatomical MS. C, and so datable, *c.* 1513.

3. Cf. Richter, para. 1210, and *Trattato*, para. 29.

futility of religious conflicts, and to have held that new faith in mathematical science, which in the seventeenth century was to replace, in the finest minds, the lost certainties of revealed religion. This does not mean that Leonardo was a great mathematician. To him figures were the most incontrovertible facts, and facts were good in themselves. They should not be made to create hypotheses. He therefore used mathematics as a means of proof rather than a technique of speculation; and it must be confessed that he also used them in those games and puzzles on which so many early mathematicians wasted their abilities.

Leonardo's lack of synthetic faculty, perceptible in the notebooks as a whole, is partly responsible for their complete lack of order. Perhaps it would have been impossible at that date to give such an accumulation of facts any rational structure. The logical system of scholasticism, which compelled all facts into the service of God, had broken down under the weight of its own elaboration. The philosophical system of the seventeenth century with its faith in the laws of nature had yet to be evolved. But Leonardo's observations are not simply devoid of a controlling plan; they are put down at random with a capricious, or even wilful inconsequence, which students have found difficult to explain. Some writers have claimed that his sense of natural order was so great as to make all observations equally relevant to a central scheme. *Il a un sens extraordinaire de la symétrie*, says M. Valéry, *qui lui fait problème de tout*. This is the idealistic view of Leonardo, by which his defects, like disreputable Old Testament stories, are interpreted in the light of later spiritual experience and given a symbolical value. In contrast is the recent view that Leonardo was the victim of psychological frustrations, which prevented him from concentrating on a single theme: a poor theory by which to explain the author of the 'Last Supper', but perhaps nearer the truth than the first, for there was something abnormal about Leonardo's appetite for information, which led him to gobble up every fact with almost equal relish. Perhaps the chief reason for the lack of order in Leonardo's manuscripts is the one he himself gives in a kind of introductory note to the British Museum MS. He could not arrange his notes for lack of time. It is a miracle that any man should have observed, read, and written down so much in a single lifetime; and we should not complain that in the urgency of his appetite for facts he did not always stop to consider their order or ultimate purpose.

Having outlined the character of Leonardo's notebooks as a whole, let me examine those which date from his first residence in Milan. The earliest of these, MS. B, I have already mentioned as containing the drawings for engines of war with which he hoped to win Ludovico's favour. In addition to these it contains a number of drawings which prove that in about the year 1487 Leonardo was seriously interested in the problems of architecture. Unfortunately, Leonardo's architecture has never been properly studied and

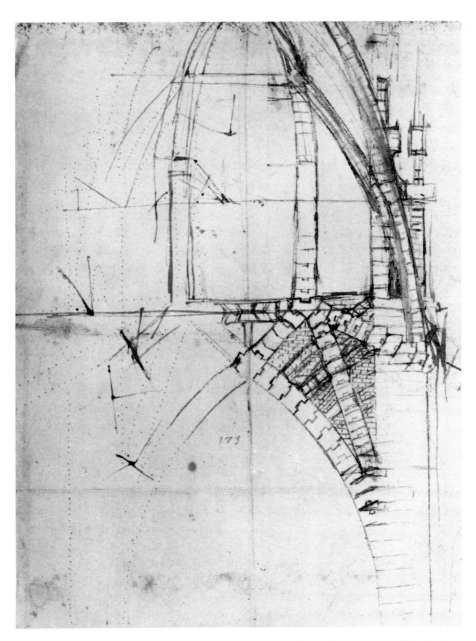

42. *Study for the dome of Milan Cathedral, 1488. Codice Atlantico, Ambrosiana, Milan*

I can only treat it here in a superficial way. At this date we can distinguish between two kinds of architectural employment, practical and real. The former arose out of his position at court, and consisted chiefly in the renovation or completion of buildings in which the Sforzas were interested. For example, he made one of the many attempts to design a central tower or dome for the Cathedral of Milan (Pl. 42), and in 1488 presented a model of his proposals, as also did Bramante, Luca Fancelli, and Pietro da Gorgonzola. In 1490 he was summoned to Pavia where, in company with Amadeo and Francesco di Giorgio, he was consulted about the completion of the Cathedral. Writers on Leonardo have suggested that some drawings of churches in M S. B were connected with this work, and certainly the manuscript dates from this period[4]; but there is no substantial evidence that any of Leonardo's designs were used. We may speculate on Leonardo's relations with Francesco di Giorgio, who more than any of his older contemporaries shared his range of interests; but although he owned one of Francesco's MSS., no record of their intercourse remains. M S. B also shows that he was continually occupied with the great castle of the Sforzas in Milan, on which, to a large extent, their power depended. In several drawings we see one of its towers raised to an unprecedented height in order to command the surrounding plain; in others new bastions, escarpments, moats, and trenches. How far any of these grandiose projects were carried out, it is impossible to say. They were largely engineering jobs, and as such have remained anonymous. Leonardo's name is not connected by tradition with any building in the Milanese, and he probably contributed by giving rough sketches or verbal advice, rather than working plans. We can infer from the notebooks that he did supervise personally some modest architectural work for his patrons, a pavilion for the Duchess's garden and a heating system for her bath.

At the same date we have our first evidence of Leonardo's interest in town planning. The idea of building a model city was familiar to the Renaissance and had already been carried out in Ferrara and Pienza. The motive was partly aesthetic, partly practical, for it was hoped in this way to avoid the plagues which ravaged Italian towns once at least in every decade. Leonardo's plans for Milan were made in consequence of the terrible plagues of 1484–5, and his intention was to produce an efficient rather than a beautiful city (Pl. 43). They should, however, be classed as ideal rather than practical, for they show a strain in Leonardo's character, to which I shall often refer – the romantic colouring which he gave to utilitarian undertakings. In all his engineering work he wished to achieve grandiose and improbable results, to remove mountains and divert huge rivers. And so his replanning of Milan was to involve a town on two levels: 'No vehicles,' he says, 'should go in the upper streets; these should be reserved for the use of gentlemen. And through the lower streets would go the carts and barrows and things used by the populace.' This plan also allows for subterranean canals. Town planning was to be one of his last recorded activities during his residence in France (see p. 253), but there again, we do not know how far his designs were carried out.

4. E. Solmi, *Scritti Vinciani* (1924), pp. 17 *et seq.*

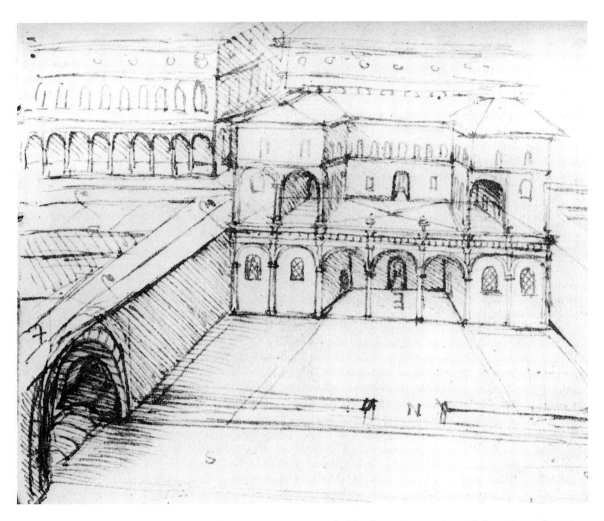

*43. Scheme for Palaces and Roads at Various Levels, c. 1488. MS. B, Bibliothèque de l'Institut de France, Paris*

Lastly, and most important of all, there is a series of drawings showing the plans and elevations of domed churches (Pl. 44). As far as we can tell, these were not intended to be built, but were simply solutions of the architectural problem, how to construct a church which should achieve its spiritual quality by uniting the two 'perfect' geometrical forms, the square and the circle. It was a problem that had occupied the greatest contemporary architects from Alberti to Bramante. Leonardo was familiar with Alberti's *De re aedificatoria* (written about 1450) and was the close friend of Bramante. The drawings in MS. B probably reflect Bramantesque ideas otherwise unknown to us, projects which found fulfilment later in works of Bramante's disciples, such as 'Santa Maria della Consolazione' at Todi.[5] Leonardo's elevations are not all

5. Begun by an architect named Cola da Caprarola in 1508. The drawing by Leonardo which it resembles most closely is actually in the Bibliothèque Nationale, Paris, no. 2037.

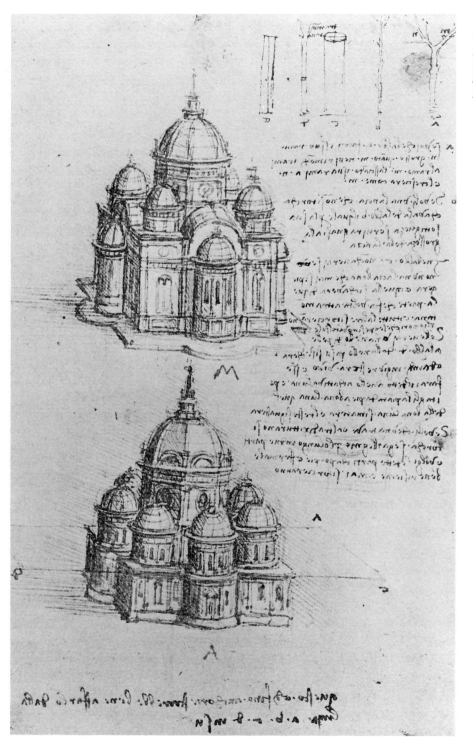

44. *Studies for a domed Church, 1485–90. MS. B, Bibliothèque de l'Institut de France, Paris*

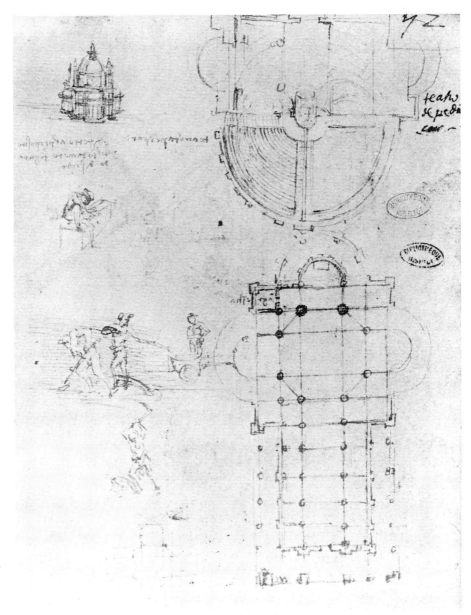

*45. Plan for a Church as a 'Theatre for Preaching' and other studies, c. 1488. MS. B. Bibliothèque de l'Institut de France, Paris*

successful. In some his ingenuity has outrun his sense of proportion. The North Italian tradition which permitted an accumulation of domes and turrets has appealed too strongly to his own *horror vacui*, and some of his designs recall the Church of S. Front at Périgueux or the Santo at Padua. A few even give the impression of those Russian churches in which every inch is covered with excrescences till the sense of scale is lost and a large building looks the size of a pepper-pot. We feel that Leonardo lacked the native sense of interval, of allowing one space to tell against another, which the simplest Tuscan *muratore* can give to a farm building, and which remains the essential quality of classical architecture. But then, as I shall often repeat in these pages, Leonardo's true taste was not classical and could have been more fully displayed a hundred years later, when the Baroque style would have allowed him to indulge his love of curves without loss of unity. The ground plans are done with more conviction, since they afforded the kind of geometrical puzzle which always interested him. To the end of his life he continued to draw patterns of squares, circles, and arcs, trying to exhaust every possible combination rather as an alchemist might try every possible combination of fluids in order to discover the elixir of life; and this passion, disciplined to the service of architecture, produced plans of great originality. In some the church is thought of as a circular hall for preaching (Pl. 45) (he actually describes it as *teatro da predicare*), an idea rarely attempted until a much later date, for example, in the Frauenkirche at Dresden. In others, the cluster of chapels round the central space reminds us of advanced Baroque design like Borromini's earlier drawings for Sant' Agnese.

In studying the architecture and even the painting of the Renaissance, we must always remember that one whole branch of each is almost completely lost to us – the architecture and decoration which was designed for pageants and masquerades. We know from Vasari how many of the greatest artists whose lives he records seem to have given a considerable part of their time to such ephemeral work. It was in these lath and plaster designs that a man could show his invention, his fantasy, unimpeded by cost and the painful process of construction: and we know that Leonardo did such work with pleasure. Our only series of drawings for masquerade costumes belongs to a later period, but we have written record of several pageants which he ordered with great ingenuity – in particular the Masque of the Paradiso of 1490 and the performance of Jupiter and Danaë of 1496. Leonardo's notes and sketches of stage machinery include a revolving stage and a lift; but, once more, we do not know how far these were his inventions or current theatrical usage.

These masquerades were performed as a means of glorifying the ruling powers – in this instance, Ludovico, his wife and mistresses – and like all Renaissance ideas of fame, they involved participation in elaborate allegories by which, for a few hours, the individual assumed the immortality of a work of art. Much of Leonardo's time was spent on the invention of allegories and emblems expressive of Ludovico's greatness. This work seems to have appealed to him, for the manuscripts contain many fabulous or allegorical writings. In MS. H Leonardo has compiled a bestiary,[6] one of his longest

6. Reprinted in Richter, vol. II paras. 1220–64. For the sources of this bestiary cf. Calvi in the *Archivo*

pieces of coherent prose, which is partly taken from a popular medieval compilation called the *Fiore di Virtù*, partly from a similar work, the *Acerba*, by the so-called Cecco d'Ascoli. Leonardo also quotes from Pliny, but it is significant that although he had before him this relatively scientific source for the life and habits of animals, the greater part of his bestiary is taken from those fanciful medieval writers to whom natural history was only a pretext for moral allegory.

Closely allied to this bestiary, and inspired by similar sources, are the fables which are scattered throughout the *Codice Atlantico*. Although many of these must be derivative, they have, when read as a whole, a certain unity expressive of Leonardo's point of view. Almost all are pessimistic. The animals, plants, or inanimate objects, who are the heroes of the fables, are no sooner confident of success and security than they are utterly destroyed by some superior and usually unconscious agency. If they avoid one misfortune, they immediately fall victim to a far greater as a result of their previous cunning. We see reflected Leonardo's view of contemporary politics, and indeed of life in general, where nature only allows man to reach some pinnacle of self-esteem in order to deal him a more shattering blow. The most personal of all these emblematic writings is a series in the *Codice Atlantico*[7] which Leonardo has entitled 'Prophecies'. These are in a form which seems to have been popular among the wits of Milan, and we read that Leonardo's prophecies[8] were written in competition with those of Bramante. They consist of descriptions of ordinary everyday happenings, so worded as to sound like appalling catastrophes. Thus 'many people by puffing out a breath with too much haste will thereby lose their sight and soon after all consciousness'; to which Leonardo supplies the explanation 'of putting out the light when going to bed'. Here the intention is solely humorous, and the 'prophecy' is really a sort of riddle. But in some instances I believe that Leonardo has taken advantage of this form to express his own convictions. Many describe acts of cruelty and injustice which sound unbelievable, until the 'key' tells us that they refer to animals. 'Endless multitudes will have their little children taken from them, ripped open and flayed and most cruelly cut in pieces (of sheep, cows, goats, and the like).' 'The severest labour will be repaid with hunger and thirst, blows and goadings, curses and great abuse (of asses).' Knowing from contemporary sources Leonardo's love of animals, we can be sure that such 'prophecies' as these are not mere jokes, but represent his refusal to take

---

*Storico Lombardo*, sec. 3, vol. 10 (1898), Anno 25, p. 73, and Kenneth McKenzie in *Giornale storico della letteratura italiana*, vol. LXIV (1914), p. 358.

7. Richter, paras. 1293–1313.

8. Cf. E. Solmi, 'Le fonti manoscritti di Leonardo da Vinci', in *Giornale storico della letteratura italiana*, suppl. 10, 1908, p. 109.

as a matter of course the suffering which man's technical skill has allowed him to inflict on the other animals.

The love of allegory revealed in the notebooks is also expressed in some very beautiful drawings. They date from about the period of the bestiary in MS. H 1494, and several of them illustrate fabulous events of natural history, the ermine, the lizard (Pl. 46), and others which I cannot interpret. These differ from most of Leonardo's drawings in that they are complete compositions: that of the lizard, in particular, has a suggestion of atmosphere and the vibration of light which was one of Leonardo's most precious gifts when he chose to use it. In contrast to these charming fables is a series of macabre allegorical drawings at Christ Church, Oxford. They seem to have some political meaning which is lost to us, and may have attracted Leonardo chiefly as an outlet for his bizarre fancies. We see two witches seated on a gigantic toad, while a third rides a skeleton with a load of arrows: there are two-headed monsters, wild pursuits, unexpected checks and repulses, all the inhabitants of a nightmare drawn with the flashing, flickering touch which Leonardo only used when the subject really interested him (P. 104–8).

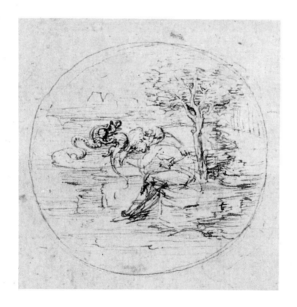

46. *Study of the 'Allegory of the Lizard Symbolizing Truth', c. 1496. Metropolitan Museum of Art, New York*

Closely connected with such fantasies are those once popular specimens of Leonardo's art – the grotesques or caricatures (Pl. 47). For three centuries these were the most typical of his works, familiar in numerous engravings. Today we find them disgusting, or at best wearisome. But Leonardo's immediate successors were right in recognizing the caricatures as essential to his genius, concentrating many elements of his spirit. In the first place, they express his love of phenomena – of eccentric nature. They are part of the same curiosity which led Dürer to make an engraving of a pig with eight legs. Vasari describes how Leonardo would follow extraordinary types for a whole day in order to memorize their features. We know that he even took the address of those which had interested him, 'Giovanina, fantastic face, is at Saint Catherine's hospital'.[9] It is one of the very few references to a woman in all Leonardo's notebooks. Given this interest in freaks, we can see that many of the so-called caricatures are much more realistic than at first sight we believe. In a humanitarian age we instinctively shut our eyes to such horrors, and lunatic asylums, good doctoring, and false teeth have greatly reduced their number. *'Monsieur Degas, Pour-quoi faîtes-vous toujours les femmes si laides?' 'Madame, parceque la femme en générale est laide.'* Mixed with his motive of curiosity lay others, more profound: the motives which led men to carve gargoyles on the gothic cathedrals. Gargoyles were the complement to saints; Leonardo's caricatures were complementary to his untiring search for ideal beauty. And gargoyles were the expression of all the passions, the animal forces, the Caliban gruntings and groanings which are left in human nature when the divine has been poured away. Leonardo was less concerned than his gothic predecessors with the ethereal parts of our nature, and so his caricatures, in their expression of passionate energy, merge imperceptibly into the heroic. Most typical of such creations is the bald, clean-shaven man, with formidable frown, nut-cracker nose and chin, who appears sometimes in the form of a caricature, more often as an ideal (Pl. 48). His strongly accentuated features seem to have typified for Leonardo vigour and resolution, and so he becomes the counterpart of that other profile which came with equal facility from Leonardo's pen – the epicene youth. These are, in fact, the two hieroglyphs of Leonardo's unconscious mind, the two images his hand created when his attention was wandering, and as such they have an importance for us which the frequent poverty of their execution should not disguise. Virile and effeminate, they symbolize the two sides of Leonardo's nature, a dualism I have already suggested in the contrast between his life in Florence and in Milan. It is no accident that the heroic type appears with almost caricatural emphasis in the masterpiece of his Florentine period, the 'Battle of Anghiari'; and that the epicene type is drawn with the greatest affection in those Milanese years, soon after 1490, when Salai entered Leonardo's studio. But as usual both types go back to his earliest Florentine years, were indeed taken from Verrocchio, the elegant youth from such a head as the David (Pl. 2), the warrior from the lost Darius relief. Both types appear, contrasted for the first time, on the famous sheet at Windsor of about 1478, but there they have a Florentine *quattrocento* character, which they lose as they become more expressive. The warrior is still classical, the boy still young.

9. Richter, para. 1401, from *S.K.M.* (Forster) II, 2, 78b.

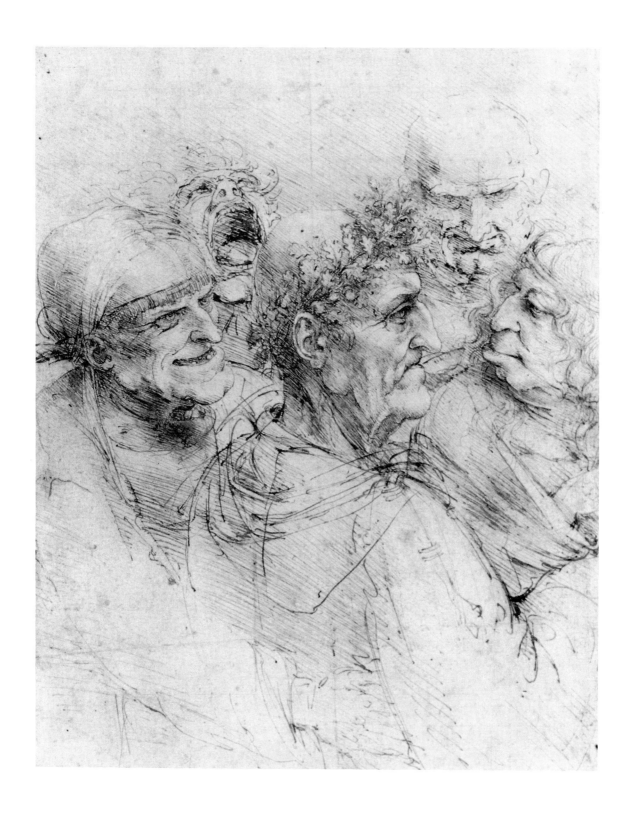

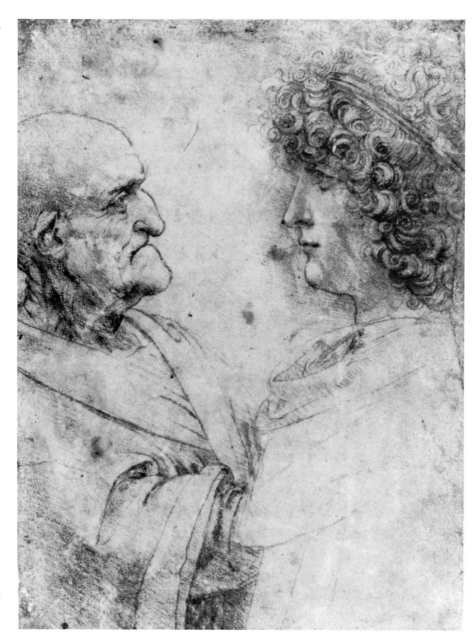

47. *Grotesque Heads,*
*1485–90. Royal*
*Library, Windsor* (RL
*12495r)*

48. *Study of a*
*'Nutcracker' man and*
*a beautiful youth,* c.
*1500. Uffizi, Florence*

Later the warrior's profile is distorted by the violence of his resolution, the boy becomes blowsy and self-satisfied. Yet the change is slight and subtle, more one of expression than of morphology, and shows that these two images reflect deep and fixed necessities in Leonardo's nature. Even in his most conscious creations, even in the 'Last Supper', they remain, as it were, the armature round which his types are created.

The two most important of Leonardo's studies at this period remain to be mentioned. They are anatomy and the action of light. His treatment of these subjects springs from his belief in painting as a science. They are two of the means by which the uncertainty of mere appearances may be given some of the certainty of measured facts. They are therefore best considered in relation to his theory of art, which, from its importance and complexity, I shall treat in a separate chapter.

# CHAPTER FOUR

# THE 'TRATTATO DELLA PITTURA'

L EONARDO is one of the few great painters to leave us a quantity of
writing about his art. I put it in this way, rather than saying a treatise
on art, because his numerous notes on painting are hardly more
systematic than his other observations. We have, however, more reason to
believe that he intended a definite treatise on the subject, and he may even
have given some shape to the part dealing with the human figure, since in his
introduction to the *Divina Proportione*, written in 1498, Pacioli says that
Leonardo had 'finished with great diligence an admirable book on the depic-
tion and movements of men' (*de pictura et movimenti humani*). This book
is lost, but amongst Leonardo's anatomical drawings at Windsor are several
studies of the human body in movement which date from this period and
must be connected with the treatise; and it was probably known to the author
of a treatise on the art of drawing known as the *Codex Huygens*, much of
which is clearly derived from Leonardo.[1] A great many of his original notes
on the science of painting have also survived. Some of the manuscripts deal
with the subject almost exclusively: the MS. C is concerned with light and
shade, and MS. E with the understanding of plants and trees. The Ashburnham MS. No. 2 (now Bibliothèque Nationale, 2038 Italien) contains so
many and varied instructions on painting that when it was discovered it was
at first taken for the lost treatise. But the majority of such notes are scattered
throughout the manuscripts in the pages of the *Codice Atlantico* and on
individual drawings. These notes on painting, with a certain amount of
writing on other subjects loosely related to it, were collected by J. P. Richter
and published in 1883 under the somewhat misleading title, *The Literary*

1. Now in the Morgan Library, New York. Cf. E. Panofsky, *The Codex Huygens* (London, 1940).

*Works of Leonardo da Vinci.* A number of Leonardo's writings on art have not survived in their original form. Vasari tells us that beside the main body of the manuscripts which in his day were in the possession of Francesco Melzi, there were 'in the hands of N. N., a painter of Milan, some writings of Leonardo likewise in characters written with the left hand, backwards, which treat of painting and of the methods of drawing and colouring. This person, not long since, came to Florence to see me, wishing to print this work; and he took it to Rome in order to give it effect, but I do not know what may afterwards have become of it.'[2] It seems reasonable to suppose that these papers in the possession of N. N. formed the first part of a selection from Leonardo's notes on art which was made about the middle of the sixteenth century and has come down to us in several manuscripts.[3] The best of these comes from the Urbino library and is now in the Vatican library. This is the transcript of Leonardo's notes, known as the *Trattato della Pittura* – and as such I shall refer to it. Some of the matter it contains can also be found in Leonardo's original autograph, and we can see that the copyist was, for the date, remarkably faithful in following Leonardo's actual word. It is important to be sure of this, since a great part of his transcript reproduces notes by Leonardo which are lost to us in the original, and which greatly enlarge our knowledge of his aims and character. The *Trattato* was copied and recopied with diminishing accuracy throughout the sixteenth century. One copy belonged to Benvenuto Cellini,[4] another to Annibale Carracci, who said that if he had known it earlier it would have spared him twenty years of labour; yet another, in the Barberini library, was edited by Cassiano del Pozzo, who induced Poussin to draw illustrations to it.[5] In 1651 it served as a basis for the first printed edition published by Raphael du Fresne. Other editions followed; but under the influence of contemporary art theorists they drifted farther and farther from Leonardo's original text, became, in fact, little more than case-books of academic classicism. This the *Trattato* remained until the rediscovery of the earlier manuscripts, with their relation to Leonardo's original notes, which showed how far were the real workings of his mind from the formulas of Du Fresne, Roland Freart, and Francesco Fontani.

The *Trattato della Pittura* is not an easy book to read. In the Vatican MS.[6]

2. This passage does not occur in the first (1550) edition of Vasari's *Vite*. The manuscript was therefore shown to Vasari after that date and before 1568.

3. This same section, consisting largely of the so-called *Paragone*, is referred to by G. Paolo Lomazzo in *Trattato dell'arte della pittura*, Milan, 1584, p. 158.

4. It seems possible that Cellini's copy also contained Leonardo's treatise on perspective now lost. Cf. John White in *Warburg and Courtauld Journal* (1979), p. 70.

5. In the library of the Comtesse de Béhague, Paris.

6. Cod. Vaticano Urbinate 1270. I have used the convenient edition of Angelo Borzelli (Lanciano, 1914).

it consists of eight books and 935 'chapters', some no more than a few lines, some covering several pages. Although the compiler has tried to arrange the entries under their subjects, very few have any sequence, and many repeat each other in slightly varying form. In a short summary we may say that the contents are valuable in four different ways. First, they give Leonardo's general views on the nature of art; secondly, there are notes on the science of painting; thirdly, there are notes on studio practice; and fourthly, there are entries scattered through the *Trattato*, in which Leonardo expresses, sometimes half-unconsciously, his personal tastes and feelings as a painter.

Leonardo's general views on the art of painting are found for the most part in the first book of the *Trattato*, where he compares it to the arts of poetry, music, and sculpture.[7] These comparisons, or *paragoni* as they were called, were a standard form of critical literature at the time, and something of what they contain is derivative; but the presentation of the argument and, above all, the illustrative examples quoted are characteristic of Leonardo and of immense interest, since nowhere else does he allow himself to write in such generalized or such personal terms of the things which concerned him most deeply.

Since classical times painting had been classed among the mechanical arts,[8] and Leonardo, like Sir Joshua Reynolds in his *Discourses*, is concerned to establish its respectability by proving that it is a mental activity and a science. The destruction of such an artificial premise naturally involves him in some artificiality himself, but above these sophistries, which are harmless enough if judged by the standards of contemporary literature, there towers a noble and thrilling conception of what painting should be. In the first place, it is a recreation of the visible world. Leonardo always insists on this godlike quality of the painter's imagination. From the divine element in the science of painting it follows that the mind of the painter is transformed into the likeness of the mind of God. It is this view of art as creation which makes him insist that the painter must be universal, must neglect no aspect of nature; and for the same reason he must be a scientist, that is to say, must understand the inner nature of what he paints almost as if he had created it himself. 'If you despise painting,' he says,[9] 'which is the sole means of reproducing all the known

---

The standard critical edition is by H. Ludwig, *Quellenschriften für Kunstgeschichte*, vols. XV–XVIII (Vienna, 1882). See also now, *Treatise on Painting*, ed. P. McMahon, 2 vols. (Princeton, 1956), containing facsimile and translation.

7. G. P. Lomazzo, *Trattato* (1584), p. 158, says that this was written at the request of Ludovico Sforza to answer the question which was the nobler, painting or sculpture. Leonardo's *Paragone* has been printed separately with an English translation and introduction by Irma A. Richter (Oxford, 1949).

8. Indeed it was not even one of the seven canonical Mechanical Arts, though usually thought to be subsumed under them, cf. Cennino Cennini.

9. *Trattato*, para. 8.

works of nature, you despise an invention which with subtle and philosophic speculation considers all the qualities of forms: seas, plants, animals, grasses, flowers, all of which are encircled in light and shadow.' But the painter must not only recreate the semblance of things seen: he must select and dispose them with harmonious intention. Painting, he says, depends on *'l'armonica proporzionalita delle parti che compongono il tutto, che contenta il senso'*.[10] Here Leonardo shows himself touched by the predominant Platonism of his time, for the idea that the visual arts were a sort of frozen music was familiar to many theorists of the Renaissance, and had been given superb expression by Leon Battista Alberti, to whose treatise on painting, written in 1435, Leonardo was greatly indebted. But in his enthusiasm for painting, Leonardo goes farther and claims that painting is superior to music in so far as it *is* frozen, since its sequences are not fleeting sounds or images, *si volece nel nascere come nel morire*, but can be apprehended immediately and contemplated indefinitely.[11] This exposition of the relative immediacy and permanence of the sensations aroused by the arts, anticipating to some extent the theories of Lessing, is, from a critical point of view, the most valuable part of the *Trattato*. But strict logic was no part of Leonardo's equipment, and when he comes to compare painting with sculpture his personal prejudices rush in, to the confusion of his aesthetic theories, but to the vast enrichment of our knowledge of his character.

For that side of painting which consists in the harmonious composition of proportionate parts Leonardo gives no rules, though in one abstruse passage he hints at a means of establishing an equivalent to certain musical intervals.[12] The academic advice and instruction which fill a great part of the *Trattato* are concerned with painting as the science by which visible objects are recreated in permanent shape. And since the exact sciences must be stated in mathematical terms, Leonardo insists that the student of painting must be grounded in mathematics. This union of art and mathematics is far from our own way of thinking, but it was fundamental to the Renaissance. It was the basis of perspective, that article of faith of the fifteenth-century painters, through which they hoped to surpass even the painters of antiquity. By perspective they sometimes meant the whole science of vision, the means by which a visual impression is received in the retina; more frequently they limited the word to the scientific representation of receding figures in space. But even in this narrower interpretation, the study of perspective involved a real mastery of mathematics: and this the great artists of the *quattrocento* – Brunelleschi, Masaccio, Uccello, Mantegna, Bramante, above all Piero della

10. *Trattato*, para. 19.

11. *Trattato*, paras. 25, 26.

12. *Trattato*, para. 27.

Francesca – had evidently possessed. All this must be borne in mind when studying the diagrams and calculations which fill the pages of Leonardo's writings on art. His chief treatise on perspective seems to be lost; such notes on the subject as have come down to us derive from Alberti and perhaps from Piero della Francesca. His notes on the perspective of colour, however, and what he calls the perspective of disappearance contain many of those acute observations in which he anticipated the doctrines of impressionism; but he was so far from carrying out these delicate observations of colour and atmosphere in his painting that they were entirely without influence. The reverse is true of his observations on light and shade. Like all good Florentines he felt the importance of relief, but he was not content to achieve it by the subtle combination of drawing and surface modelling which the painters of the *quattrocento* had brought to perfection. He wished to achieve relief through the scientific use of light and shade. In the *Trattato* he says – under the heading 'which is the more difficult, light and shade or good drawing' – 'Shadows have their boundaries at certain determinable points. He who is ignorant of these will produce work without relief; and the relief is the summit and the soul of painting.'[13]

It was in order to establish scientifically the determinable boundaries of shadows on curved surfaces that he drew the long series of diagrams showing the effect of light falling on spheres and cylinders, crossing, reflecting, intersecting with endless variety, which we find in MS. C of about 1490. The calculations are so complex and abstruse that we feel in them, almost for the first time, Leonardo's tendency to pursue research for its own sake, rather than as an aid to his art. How far, in fact, his art was affected we cannot determine. The drawings which show his greatest mastery of chiaroscuro from a naturalistic point of view belong to the years just before this period. He never surpassed the rendering of light passing over curved surfaces in the studies of skulls dated 1489. But it is characteristic of his development that he should grow dissatisfied with this empirical mastery and wish to reduce it to rule. Critics have complained that the scientific study of light and shade led to a kind of academism in Leonardo's later work, and was ultimately responsible for the artificiality of the Louvre 'St John'. This is certainly untrue. Much of Leonardo's most sensitive and unacademic use of chiaroscuro dates from long after his investigations into its nature. And to those who maintain that the innumerable patient diagrams of criss-cross rays were a tragic waste of time, Leonardo might well have replied that between the 'Ginevra de' Benci' and the 'Mona Lisa' there is a difference in fullness and continuity of modelling which he, at any rate, could only have achieved by the scientific study of light striking a sphere.

13. *Trattato*, para. 121; see also *ibid*. para. 133.

The effect of Leonardo's passion for chiaroscuro, both in his own art and in that of his followers, I shall discuss later on. But while dealing with the *Trattato* I must quote one passage which has a bearing on his whole feeling for the subject.

Very great charm of shadow and light, [he says] is to be found in the faces of those who sit in the doors of dark houses. The eye of the spectator sees that part of the face which is in shadow lost in the darkness of the house, and that part of the face which is lit draws its brilliancy from the splendour of the sky. From this intensification of light and shade the face gains greatly in relief ... and in beauty.[14]

Here is the description of a *seicento* picture, a Caravaggio or a Rembrandt, as far as possible from the theory and practice of Leonardo's day, or, as we shall see, his own academic theory.

Next to perspective the branch of science which played the greatest part in the traditional discipline of the Florentine school was anatomy. To Castagno it had seemed to offer the basis of scientific realism, to Pollaiuolo the mastery of movement. With proportion it lay at the root of Renaissance aesthetics, for if man was the measure of all things, physically perfect man was surely the measure of all beauty, and his proportions must in some way be reducible to mathematical terms and correspond with those abstract perfections, the square, the circle and the golden section. It is not surprising, therefore, that Leonardo studied anatomy with passion throughout his life, and applied his knowledge in painting the great composition of the 'Battle of Anghiari', and in preparing the lost treatise on the human figure referred to by Pacioli. But quite early his intellectual curiosity led him to investigate aspects of anatomy which could not conceivably benefit his painting. The anatomical drawings in the Windsor MS. B, dated 1489, are studies of skulls, done with a delicacy which makes them works of art, but with scientific intention (Pl. 49). This intention is made even clearer in some drawings, done perhaps a year or two later, showing the structure of a bear's foot. Quite recently three drawings by Leonardo have been discovered representing the actual bear (P. 78–9). Leonardo had drawn its paws while alive; on its death he dissected it in order to compare them to the human foot. This idea of comparative anatomy appears again in his drawings – he compares the arms of men and monkeys,[15] the legs of men and horses[16] – and is typical of the workings of his mind. It springs from his conception of man as a part of nature, subject to the same laws of growth, controlled by the same chemistry,

14. *Trattato*, para. 90.

15. P. 214. Dürer copied some of the drawings on this sheet in his Dresden Sketch Book, ff. 130 *verso* and 133 *verso*. His copies are in reverse and differently distributed on the page.

16. MS. K, 109 *verso* (so datable *c.* 1505).

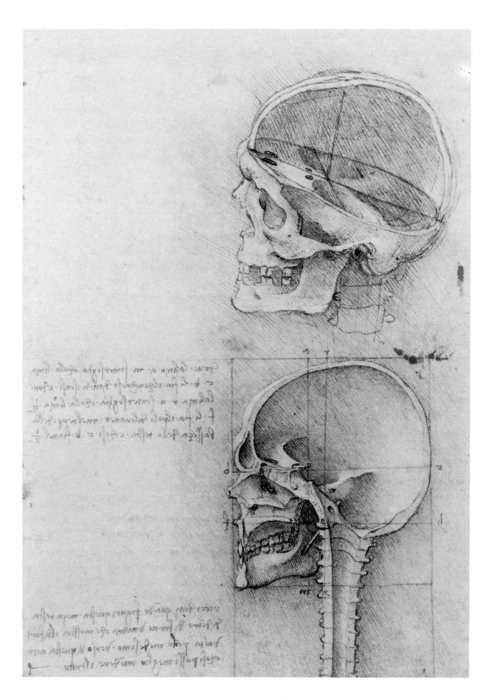

a conception which transcended his scientific researches, and is one of the
roots of his art.

  The third branch of the art of painting on which Leonardo insists is proper treatment of the subject. It must be natural, circumstantial, and dramatic. He is continually advising the painter to study appropriate gestures and expressions. The student is warned against monotonous attitudes, and in particular against the danger of reproducing his own physical characteristics,[17] a danger more real than might be supposed. Of dramatic impropriety he gives an amusing example: 'I recently saw an Annunciation in which the Angel looked as if he wished to chase Our Lady out of her room with movement of such violence that she might have been a hated enemy. And Our Lady seemed as if in despair she was about to throw herself out of the window. Remember not to make such a mistake as this.'[18] We may speculate with interest on the author of this picture seen *a questi giorni*, a probable answer being Botticelli, who in the enthusiasm of his later work was carried beyond classical decorum. This aspect of Leonardo's teaching is easily remembered in front of the 'Last Supper', and we shall have reason to refer to it again. But we must also keep it in mind when we come to look at those of his compositions in which the treatment of the subjects is less obvious, in the 'St Anne', in the 'Leda', and, above all, in the 'St John'. Strange and perverse as his presentations of these themes may seem, we cannot, with the *Trattato* before us, dismiss them as merely capricious.

In addition to defining the principal aims of painting, Leonardo gives us practical hints as to how they can be achieved, interesting to us as indications of his own studio practice. He tells the student to avoid above all light which casts a dark shadow, so that even if he is painting in the open air he must do so as if some mist or transparent cloud was between his object and the sun.[19] In sunlight it is better to paint in a courtyard with high walls painted black and a linen curtain stretched over it. The ideal light falls on the object at an angle of 45 degrees. This last shows Leonardo at his most academic, and is a contrast to the Rembrandtesque figure looking out of a dark interior, described above. More sympathetic are his numerous instructions as to how to catch that degree of animation in figures which he valued so highly (Pl. 50).

When you are out for a walk, [he tells the painter][20] see to it that you watch and consider men's postures and actions as they talk, argue, laugh, or scuffle together: their own actions, and those of their supporters and onlookers: and make a note of these with a few strokes in your little book which you must always carry with you. This book should be of tinted paper so that you cannot rub out, but always go on to a new page.

He also gives the very sound advice that any student drawing a detail of a

17. *Trattato*, para. 105.

18. *Trattato*, para. 35.

19. *Trattato*, para. 87.

20. *Trattato*, para. 169. See also *ibid.* para. 175.

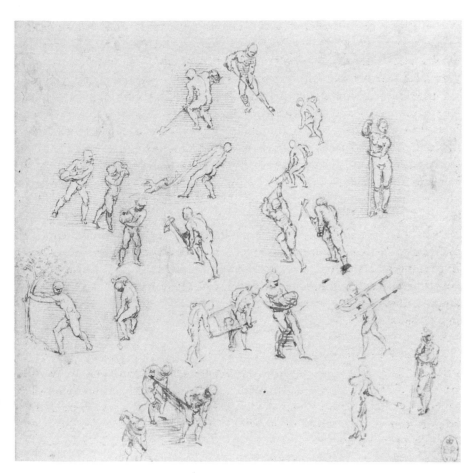

*50. Studies of Figures, Digging, Carrying etc., c. 1503. Royal Library, Windsor (RL 12644r)*

figure should first sketch in the figure as a whole, so that the real meaning of the finished part should not be lost sight of. Good examples of his own practice are the studies of the nude at Windsor. These practical hints show how far he was in revolt against the decorative style of the *quattrocento*. Painters are warned not to surround their figures with dark outlines;[21] rows of frescoes one above the other, the time-honoured Italian way of telling a story in pictures, is blamed on grounds of reason (*ragionevolmente biasimato*), and as an alternative Leonardo suggests putting several scenes in the same composition, but cutting them off from one another by 'large trees, or angels if they are suitable to the story, or birds or clouds or similar devices'.[22] Scorn is reserved for mere decorators. 'There is a certain race of painters,' he says, 'who from their lack of science have to live by the beauty of blue and

21. *Trattato*, para. 113.
22. *Trattato*, para. 116.

gold – *vivano sotto la bellezza dell'oro e dell'azzuro*. With supreme folly these men allege that they cannot do anything good except at a high cost.' I think there can be little doubt that Leonardo was actually thinking of Pintoricchio, who was notoriously extravagant – *Consuma*, said the papal secretary of him, *troppo vino, troppo oro e troppo azzuro*. In any case, these maxims foreshadow that great stride in the history of art which the visitor to the Vatican can take by climbing the stairs from Pintoricchio's Borgia Apartments to Raphael's Stanze.

Interesting as are the theories and precepts propounded in the *Trattato*, and important in their bearing on Leonardo's painting, it contains entries of a far deeper significance. These are the passages in which he reveals his own preferences, prejudices, and the real colour of his imagination. His manuscripts, for all their enormous bulk, so seldom contain the least expression of personal feeling that the passages preserved by the unknown editor of the *Trattato* are worth examining at length. In the first place, Leonardo makes fairly frequent reference to the sort of subject the painter might wish to treat. Here is one of them, the 65th chapter of the *Trattato*, headed 'Piacere del Pittore'.

The painter can call into being the essences of animals of all kinds, of plants, fruits, landscapes, rolling plains, crumbling mountains, fearful and terrible places which strike terror into the spectator; and again pleasant places, sweet and delightful with meadows of many-coloured flowers bent by the gentle motion of the wind which turns back to look at them as it floats on; and then rivers falling from high mountains with the force of great floods, ruins which drive down with them uprooted plants mixed with rocks, roots, earth, and foam and wash away to its ruin all that comes in their path; and then the stormy sea, striving and wrestling with the winds which fight against it, raising itself up in superb waves which fall in ruins as the wind strikes at their roots.

The rest of the passage is a description of the struggle between wind and water, in which the water takes the form of rain to assault the sea from above, but finally 'pressed back it turns into thick clouds, and these become the prey of the conquering winds'. Here is Leonardo carried away by his true feelings. He begins to enumerate the subjects that delight a painter, and instead of compositions of figures, classical and religious legends, beautiful faces and draperies, all the subjects which pleased the patrons and artists of his time, he describes this combat of the elements, a subject for Turner, in the language of Herman Melville. Nor was this an isolated freak. All his longest and fullest descriptions of pictorial subjects are of great battles, storms, and deluges[23] and, as we shall see, he carried out these subjects in the

23. *Trattato*, paras. 144, 145, from the Ashburnham Codex, given in Richter, paras. 601, 606.

most personal of all his designs (see p. 244). Unfortunately, we have no hint of how he would have executed another subject, which he describes with equal pleasure, a night piece with a fire,[24] and when we try to picture it our eye cannot rid itself of the strong images created by an artist at the farthest remove from Leonardo, the night pieces of Rembrandt.

The figures which are seen against the fire look dark in the glare of the firelight; and those who stand at the side are half dark and half red, while those who are visible beyond the edges of the flames will be feebly lighted by the ruddy glow against a black background. As to their gestures, make those which are near it screen themselves with their hands and cloaks, to ward off the intense heat, and some with their faces turned away as if drawing back. Of those further off, represent some of them with their hands raised to screen their eyes, hurt by the intolerable splendour of the flames.

These descriptions not only show the deeply romantic colour of Leonardo's imagination: they imply a sense of form completely at variance with that of his contemporaries. Instead of the firmly defined forms of the *quattrocento* or the enclosed forms of the high Renaissance, the subjects he describes could only be treated with the broken, suggestive forms of romantic painting. That Leonardo felt the full evocative power of such forms is proved by a famous passage in the *Trattato*:[25]

I shall not refrain [he says] from including among these precepts a new and speculative idea, which although it may seem trivial and almost laughable, is none the less of great value in quickening the spirit of invention. It is this: that you should look at certain walls stained with damp or at stones of uneven colour. If you have to invent some setting you will be able to see in these the likeness of divine landscapes, adorned with mountains, ruins, rocks, woods, great plains, hills, and valleys in great variety; and then again you will see there battles and strange figures in violent action, expression of faces, and clothes, and an infinity of things which you will be able to reduce to their complete and proper forms. In such walls the same thing happens as in the sound of bells, in whose strokes you may find every named word which you can imagine.

Later he repeats this suggestion in slightly different form, advising the painter to study not only marks on walls, but also 'the embers of the fire, or clouds, or mud, or other similar objects from which you will find most admirable ideas ... because from a confusion of shapes the spirit is quickened to new inventions.' 'But,' he adds, 'first be sure you know all the members of all the

24. *Trattato*, para. 143, from the Ashburnham Codex, 17a, given in Richter, para. 604.
25. *Trattato*, para. 63.

things you wish to depict, both the members of animals and the members of landscapes, that is to say, rocks, plants and so forth.'

I have quoted this passage at length, familiar as it is, because it is profoundly characteristic of Leonardo. Nothing could be farther from the precepts of academic classicism than the use of stains in walls as a stimulus to the imagination. This procedure was followed by Goya, one of the most anti-classical of all painters; and Victor Hugo, whose name is the first to come to mind when we read Leonardo's descriptions of a deluge, made many of his strangely exciting drawings out of accidental blots and smears of coffee. Yet although Leonardo would admit such aids to the imagination, his conception of art as a science forced him to add a warning that the painter must understand the detailed structure of all that he wished to represent.

Before leaving the *Trattato* I will take the opportunity of quoting from it a few of the passages which throw some light on Leonardo's character apart from his ideas on painting. First of all, we have some first-hand confirmation of those early authorities who tell us that he was elegant, solitary, and calmly aware of his superiority to the average of mankind. This is apparent in his perfectly illogical attacks on sculpture. Sculpture, he says, is not a science, but an *arte meccanicissima*, for

the sculptor in creating his work does so by the strength of his arm by which he consumes the marble, or other obdurate material in which his subject is enclosed: and this is done by most mechanical exercise, often accompanied by great sweat which mixes with the marble dust and forms a kind of mud daubed all over his face. The marble dust flours him all over so that he looks like a baker; his back is covered with a snowstorm of chips, and his house is made filthy by the flakes and dust of stone. The exact reverse is true of the painter (taking the best painters and sculptors as standards of comparison); for the painter sits before his work, perfectly at his ease and well dressed, and moves a very light brush dipped in delicate colour; and he adorns himself with whatever clothes he pleases. His house is clean and filled with charming pictures; and often he is accompanied by music or by the reading of various and beautiful works which, since they are not mixed with the sound of the hammer or other noises, are heard with the greatest pleasure.[26]

We are reminded of the description by Jusepe Martinez of El Greco in a great house with twenty-four rooms and a band of musicians to play to him while he took his meals. But with Leonardo (as, indeed, with El Greco) this elegant way of life was combined with great austerity.

In order that the prosperity of the body, [he says] shall not harm that of the spirit the painter must be solitary, especially when he is intent on those speculations and

26. *Trattato*, para. 32.

considerations, which if they are kept continually before the eyes give the memory the opportunity of mastering them. For if you are alone you are completely yourself but if you are accompanied by a single companion you are only half yourself.[27]

And we know that Leonardo showed that perfect contempt for riches which he counsels so eloquently in chapter 62 of the *Trattato*.

Leonardo's description of the sculptor has a further significance for us. It is an unmistakable reference to his hated rival, Michelangelo. The very hardships which Leonardo describes in derision are recorded with a kind of sardonic pride in Michelangelo's letters and sonnets. We see that the antipathy, the *sdegno grandissimo* as Vasari calls it, which existed between the two men was something far more profound than professional jealousy; sprang, in fact, from their deepest beliefs. In no accepted sense can Leonardo be called a Christian. He was not even a religious-minded man. It is true that he allowed himself an occasional reference to superstitious observances; thus he writes 'of Worshipping the pictures of Saints. Men will speak to men who hear not. . . . They will implore favours of those who have ears and hear not; they will make light for the blind.' Here and in a few other passages he seems to associate himself with the precursors of the Reformation. But these protests spring from his dislike of mumbo jumbo and loose thinking in general rather than from any real religious conviction. Michelangelo, on the other hand, was a profoundly religious man, to whom the reform of the Roman Church came to be a matter of passionate concern. His mind was dominated by ideas – good and evil, suffering, purification, unity with God, peace of mind – which to Leonardo seemed meaningless abstractions, but to Michelangelo were ultimate truths. No wonder that these ideas, embodied in a man of Michelangelo's moral, intellectual, and artistic power, gave Leonardo a feeling of uneasiness thinly coated with contempt. Yet Leonardo held one belief, implicit in his writings, and occasionally expressed with a real nobility: the belief in experience. Such an expression is to be found in chapter 29 of the *Trattato*, in which Leonardo denies with passion the old scholastic belief that only those sciences which have their origin in abstract intellectual speculation can escape the charge of being 'mechanical'.

To me it seems that those sciences are vain and full of error which are not born of experience, mother of all certainty, first-hand experience which in its origins, or means, or end has passed through one of the five senses. And if we doubt the certainty of everything which passes through the senses, how much more ought we to doubt things contrary to these senses – *ribelli ad essi sensi* – such as the existence of God or of the soul or similar things over which there is always dispute and contention. And in fact it happens that whenever reason is wanting men cry out against one

---

27. *Trattato*, para. 48.

another, which does not happen with certainties. For this reason we shall say that where the cry of controversy is heard, there is no true science, because the truth has one single end and when this is published, argument is destroyed for ever. But true sciences are those which, impelled by hope, have been penetrated by the senses so that the tongues of argument are silenced. They are not nourished on the dreams of investigators, but proceed in orderly sequence from the first true and established principles through successive stages to the end; as is shown by the elements of mathematics, that is to say number and measure, called arithmetic and geometry, which with complete truth treat of quantities both discontinuous and continuous. In them one does not argue if twice three makes more or less than six, or that the angles of a triangle are less than the sum of two right angles: all argument is reduced to eternal silence, and those who are devoted to them can enjoy them with a peace which the lying sciences of the mind can never attain – *con eterno silenzio resta distrutto ogni arguizione, e con pace sono fruite dai loro devoti il che far non possono le bugiarde scienze mentali.*

# CHAPTER FIVE
# 1485-1496

WE have seen Leonardo fulfilling the chief duties of an artist at a Renaissance court, painting portraits, supervising pageants, and doing those small engineering jobs which demanded unusual resource and skill in the handling of materials. In addition to these duties he undertook for the Duke two works which exacted the whole measures of his genius, the 'Horse' and the 'Last Supper'.

'The Horse' is the title by which contemporaries always referred to his model for the equestrian monument to Ludovico's father, the great *condottiere* Francesco Sforza. Such a monument had first been attempted in 1473 under Duke Galeazzo Maria, and after his death in 1476 the idea was taken up with enthusiasm by Ludovico. By the time Leonardo went to Milan it had become a symbolic undertaking, involving group prestige, like the building of a giant liner today. Leonardo may have had some hope of being employed on the work, since he mentions it at the end of the letter to Ludovico in which he recommends himself as a military engineer. 'Again, I can undertake to work on the bronze horse which will be a monument to the immortal glory and eternal honour of your father the Prince, and the illustrious house of Sforza.' There is no evidence that he had been offered the commission or that it was the chief motive of his journey to Milan, but when he had proved his competence in various kinds of work he was evidently ordered to try his hand at the monument. If Sabba Castiglione is right in saying that he worked on it for sixteen years, he must have begun it in 1483.[1] His first conception is known to us from an engraving and two drawings which on grounds of style are datable before 1490 (Pl. 51). They show that in this early stage Leonardo

---

1. Sabba Castiglione, *Ricordi* (Venice, 1560), f. 57r.

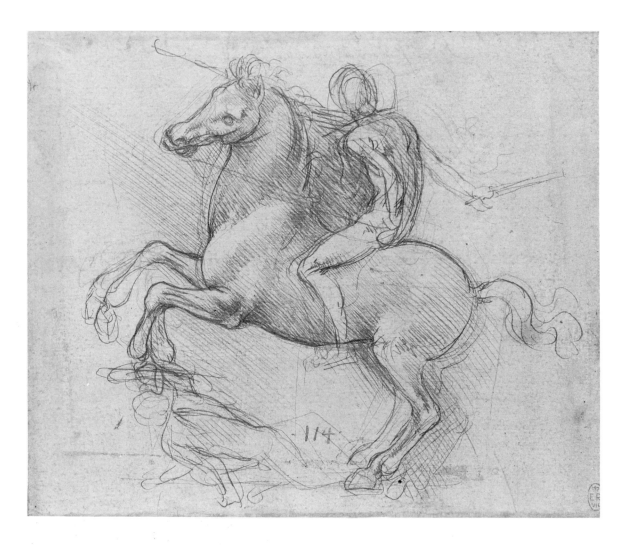

51. *Study for the Sforza monument*, c. 1488. Royal Library, Windsor (RL 12358r)

had conceived the horse as prancing, in a pose similar to those which he had just studied in the background of the 'Adoration', but simpler and less twisted. We know how strongly this sequence of forms appealed to him and we can imagine how eager he was to carry it out in sculpture, where its full plastic possibilities could be realized. At that date no equestrian statue with a prancing horse can have been known, and if he could have executed one Leonardo would have surpassed in technical skill not only the recent glories of the Gattamelata and Colleoni monuments, but even the masterpieces of antiquity. But his ambition far outran his experience. The two drawings mentioned show no attempt to meet the problems of monumental sculpture. In one the horse's raised forefeet are supported by an inadequate and unconvincing tree-trunk; in the other they rest on a prostrate foe, a motif common

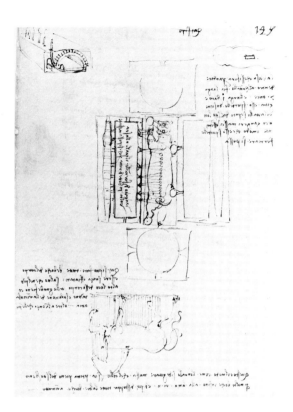

52. *Study for the Casting of the Sforza monument showing a Walking Horse*, c. 1493. *Biblioteca Nacional, Madrid*

in antique reliefs, but far too complicated and unsubstantial for large-scale sculpture in the round. Even if Leonardo's designs had been more sculptural, such a complete group could hardly have been cast in bronze at that date, and it is surprising that Leonardo, with his experience of casting cannon, did not realize this. But this disregard for media of execution marked all his most important works. The 'Last Supper', the 'Battle of Anghiari', the canalization of the Arno were all damaged or even annihilated by this defect, which sprang not only from impatience and experimentalism but from a certain romantic unreality. By 1489 Ludovico had either realized or been informed of the impracticability of Leonardo's design, and through the Florentine ambassador in Milan he wrote to Lorenzo de' Medici asking him to recommend one or two masters more apt for the work. At about this period Leonardo gave up work on the horse. Apparently Lorenzo made no satisfactory recommendation; and on 23 April 1490 Leonardo notes, 'I began the horse again.' This time he seems to have realized that the project of a rearing horse was too ambitious, and returned to the traditional pose of a horse walking. There is good evidence of what this horse was to be like. It is shown complete in a small sketch in the right-hand bottom corner of a drawing at Windsor (12346), on a page in Madrid (Pl. 52) and in a red chalk sketch in the *Codice*

*Atlantico*, f. 216 *verso*, a, where it is shown packed for transport, Leonardo taking his usual delight in the technical devices involved. Some drawings from nature at Windsor indicate the disposition of its limbs, and these hints of the pose are confirmed by representations of horses in contemporary bronzes and illuminated manuscripts which are almost certainly derived from the Sforza monument. The most interesting of all these reminiscences is the horse in Dürer's engraving of the 'Knight and the Devil' which was probably inspired by one of Leonardo's final drawings for the monument. All these indications show a pose in strong contrast with the original project. Leonardo has not attempted to rival the recent triumph of his master, the nervous swaggering Colleoni, but has gone back to Donatello's 'Gattamelata', with its slow-pacing horse giving the authority of movement appropriate to a great commander. But Leonardo's horse is lighter and more classical, partly owing to the influence of certain antique bronzes, an equestrian statue in Pavia, known as the Regisole and the horses of St Mark, and partly to the living models which he found in the Sforza stables. Some of the beautiful drawings done from nature at this time show that horses could be found as well-knit and delicate as those idealized by antiquity (Pl. 53). This series of nature studies, for the most part in silverpoint, shows Leonardo's style at its most attractive.[2] The observation is delicate and direct; the handling fresh and decisive, without the slow deliberation that takes the bloom from his later drawings of horses. They were made between 1490 and 1493. In July 1493 Leonardo was still taking notes of horses worth drawing,[3] and that autumn he constructed a full-scale model in clay. On 30 November this model was exhibited at festivities held on the marriage of Bianca Maria Sforza to the Emperor Maximilian.

Leonardo had for some time been considering the casting of his colossus and in the recently discovered Madrid MS., gave a detailed account of the method to be followed. He noted that it would take place on 20 December 1493, but for some unknown reason nothing was done, and on 17 November 1494, Ludovico sent the whole of the bronze collected for the horse to his father-in-law, Ercole d'Este. It was made into cannon. The full-scale model continued to stand in the Corte Vecchia of the Castello, where it was seen and admired by many famous visitors to Milan, who refer to it and the 'Last Supper' in almost equal terms. According to Bandello Leonardo continued to work on it while painting the 'Last Supper', and this is confirmed by Sabba Castiglione's statement quoted above. We have no evidence that Ludovico revived the project of casting it in bronze, and Leonardo does not again refer

2. Those at Windsor are 12,289, 12,294, 12,304, 12,317, 12,319, 12,320, 12,321. Of these 12,294 and 12,304 are in pen and ink; 12,297 may be a copy. Another drawing of the same type and date is in the Royal Library, Turin, 15,580.

3. 'A di 16 di luglio 1493 ... *Morel Fiorentino di messer Mariolo cavallo grosso a bel collo e assai bella testa.*' Forster MS. III, i *verso*.

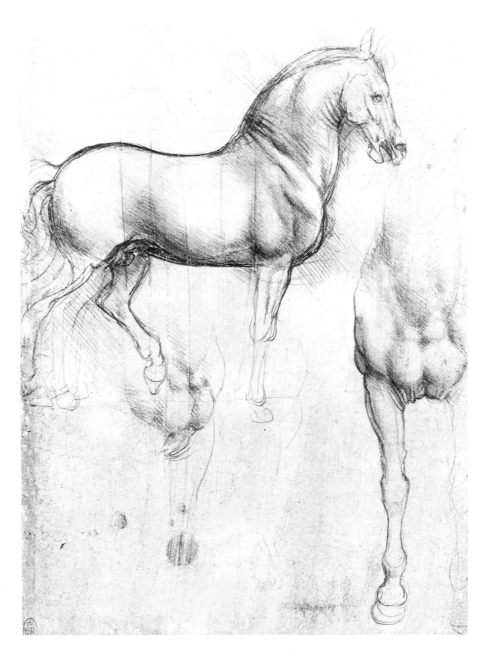

*53. Study from
Nature for the Sforza
monument, 1490.
Royal Library,
Windsor (RL 12321)*

to work on it, but in an incoherent and fragmentary letter to the Duke he
wrote 'of the horse I say nothing because I know that times are bad'. When
the French entered Milan the connoisseurs expressed much admiration for
the model: but the soldiers used it as a target. Finally it was taken to the
Court of Ferrara, where it fell to pieces.

It is difficult for us to understand contemporary enthusiasm for the monument. Apart from the fact that it no longer exists, we can hardly believe that the model of a walking horse, however large and well contrived, could have given Leonardo the opportunity of displaying that gift of poetical evocation which seems to us the peculiar beauty of his work. But to the Renaissance, who valued his mastery of the means of expression more, perhaps, than the spirit expressed, the mere size of the horse was an impressive achievement. A great mass of inert matter had been given form and life. Moreover, he had established for the animal, which was second only to man in importance and 'nobility', a canon of perfection. His studies of the ideal proportion of the horse were known to his contemporaries, and seemed to invest his model with that final authority which the Renaissance hoped to find in a union of antique art and mathematics. All this we can hardly realize from the few surviving drawings for the Sforza memorial:[4] but when, twenty years later, Leonardo returned to the problem with the design for a monument to Marshal Trivulzio, we can follow in a relatively large series of drawings some of the calculations by which he strove for perfection.

We have now reached what is commonly held to be the climax of Leonardo's career as a painter, the 'Last Supper' (Pl. 54). It is a point at which the student of Leonardo must hesitate, appalled at the quantity of writing which this masterpiece has already evoked, and at the unquestionable authority of the masterpiece itself. And almost more numbing than this authority is its familiarity. How can we criticize a work which we have all known from childhood? We have come to regard Leonardo's 'Last Supper' more as a work of nature than a work of man, and we no more think of questioning its shape than we should question the shape of the British Isles on the map. Before such a picture the difficulty is not so much to analyse our feelings as to have any feelings at all. But there are alternatives to the direct aesthetic approach. We may profitably imagine the day when the 'Last Supper' did not exist, and Leonardo was faced with a blank wall and an exacting patron.

The 'Last Supper' was painted at the command of Ludovico il Moro for the refectory of the Convent of Dominican friars at Santa Maria delle Grazie, Milan. It was probably begun in 1495, but the archives of the convent have been destroyed and our meagre documents date from 1497 when the painting was nearly finished. On 29 June in that year the Duke sent a memorandum

4. *The Codex Huygens* (see p. 125) contains fourteen drawings of horses copied from Leonardo, of which only three survive in the original. The extreme complexity of the system may be judged from the fact that he dealt in fractions $\frac{1}{900}$ of the total length of the horse. There are frequent references in the early sources to a treatise on the anatomy of the horse. Lomazzo says that it was burnt during the troubles in Milan in 1499. Vasari says: 'By Leonardo we have the anatomy of the horse.' No anatomical drawings of horses, in the strict sense of the word, have come down to us, and it is possible that Vasari was thinking of the measured drawings.

*54. The 'Last Supper', 1497. Sta Maria delle Grazie, Milan*

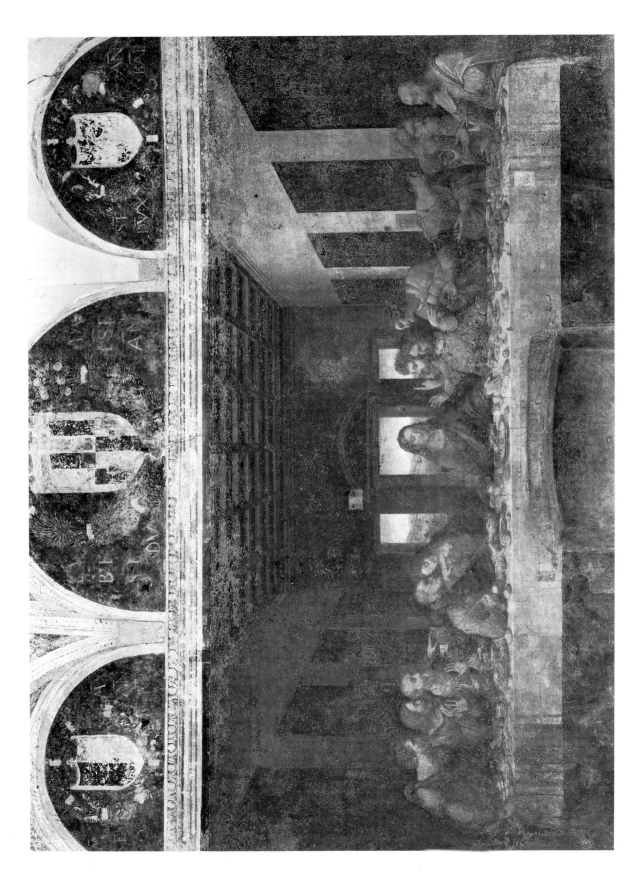

to his secretary Marchesino Stanga, asking him to order Leonardo the Florentine to finish the work begun in the refectory of the Grazie and then to see to the other end wall of the refectory.[5] This implies that the 'Last Supper' was far advanced; and Pacioli, in the dedication of his *Divina Proportione*, dated 9 February 1498, speaks of it as if it had been completed. In compensation for the dearth of documents, we have several accounts of the work by eye-witnesses, including one by the novelist, Bandello, which, familiar as it is, I must quote again, for nothing else gives such a vivid idea of Leonardo at work.

Many a time [he says] I have seen Leonardo go early in the morning to work on the platform before the 'Last Supper'; and there he would stay from sunrise till darkness, never laying down the brush, but continuing to paint without eating or drinking. Then three or four days would pass without his touching the work, yet each day he would spend several hours examining it and criticizing the figures to himself. I have also seen him, when the fancy took him, leave the Corte Vecchia when he was at work on the stupendous horse of clay, and go straight to the Grazie. There, climbing on the platform, he would take a brush and give a few touches to one of the figures: and then suddenly he would leave and go elsewhere.

Such irregular methods meant that the painting could not be *al fresco*; and in fact, we know that Leonardo used a medium containing oil and varnish. The wall was damp and as a result the painting very soon began to suffer. Already in 1517 Antonio de Beatis noted that it was an excellent work although it had begun to perish, either through the dampness of the wall or some other mischance;[6] and Vasari, who saw it in May 1556, describes it as 'so badly handled that there is nothing visible except a muddle of blots'. By 1642 Scanelli can write that of the original there remain only a few traces of the figures and those so confused that it is only with great pains that one can make out the subject.[7] In face of such evidence it is hard to resist the conclusion that what we now see on the wall of the Grazie is largely the work of restorers. We know that the painting has been restored four times since the beginning of the eighteenth century, and was probably restored several times before. In 1908 it was thoroughly cleaned by Cavenaghi, who gave a most optimistic report on the picture, saying that only the Christ's left hand was seriously repainted. He adds ingenuously that Leonardo was ahead of his time in that

5. Only two years earlier this wall had been covered with a fresco of the Crucifixion by a provincial Lombard named Montorfano; and dry and incompetent as this is, Ludovico can hardly have wanted Leonardo to paint over it. He probably refers to the portraits of himself and his family which occur in the fresco and seem to have been executed by Leonardo. These are now so completely effaced that no certainty is possible.

6. L. Pastor, *Die Reise des Kardinals Luigi d'Aragona* (Freiburg, 1905), p. 176.

7. Francesco Scaneli, *Microcosmo della pittura* (Cesena, 1657), lib. II, cap. 6, p. 41. Scaneli saw the 'Last Supper' in 1642, although his work was not published till fifteen years later.

he seems to have employed a medium not usually found till the late sixteenth century. Cavenaghi was such a brilliant technician that his word is usually accepted, but in this case there is overwhelming evidence to prove that he was mistaken. It is inconceivable that a painting which by all accounts was a hopeless wreck in the sixteenth and seventeenth centuries could still have survived till our own day more or less intact, and concrete evidence of restoration is provided by a comparison of the Apostles' heads in the fresco with those in early copies. Perhaps the best examples are the two independent series of drawings at Weimar and Strasbourg,[8] which were done direct from the original by Leonardo's pupils and show none of the personal variations which occur in a painted copy. Now these drawings agree in certain differences from the painting as we now have it, and in each case the drawing is clearly superior both in sentiment and design. Take four of the Apostles on the left of Christ. In the original, St Peter, with his villainously low forehead, is one of the most disturbing figures in the whole composition; but the copies show that his head was originally tilted back in foreshortening. The restorer was unable to follow this difficult piece of drawing and has rendered it as deformity. He shows a similar failure to cope with an unusual pose in the heads of Judas and St Andrew. The copies show that Judas was originally in *profil perdu*, a fact confirmed by Leonardo's drawings at Windsor (Pl. 55). The restorer has turned him round into pure profile, with considerable damage to his sinister effect. St Andrew was almost in profile; the restorer has turned him into the conventional three-quarters. He has also made the dignified old man into an appalling type of simian hypocrisy. The head of St James the Less is entirely the restorer's invention, and gives the measure of his ineptitude.

It is worth insisting on these changes because they prove that the dramatic effect of the 'Last Supper' must depend entirely on the disposition and general movement of the figures, and not on the expression of the heads. Those writers who have complained that the heads are forced or monotonous have been belabouring a shadow. There can be no doubt that the details of the fresco are almost entirely the work of a succession of restorers, and the exaggerated grimacing types, with their flavour of Michelangelo's 'Last Judgement', suggest that the leading hand was that of a feeble mannerist of the sixteenth century.[9]

8. Reproduced in Francesco Malaguzzi Valeri, *La Corte di Ludovico il Moro*, vol. II (Milan, 1915) figs. 586-9, 590-3, 599-603.

9. Since this was written the fresco has been cleaned once more by Mauro Pellicioli, and this time the early restorations have really been removed and the little that remains seems to have been painted by Leonardo, but it is too faint and discontinuous to give much idea of its original effect. (Ed. note: for the even later campaign of restoration from 1976 onwards, see Introduction, p. 31, and the report by D. A. Brown listed in the Bibliography.)

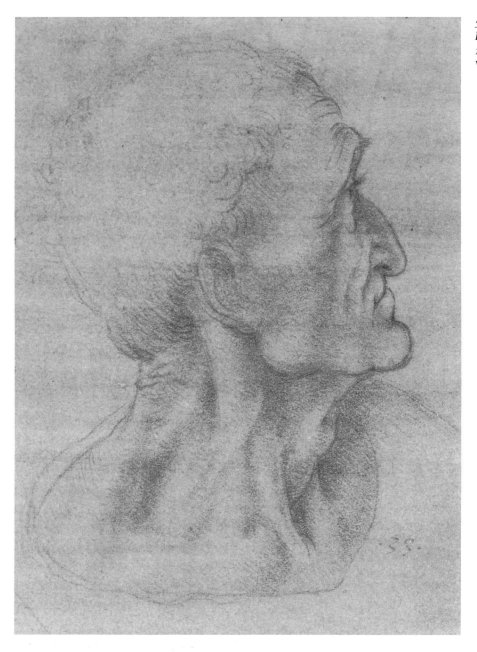

*55. Study for the Head of Judas,* c. *1496. Royal Library, Windsor (*RL *12547)*

But in spite of the depressing insistence of these facts, some magic of the original remains, and gives the tragic ruin in Santa Maria delle Grazie a quality lacking in the dark smooth copies of Leonardo's pupils. Luminosity, the feeling for atmosphere, which distinguishes all Leonardo's genuine work from that of his pupils, must have distinguished the 'Last Supper' also: and the fresco, perhaps from its very vagueness, has kept a certain atmospheric quality. As we look at them, these ghostly stains upon the wall, 'faint as the shadows of autumnal leaves', gradually gain a power over us not due solely to the sentiment of association. Through the mists of repaint and decay we still catch sight of the superhuman forms of the original; and from the drama of their interplay we can appreciate some of the qualities which made the 'Last Supper' the keystone of European art. We can recognize Leonardo's power of invention by the simple means of comparing his treatment of the subject with any other which had preceded it. The Last Suppers of Ghirlandaio and Perugino, painted only a year or two earlier, show fundamentally the same composition as that which had satisfied the faithful for almost a thousand years. Eleven apostles sit on the far side of a table, each one quiet and separate. Sometimes they talk to each other, or drink their wine. Our Lord sits in the middle with St John reclining uncomfortably on his lap. Alone, on the near side of the table, is Judas. We have seen how Leonardo's departure from the traditional iconography of the 'Adoration' involved a change in his whole interpretation of the drama. The same is true of the 'Last Supper'. The older painters had represented the moment of communion, a moment of calm in which each apostle might wish to sit alone with his thoughts. Leonardo, as is well known, chose the terrible moment in which Jesus says, 'One of you will betray me.' Immediately this row of quiet individuals is unified by emotion.

Unity and drama, these are the essential qualities by which Leonardo's 'Last Supper' is distinguished from earlier representations of the subject. It is worth analysing the means by which these qualities have been achieved. To begin with the setting: we notice that there is nothing to distract the eye from the main theme. 'In history painting,' says Leonardo in the *Trattato* (para. 178), 'do not ever make so many ornaments on your figures or their setting as will confuse the form and attitudes of the figures or the essential character of the setting.' Instead of the fanciful, decorative architecture which earlier interpretations of the subject include, the scene of Leonardo's 'Last Supper' is so bare and severe that most copyists felt bound to invent a more attractive setting. There are no incidental motifs – no flying birds, nor gossiping disciples. The vanishing point of the perspective is the principal figure. Every form and every gesture is concentrated. The problem of dramatic and formal concentration, always difficult, is almost insoluble when the subject is thirteen men sitting at a table. The earlier painters did not attempt to subordinate their figures to a single motif, but relied on a purely decorative arrangement. The painters of the Baroque, to whom unity of composition was essential, solved the problem by ingenious tricks of lighting and fore-shortening, but in so doing they sacrificed the quietness and clarity of statement suitable to the subject, sometimes turning it, as Tintoretto in S. Paolo, into a scene of violence and confusion in which the Apostles reel and struggle among the servants and unknown onlookers. Leonardo's solution is in some respects the same as that used in the 'Adoration', two dynamic masses united and kept in repose by a single point of balance. This seemingly simple arrangement involved the feat of composing the twelve Apostles into two groups of six: which groups should be perfectly coherent, and yet have sufficient movement to give them an interesting relation to the centre. The steps by which Leonardo arrived at his final solution are lost to us. We have very few drawings for the 'Last Supper' and for the composition only two studies. The more elaborate of these, a red chalk drawing in the Venice Academy, is one of the most puzzling of all Leonardeque relics (Pl. 56). It is badly drawn – the Christ's right arm and hand are childish; and in spite of the factitious animation of the figures they lack the inner life which redeems Leonardo's most careless scribbles: they are stiff, almost archaic. For these reasons some of the best judges have doubted its authenticity; but the writing above the figures done in the same chalk as the drawing seems to be genuine and we may surmise that Leonardo was interested solely in noting down the order and characteristics of the Apostles. It tells us nothing about the composition, except that, although the drawing must date from about 1495, Leonardo has not yet begun to think of the two groups as wholes, and Judas

*56. Study for the 'Last Supper', c. 1495. Accademia, Venice*

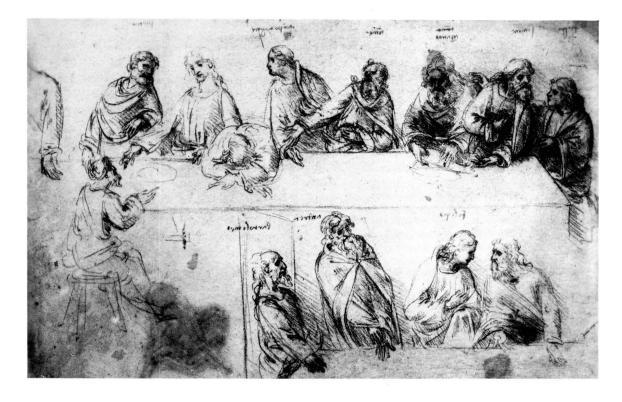

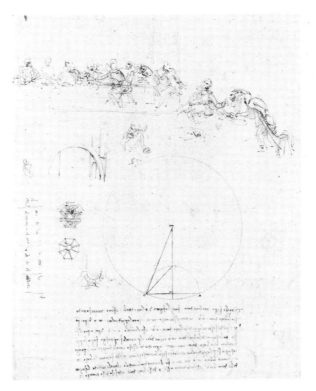

57. *Study for the 'Last Supper'*, c. 1496.
*Royal Library,*
*Windsor* (RL 12542r)

is still placed on the near side of the table. This last motif also appears on the other surviving study, a pen and ink drawing at Windsor (Pl. 57); but here Leonardo is already aiming at dramatic unity, and in a subsidiary sketch on the same sheet he considers the almost unbearably dramatic subject of Our Lord giving the sop to Judas.

Between these sketches and the final composition an immense labour must have intervened; but unfortunately the drawings and studies in which the great construction gradually took its inevitable shape are almost entirely lost. It is perhaps a criticism of the 'Last Supper' that in the groups of Apostles the evidence of this labour is still too apparent. We can see how Leonardo has varied each action, calculated each interval, balanced every change in direction. He has given us the ideal demonstration of his treatise on painting. What could be more in keeping with his theories than the two groups of Apostles on either side of Christ, turned inwards so that their axes form a kind of echelon of perspective around the central figure: or the way in which, having made the three Apostles on the extreme left look eagerly inward, he makes two on the right look outward, but point inward, so that their intention, meeting the formidable glare of St Simon, seems to ricochet back along the line of their hands? The building up of such sequences is, no doubt, one of the greatest manifestations of intellectual power in art, but, seen

through the medium of copies it remains an intellectual achievement, stupendous, but cold and academic. The centre of the composition upon which
these two masses rest, the figure of Christ, springs from a deeper source. It
is the unfathomable mystery of Leonardo that with all his apparent coldness,
his aloofness from ordinary human feelings, his essential strangeness, he could
yet create this figure so simple, so touching, and so universal in its appeal.

Evidently one cannot look for long at the 'Last Supper' without ceasing to
study it as a composition, and beginning to speak of it as a drama. It is the
most literary of all great pictures, one of the few of which the effect may be
largely conveyed – can even be enhanced – by description. It is the opposite
of a picture by one of the great decorative artists, by Paul Veronese, for
example, where the actions, distractions, costumes, and expressions of the
actors may be quite unsuitable to the subject and simply chosen for their
pictorial effectiveness.

I need hardly describe, what has been described so often, the variety of
gesture which Leonardo has given to the disciples, and the way in which the
effect of these gestures is enhanced by contrast; how, for example, the rough
impetuous Peter, pugnaciously eager to declare his innocence, contrasts with
the resigned St John, content to sit quietly, because he knows that no one
will suspect him, and how St Peter's hand, forming a bridge between the
heads of St John and Judas, underlines the contrast between innocence and
villainy – *le bellezze con le bruttezze*, says Leonardo, *paiono più potenti l'una
per l'altra*.[10] All these penetrations, these dramatic inventions, have been
analysed once and for all by one of the few men who, by the scale of his
genius, was in a position to judge Leonardo – by Goethe. His essay on Bossi's
*Cenacolo* remains the best literary interpretation of the 'Last Supper'. Very
often in reading the description of a picture by a man of letters we feel that
what the writer takes to be a stroke of dramatic genius is an accident of
which the painter was quite unaware. With Leonardo this is not the case. We
know from his notebooks and his theoretical writings on art how much
thought he gave to the literary presentation of his subject. He is continually
advising the painter to study expressive gestures and suitable actions, and to
combine them with effects of variety and contrast. 'That figure is most
praiseworthy,' he says, 'which, by its action, best expresses the passions of
the soul.' With unusual good fortune we have in one of his pocket-books[11] a
note of the gestures suitable to the 'Last Supper'.

One who was drinking has left his glass in its position and turned his head towards
the speaker. Another twists the fingers of his hands together and turns with a frown

10. *Trattato*, para. 136.

11. Victoria and Albert Museum, Forster MS. no. II, ff. 1 *verso* and 2 *recto*.

(*con rigide ciglia*) to his companion. Another with hands spread open showing the palm, shrugs his shoulders up to his ears and makes a grimace of astonishment (*fa la bocca della maraviglia*). Another speaks into his neighbour's ear and the listener turns to him to lend an ear, while he holds a knife in one hand and in the other the loaf half cut through by the knife; and in turning round another, who holds a knife, upsets with his hand a glass on the table.

In the note these gestures are, so to say, unallotted, and it is interesting to see which ones Leonardo has retained. There is no difficulty in recognizing in St Andrew the man who shrugs his shoulders and makes the *bocca della maraviglia*; and St Peter, who speaks into his neighbour's ear, still holds the knife. The gesture of the man twisting his fingers together did not sufficiently add to the movement of the composition and has been dropped out; and so has the man with his glass half-way to his lips. Leonardo's note was made from observation, and as the conception of the 'Last Supper' grew more heroic, these everyday gestures became too trivial. But the man who turns round suddenly and upsets a glass has suffered a curious transformation. The motif has been given to Judas, only instead of a knife he holds the bag, and instead of a glass he upsets the salt, an accident still commemorated by the superstitious.

This abundance and variety of gesture on which Leonardo expended so much thought is not the characteristic of the 'Last Supper' which appeals most strongly to modern sensibility. Nor do I believe that our lack of appreciation springs solely from a Northern embarrassment in face of the more expressive manners of the South. We feel no uneasiness before the Uffizi 'Adoration'. In part this may be due to the fact that the 'Adoration' is unfinished. The movement of the figures is communicated by the still perceptible movements of the painter's brush. In the 'Last Supper' the movement is frozen. There is something rather terrifying about all these ponderous figures in action; something of a contradiction in terms in the slow labour which has gone to the perfection of every gesture. And beyond this is a deeper cause. The whole force of gesture, as an expression of emotion, lies in its spontaneity: and the gestures in the 'Last Supper' are not spontaneous. Leonardo, as we have just seen, consciously excluded those motions which approached the nature of *genre*. He intended the whole scene to be carried through in the highest mood of classical art, and this imposition of classicism on his innate feeling for life is slightly disturbing. The Apostles are too vital to be heroic, too large to be so animated.

And here we come back to the disastrous change which the whole picture has suffered from the repainting of the heads; for had the original heads been there, with all their pathos and dramatic intensity, the gestures, in a subsidiary role, might have lost some of their flavour of artifice. The coarsely painted grimaces which are all that time and restoration have left us, would have horrified Leonardo, for many passages in the *Trattato* show us the importance he gave to facial expression and describe how the painter must use every artifice to observe it and note it down. To gain any idea of what we have lost we must turn to the few surviving drawings, in particular those two masterpieces, the St James the Greater and the St Philip at Windsor (Pls. 58 and 59); and we must remember that in the painting the dramatic intensity of both heads would certainly have been increased; they would have ceased to be studies from life and have become embodiments of emotional states, as concentrated and complete as the highest creations of classic drama.

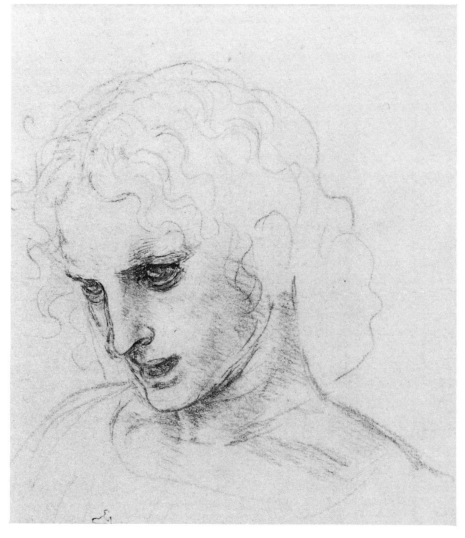

*58. Study for the Head of St James the Greater, c. 1496. Royal Library, Windsor (RL 12552)*

*59. Study for the Head of St Philip, c. 1496. Royal Library, Windsor (RL 12551)*

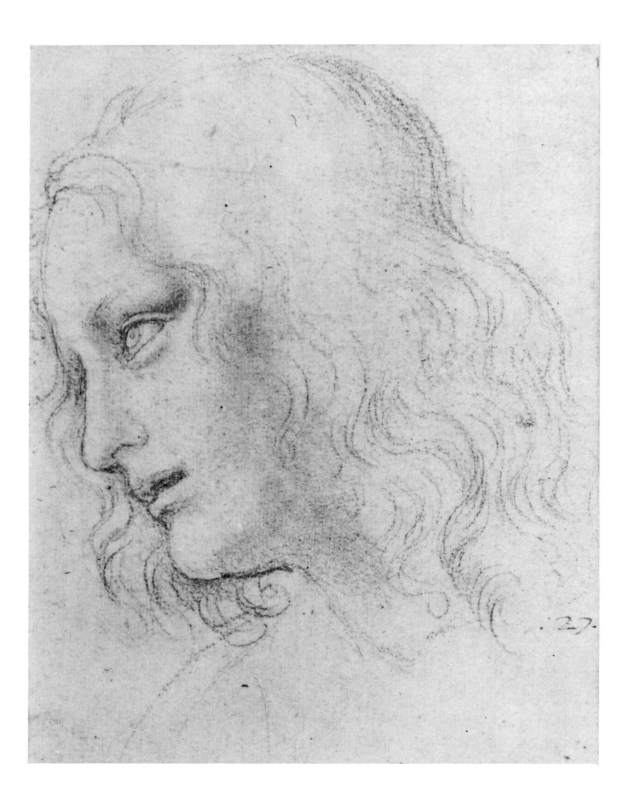

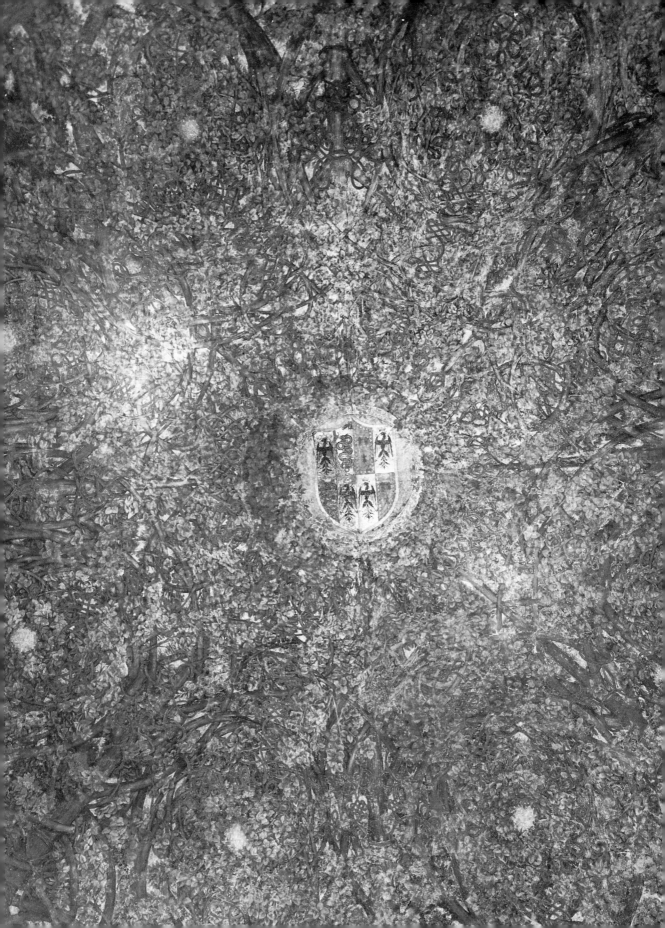

# CHAPTER SIX

# 1497 – 1503

60. *Ceiling of the Sala
delle Asse, c. 1498.
Castello Sforzesco,
Milan*

BETWEEN the completion of the 'Last Supper' and Leonardo's departure from Milan, there remained rather less than two years, and we know that these were largely filled with official employments. On 2 October 1498 Leonardo was given a property outside the Porta Vercellina of Milan, and at the same time he was appointed *ingegnere camerale*. The Duke anticipated the coming French invasion, and much of Leonardo's time was occupied in planning defences for Lombardy. Of his work as an artist, two undertakings date from these years. The first is his co-operation with Lucas Pacioli in his celebrated work *Divina Proportione*. Pacioli, one of the leading mathematicians of his time, was a native of Borgo San Sepolcro, and had been the friend and pupil of Piero della Francesca, whose researches into perspective and the five regular bodies he incorporated, without acknowledgement, into his own publications. He arrived in Milan in 1496, and we know from Leonardo's notebooks that the two men were soon on intimate terms. By 1497 they were collaborating on the *Divina Proportione*. We can trace Leonardo's influence in some parts of the text, and there is no doubt that he drew the figures that illustrate the 1509 edition: Pacioli says so more than once. These figures consist of capital letters, constructed on a system of proportion, and a number of more elaborate figures of solid geometry. That Leonardo should have devoted so much time to these abstract designs is an instance of how much his creative gifts were dominated by his intellect. I said, when referring to his architecture, that for a Tuscan he was unusually devoid of the sense of abstract harmonies. Yet Pacioli, who had known Piero della Francesca, is never tired of praising Leonardo's skill. With Piero proportion was a function of the spirit, with Leonardo of the intellect. Piero could not have drawn two lines without giving them some harmonious relationship, just as Leonardo was almost incapable of drawing a line which had not the quality of organic life. Yet by sheer intellectual power, Leonardo was able to conquer this branch of art which was naturally foreign to him.

During these years the only commission of which we can be certain is the decoration of the Castle. This must have been done in the summer of 1498, for on 23 April the scaffolding was removed from the Sala delle Asse. There is evidence that Leonardo was engaged in decorating another room, the Saletta Negra, but the Sala delle Asse (Pl. 60) is the only one which has survived. I say survived – but that is not the right word, because when the vault was freed from plaster in 1901, the remains of Leonardo's fresco were entirely and thickly repainted by an artist named Bassani. He seems to have followed closely the original traces of drawing, for it remains a complex and powerful design, worthy of Leonardo's ingenuity, but he has completely lost the feeling of light and substance which is characteristic of Leonardo's studies of plants, and is still perceptible in the damaged painting of garlands in the decorative lunettes above the 'Last Supper'.[1] In covering his ceiling with branches of foliage, Leonardo was following an ancient motif. The invention goes back to classical times and is known in many mosaics, but it must have appealed equally to the gothic mind, being in effect no more than an extension to the ceiling of the Verdure tapestry. Leonardo has given his conventional design his own character: indeed, it would be impossible to think of a decorative scheme more in keeping with his love of density – his *horror vacui* – and its accompanying hatred of abstraction. He has made the branches of his trees perform an elaborate system of interlacings similar to the well-known engravings of knots inscribed *Academia Leonardi Vinci*.[2] But in spite of their artificial twistings we may be sure that Leonardo's deep knowledge of plant life gave to the original decoration a real character of growth and movement, and that feeling for the texture of fruit and leaves which we find in Correggio's decorations in the Camera di San Paolo.

During these years Ludovico was becoming a less satisfactory patron and we have several fragmentary letters of complaint from Leonardo. 'I am aware that your Excellency is far too occupied for me to venture to remind you of my small matters, and that the arts have been put to silence.' Ludovico was indeed occupied. In spite of his frenzied diplomacy the French entered Milan on 5 October 1499, and Ludovico, after regaining the city for a few months,

1. Malaguzzi Valeri, *La Corte,* p. 562, quotes Frizzoni as having seen the vault before it was repainted, and saying that the faint traces of Leonardo's original had precisely the character of the garlands above the 'Last Supper'. It seems that the original was not photographed.

2. These engravings present two unsolved problems. Did Leonardo execute them himself? And what is meant by the inscription? It seems to me unlikely that Leonardo practised engraving, though one of his pupils seems to have done so with considerable skill. Cf. Blum in *Gazette des Beaux-Arts* (August–September 1932), pp. 89 *et seq.* The inscription has been taken to mean that Leonardo was head of an academy, but more probably means that the engraving was an academic exercise.

was defeated and sent to France as a prisoner. In December 1499 Leonardo left Milan with Luca Pacioli to seek employment elsewhere. Like a true humanist he recognized no loyalties and knew no native country but his own genius.[3] He had been intimately connected with the Sforzas for eighteen years, but when Ludovico achieved his short-lived return to Milan, Leonardo made no effort to rejoin him. In this he showed his political sense: Leonardo's most intimate friend, Giacomo Andrea da Ferrara, the architect who had loyally returned to support Ludovico, was hung, drawn, and quartered by Trivulzio. Meanwhile Leonardo, who had contrived to make friends with the French, was intriguing with Trivulzio's lieutenant, Ligny, for the return of his property in Milan, and in the following year would have been certain of employment by the French, had he not already been in the service of Cesare Borgia.

On leaving Milan he seems to have gone straight to Mantua. He did not stay there long, but we know from a letter which he received in Venice on 13 March 1500 that he had had time to draw a portrait of Isabella d'Este. He seems to have impressed her all too favourably, for during the next four years she persecuted him with commissions, commanded or entreated, through her agent at Florence. She was particularly insistent that her portrait might be coloured, but as far as we know it remained no more than a cartoon, the general aspect of which has come down to us in a number of replicas. These show her wearing a wide-necked dress, seated with her head in profile, her arms folded before her, in a pose which must have influenced Venetian portraiture for the next ten years. One of these cartoons, now in the Louvre,[4] is usually accepted as the original (Pl. 61), but it has been so much re-worked that no certain judgement is possible. It has been pricked for transfer so that we can be sure of the main outlines, and these show that the right arm was in a position anatomically false. The arm is shown correctly drawn in an otherwise feeble replica at Oxford, and the natural inference is that the Louvre cartoon never was Leonardo's original. All that is left for us to appreciate is the pose, which in its ease and breadth anticipates the Mona Lisa. It is curious that Leonardo, who always sought for movement into depth, should have chosen to represent her head in profile; but we know from his early drawings that he took a pleasure in giving this, the least plastic of poses, a remarkable feeling of relief, and in the portrait of Isabella we may suppose that the austere design of the head was intended as a check to the ample movement of the bust and arms.

From Mantua Leonardo went to Venice. No doubt he had been there before, to study the horses of St Mark or to see his old fellow-pupil, Lorenzo

3. Cf. Jacob Burckhardt, *The Civilization of the Renaissance in Italy*, trs. S. Middlemore, 2 vols., London, 1878, pp. 132, 133.

4. No. 390. Others are in the Ashmolean (black chalk), and (heads only) the Uffizi (red chalk, Cat. 11, No. 419), and the collection of Mrs Stanley Leighton (red chalk).

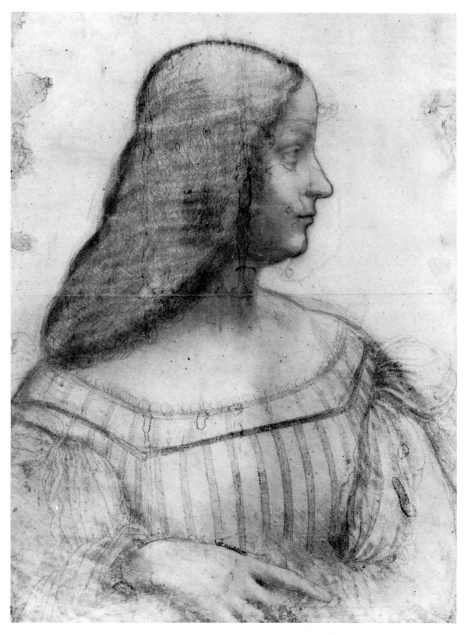

*61. 'Portrait of*
*Isabella d'Este', 1500.*
*Louvre, Paris*

di Credi, finishing the Colleoni monument. But since this is the only visit of
which we have documentary evidence, it is usually taken as the date of
Leonardo's influence on Venetian art. Vasari, in his life of Giorgione, says
that 'having seen some things from the hand of Leonardo delicately and
deeply modelled with dark shadows, they pleased him so much that as long
as he lived he made them his models, and in oil painting imitated them

greatly.'[5] Modern writers have supposed that this statement was due only to Vasari's Tuscan patriotism, but there is nothing improbable about it. Among Leonardo's most personal and spontaneous images, both written and depicted, are many which recall, by their deeply coloured romanticism, the art of early sixteenth-century Venice. Material evidence of his influence is Giorgione's picture of Christ carrying the Cross in S. Rocco which certainly derives from a design by Leonardo. This design is known to us as a whole through the replicas of Milanese pupils, evidently taken from a lost cartoon;[6] from Leonardo's own hand we have only a silverpoint drawing, now appropriately in the Venice Academy. But more important, if less easily demonstrable, is the influence on Giorgione of Leonardo's whole way of looking at forms. This is most easily seen in a change of feminine type, whereby the wide shallow features of Bellini's Madonnas were replaced by a more plastic and more regular oval. The head of the gipsy in the 'Tempesta' magnified and seen in isolation is surprisingly Leonardesque; the Giorgione portrait of a lady with laurel leaves in Vienna reflects the same sense of form as the 'Belle Ferronnière'.[7] And as a complement to this ideal beauty, Giorgione like Leonardo portrayed an ideal of ugliness. The old woman with the inscription Col Tempo in the Venice Academy, which I believe to be an authentic Giorgione, derives from Leonardo both in general conception and in the actual type. Finally, the drapery of the 'Judith', so completely unlike that of Bellini, or, it must be confessed, of Giorgione's other work, is directly inspired by Leonardo. The intricate folds which swirl out round the left side of the figure can be compared with the drawing of angels in the Venice Academy (P. 126).

These similarities of form are accentuated, as Vasari pointed out, by a similar use of light and shade. At first Leonardo's chiaroscuro seems to differ radically from that of the Venetians in that he professed to use shadow the more scientifically to render relief, they to heighten the emotional effect; or, to speak of actual practice, his shadow was an adjunct of form, theirs of colour. But Leonardo's chiaroscuro examined in the light of the *Trattato* seems less rigidly scientific; seems, in fact, to express an emotional approach to nature at least as intense as that of the Venetians. The subjects described in the *Trattato* – how to paint a night piece, how to paint a storm, how to paint a woman standing in the shadow of an open door – show that he

5. Milanesi, IV, p. 92. This passage does not appear in the 1550 edition, and so was probably added as a result of Vasari's conversations with Titian and other Venetian painters in 1566.

6. One of them by Luini in the Poldi Pezzoli presumably has the same relation to Leonardo's original as Luini's 'Virgin and St Anne' in the Ambrosiana bears to the 'Burlington House' cartoon.

7. The fact that the Vienna portrait is a doubtful Giorgione and the 'Belle Ferronnière' a doubtful Leonardo does not affect the argument since each is typical. Actually the Bellini 'Virgin and Child between St Catherine and St Mary Magdalene' with its dark background and artificial lighting may reflect Leonardo's influence although it probably dates from before 1490.

delighted in effects of light and shade of a strangeness and violence which Giorgione and his school were the first to attempt. What could be more like an illustration to the *Trattato* than the huge painting of the miracle of St Mark in the Scuola di San Marco, which was possibly designed and partly executed by Giorgione? It is true that Leonardo's paintings as they have come down to us show a much less colouristic use of shadow than his writings would lead us to expect: and no doubt he never used the full Venetian range of colour. But we must remember that of the original aspect of Leonardo's pictures we can form practically no conception, and that the traditional technique of the Milanese school, through whose copies so much of his work is known, was an opaque monochrome, to which colour was added in glazes, now frequently lost. Only the least important of his paintings, the Ambrosiana musician, is in anything like its original condition: and it is remarkable for the luminosity of the shadows. Under deep layers of repaint and varnish the shadows of the Louvre 'Virgin of the Rocks' may be equally luminous, and in the 'Last Supper' this quality is still perceptible in the still life on the table and the decorative swags of fruit. The pictures through which Leonardo was known in Venice, therefore, may have shown a treatment of light and shade far closer to Giorgione and the early Titian than we can guess from their present condition or from the replicas of Milanese pupils.

By 24 April 1500, Leonardo was in Florence again. It was almost twenty years since he had left, and during these years the atmosphere had changed. The spirit of Lorenzo was dead; and had been succeeded by a wave of revivalism in religion and republicanism in politics. In art the heroic and the ecstatic were more in demand than the daintiness and spontaneity of the *quattrocento*. Of this heroic classical style Leonardo was, in some way, the precursor and Florence was ready to appreciate his art.

When he returned [Vasari tells us] he found that the Servite brothers had commissioned Filippino to paint the altar-piece of the high altar of the Annunziata; Leonardo said that he would gladly have undertaken such a work and when he heard this Filippino, like the good fellow he was, withdrew. The friars, in order that Leonardo might paint it, took him into their house and bore the expense of himself and all his household; and so things went on for some time, and he did not even make a beginning. But at last he made a cartoon wherein were Our Lady and St Anne and a Christ, which not only filled all artists with wonder, but, when it was finished men and women, young and old, continued for two days to crowd into the room where it was exhibited, as if attending a solemn festival: and all were astonished at its excellence.

Such popular enthusiasm would hardly have been possible in Milan, and helps us to understand why the five years Leonardo spent in Florence were more productive than the preceding eighteen years spent in the north of Italy.

62. The 'Virgin and Child with St Anne and St John the Baptist', c. 1505–7 (formerly Burlington House), National Gallery, London

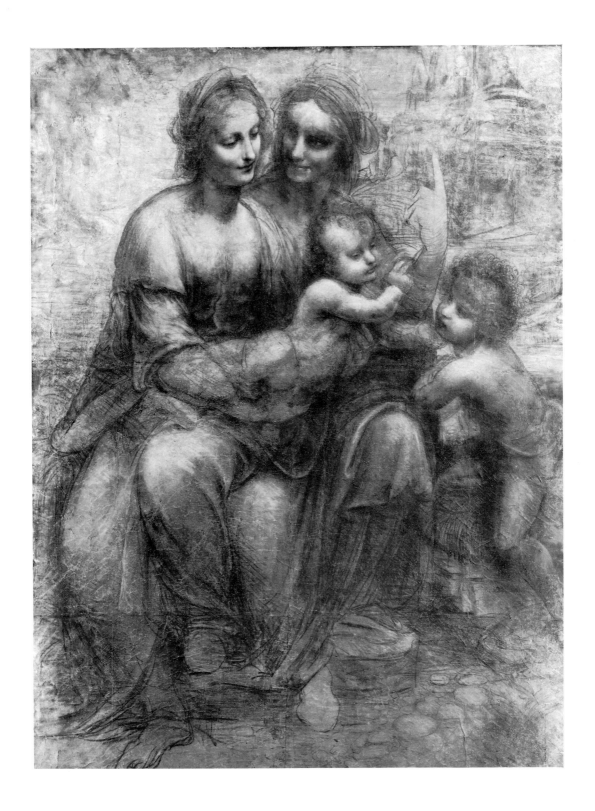

Two representations of the Virgin and St Anne by Leonardo have come down to us: the cartoon formerly at Burlington House (Pl. 62), and the unfinished painting in the Louvre. It used to be assumed that the cartoon which Vasari describes was either that from Burlington House, or a cartoon for the Louvre picture. We can be quite sure that it was not the Burlington House cartoon. During March and April of 1501 Isabella d'Este made one of her attempts to procure a picture from Leonardo. She communicated through her agent Fra Pietro da Novellara. This unhappy man was forced to write a series of letters tactfully conveying Leonardo's unwillingness to work for her, and, fortunately for us, he hid his failure under accounts of Leonardo's occupations. In one of these he describes a cartoon which must, from the date, be that mentioned by Vasari, and says that the Child Christ is leaving the arm of his Mother and has seized a lamb which he seems to be pressing to him. Now, there is no lamb in the Burlington House cartoon, and critics have therefore argued that the cartoon made for the Annunziata was the cartoon for the Louvre picture. But in so doing they did not read Fra Pietro's description carefully enough.

The mother [he goes on to say,] half rising from St Anne's lap, is taking the Child to draw it from the lamb, that sacrificial animal, which signifies the passion. While St Anne, rising slightly from her seat, seems as if she would hold back her daughter, so that she would not separate the Child from the lamb, which perhaps signifies that the Church did not wish to prevent the Passion of Christ. These figures are life-size, but they are in a small cartoon because all are seated or bent, and each one is placed before the other, to the left.

Here is a very important motif and a clear description, which do not fit the Louvre picture. St Anne is not making any attempt to restrain the Virgin; and the figures are not placed before each other to the left, but to the right. But a drawing at the Venice Academy corresponds closely enough with Novellara's description and is probably our best evidence of what the cartoon of 1501 was like.[8] At some point after his return to Florence in 1503 Leonardo took up the subject again. The result has come down to us in a large drawing, or cartoon, formerly at Burlington House, now in the National Gallery,

8. In the earlier editions of the book I accepted the hypothesis put forward by Professor Wilhelm Suida, *Leonardo und sein Kreis* (München, 1929), p. 131, that the cartoon of 1501 could be reconstructed from a painting by Brescianino in the Berlin Museum. I now believe this picture too remote from Leonardo to be admissible evidence (Ed. note: but now see Introduction, p. 32). I also accepted the current view that the Burlington House cartoon preceded the cartoon of 1501, and was executed in Milan. This was first questioned by Popham and Pouncey in their catalogue of *Italian Drawings in the British Museum* (1950), p. 67, and I am completely convinced by their reasoning. Strictly speaking, therefore, the Burlington House cartoon should have been considered in the next chapter, but I have thought it preferable not to upset too greatly the original form of the book.

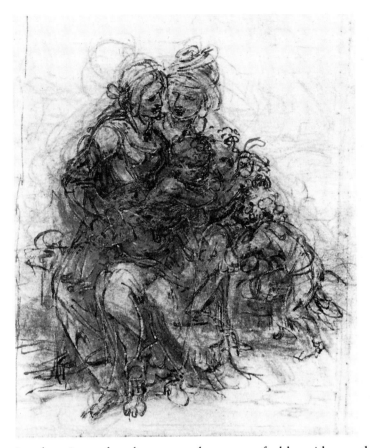

63. Study for the
'Virgin and Child with
St Anne and St John
the Baptist', c. 1505–
7. British Museum,
London

London. It used to be assumed, on very feeble evidence, that this drawing
was executed in the late 1490s, shortly before Leonardo left Milan. It now
seems to me certain that it was done considerably later, probably in about
1505. A preparatory study, now in the British Museum (Pl. 63), resembles a
drawing in Windsor for a kneeling 'Leda' which is certainly of this date; and,
apart from such questions of detail, the whole group has a sculptural largeness
that suggests Florentine art during the first heroic years of Michelangelo.
There is indeed a drawing by Michelangelo, now at Oxford, of the same
motif, although whether it was inspired by the Burlington House cartoon or
the cartoon of 1501 it is hard to say.

In the Burlington House cartoon Leonardo has made a significant change
of subject. Instead of the infant Christ leaning forward to embrace a lamb,
the symbol of sacrifice, he blesses the youthful St John, as he does in the
'Virgin of the Rocks'. St John the Baptist was especially venerated in Florence
and the fact that he is given such prominence in the Burlington House cartoon
is another indication that it was executed during Leonardo's Florentine years.
In the 'Virgin and St Anne' in the Louvre, which was painted in Milan about

five years later, he returns to the motif of the lamb, although without the human tensions described by Novellara.

By common consent the Burlington House cartoon is one of Leonardo's most beautiful works, and it is even excluded from Mr Berenson's anathema.[9] 'There is something truly Greek,' he says, 'about the gracious humanity of the ideals here embodied, and it is no less Greek as decoration. One can scarcely find draped figures contrived in a more plastic way without going back centuries to those female figures which once clustered together on the gable of the Parthenon.' Leonardo, with his love of mystery and agitation, was essentially un-Greek, and the classical elements in his work, like the geometrical, are a result of study, not predisposition. But in the cartoon the draperies have a breadth and flow remarkably similar to the group of Fates, and prove how deeply Leonardo's studies had enabled him to enter into the classical tradition. The cartoon is also the one of his works which justifies the popular notion of his art. The shadowy, smiling heads, the tender mysterious glances, the pointing hand, and those two high-sounding devices, chiaroscuro and contrapposto, all are present in their most acceptable form. This is therefore a convenient point at which to return to a question touched upon in our survey of the *Trattato*: the question of how far Leonardo's study of shadow and twisting movement led to a certain coldness and artificiality in his later work.

If theory is a true reflection of sensibility in intellectual terms, as was perspective to Piero della Francesca, it can give a painter's work an added tautness and coherency. If it is made the pretext for fantasy, as was perspective by Uccello or mannerism by El Greco, theory can actually liberate. But if, by imposing a self-created academism, it deadens the natural sensibility, as with so many painters from Raphael to Monet, it is disastrous. Leonardo, like Seurat, seems to tremble between the first and last possibility. His theories reflect his creative instincts, but by intellectual elaboration they are made dangerously stiff and pressing. For example, his love of twisting movement was an instinct, visible, as we have seen, in his earliest work; and becoming more pronounced as his sense of form becomes more liberated. His innumerable studies of waves, knots, and plaited hair were not done in pursuit of a theory, but in satisfaction of an appetite. But of this instinct he made a theory. 'Always make the figure,' he wrote, 'so that the breast is not turned in the same direction as the head. Let the movement of the head and arms be easy and pleasing, with various turns and twists.' So with chiaroscuro. He had never used the bright colours of the *quattrocento*. His early work is largely distinguishable by its mysterious twilit tones; and this instinct, too, found confirmation in the scientific investigations into the nature of light and shade,

9. In *The Study and Criticism of Italian Art*, Third Series (1916), pp. 1–37.

described on p. 129. As a result, I think that Leonardo's theories of light and shade led him to push his chiaroscuro a little further than his sensibility alone would have warranted. We shall see an example of this when we come to examine the second version of the 'Virgin of the Rocks'. The Paris picture shows Leonardo's natural feeling for darkness in the general setting, but the figures themselves are lit by more or less diffused rays: in the London picture the light comes from a single source and is concentrated on the heads so that a large part of each is in shadow. The result is a loss of colour and transparency which reminds us disagreeably of Leonardo's followers; for whatever the effect of chiaroscuro and contrapposto on Leonardo himself, on his imitators it was disastrous. He had provided them with a style, the true meaning of which they could not understand, and one which was peculiarly dangerous to mediocrities. A bad picture in the *quattrocento* style still has the merit of bright decorative colour; even its crudities may be a source of charm. A bad picture in the style of Leonardo is a horror of black shadows and squirming shapes.

These two devices had an influence far beyond Leonardo's own circle; and Vasari was right when he made them the turning point in the history of painting. The desire to lead the eye into the background by arranging the main lines diagonally to the picture plane and the theory that this movement should be achieved by smooth and continuous curves: these were to become essential qualities of Baroque. There was of course an important distinction between Leonardo and the Baroque painters. With him the movement is confined to the main group, which is detached from the background, like a piece of sculpture seen through a window; with the Baroque the diagonal serpentine movement is extended to the whole surface of the picture. But Correggio, who first conceived the true Baroque composition, never disguised his debt to Leonardo.

In his use of light and shade, Leonardo was the precursor of all subsequent European painting. Next to Giotto, it was he who put it on the road which led it away from the other painting styles of the world. After his time no one could go back to the clear tones of the old linear method – the *maniera secca e cruda*, as Vasari called it: no one, that is to say, until the youthful Ingres. This tendency in European art is usually called scientific; and we have seen that its inventor started from scientific premises. Yet, throughout, a strong contrast of light and shade has been employed, not as a branch of pictorial science but as a means of expressing an emotional attitude. Rembrandt is the least academic of great painters. And Leonardo, in all his work, most of all perhaps in the Burlington House cartoon, uses chiaroscuro with a romantic intensity unrelated to the scientific diagrams of the *Trattato*.

On 14 April 1501, a few days after his description of the St Anne cartoon, Fra Pietro da Novellara writes that he has been introduced to Leonardo and

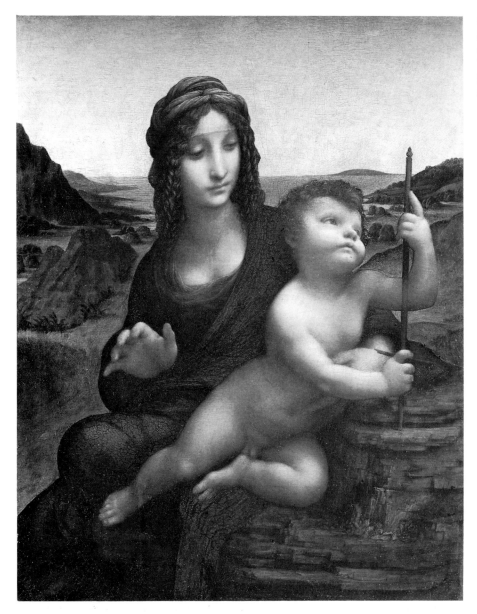

*64. Leonardo and Studio?, 'Madonna and Child with a Yarn Winder', c. 1501. Duke of Buccleuch Collection*

found him at work on a Madonna and Child for Florimond Robertet, secretary to the French King. He describes the picture with his usual accuracy – the Child has seized Our Lady's yarn winder and, holding it as if it were the Cross, gazes at it lovingly (Pl. 64). The original of this composition is lost, but the number of surviving copies shows that it must have been one of his most popular pictures; and this is easy to understand. For contemporary judgement was almost as conservative in the Renaissance as it is today, and

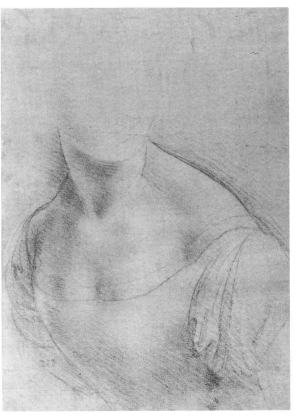

*65. Study for the
'Madonna and Child
with a Yarn Winder',
1501. Royal Library,
Windsor (RL 12514)*

Leonardo must by this time have become what is called a difficult artist.
Perugino was often spoken of as his equal, and sometimes preferred, and so
we can imagine that Leonardo's patrons were relieved when he gave them
something which rivalled Perugino in sweetness and which his earlier work
had taught them to understand. As far as we can judge from the best copies,[10]
the 'Madonna of the Yarn Winder' was close in style to the Paris 'Virgin of
the Rocks'. In spirit it is similar to the kneeling Madonna with the playing
Children, and shows that Leonardo could still relax into the happy, tender
mood of his first Florentine drawings. We must suppose that in execution it
was similar to the 'Mona Lisa', subtler and solider than the early Madonnas,
but of this our only evidence is a red chalk drawing at Windsor (Pl. 65), a
study from the model of the Virgin's shoulders, which combines firmness of
structure with the delicate pearly quality of a Watteau.

10. In a private New York collection (formerly in the collection of Robert W. Reford), and the collection
of the Duke of Buccleuch. The latter has been claimed as the original by Möller, but seems to be a fine
studio replica. The landscape, which has not been overpainted, shows that it was by a Florentine artist.
(Ed. note: Clark's later opinion, in a letter to the Duke 17.5.74, was that it originated from Leonardo's
studio and that 'the head . . . is delicate enough to be worthy of Leonardo'.)

This is the only other painting we hear of before 1502, for during these two years Leonardo was almost entirely given up to other pursuits. 'He is working hard at Geometry and has no patience with his brush' writes Fra Pietro in one letter; and in the next 'his mathematical experiments have so distracted him from painting that the sight of a brush puts him out of temper'. Finally Leonardo took the same means of escape from painting as he had attempted twenty years earlier: he took service as a military engineer. This time his engagement was more serious. His new master was Cesare Borgia.

Like Leonardo, Cesare combined extreme realism in calculation with aims so ambitious as to seem, at this safe distance of time, little more than waking

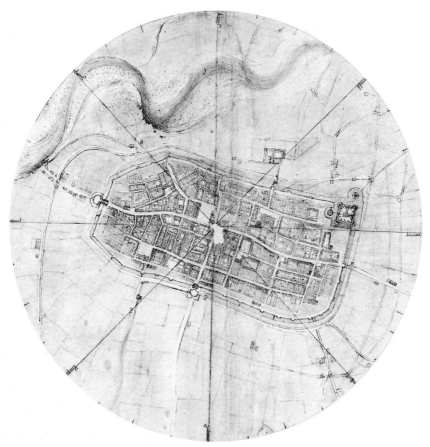

*66. Map of Imola, c. 1502–3. Royal Library, Windsor (RL 12284)*

dreams. But unlike Leonardo, he also had the will to push matters to conclusions. This new allegiance absorbed all Leonardo's energies. At the end of May he was in Piombino, making plans for draining the marsh; in June he was summoned by one of Cesare's captains, Vitellozzo Vitelli, to assist in the rebellion of Arezzo against his native Florence. To this end he made some of the beautiful maps now at Windsor. On 20 June he accompanied Cesare in his perfidious attack on Urbino; and there he remained for a month, on close terms, as it seems, with Vitellozzo and his mysterious leader. It was during this month that he first encountered another great personality of the Renaissance, with whom he was destined to become intimate, Niccolò Machiavelli, who visited Urbino as Florentine envoy in June. In August Leonardo was in Cesena, where he probably designed the canal to Porto Cesenatico and left numerous plans for fortifying the city, some of which have survived; and at this time he received a patent from Cesare which refers to him as *nostro prestantissimo et dilectissimo familiare architetto et ingegnere generale*, and gives him absolute power to command and requisition what he needs for his work. In October he and his leader were shut in Imola for several weeks (Pl. 66), and it may have been in this rare period of enforced idleness that Leonardo was able to make the red chalk drawing now at Turin of Cesare's head from three different angles. It shows his exquisitely curled, blond beard, which must have delighted Leonardo, and the curiously Northern – we might say Düreresque – look which distinguished all the Borgias. Leonardo had always aspired to the life of action, and never before had it lain open to him with such liberality and such promise. But the life of action has its drawbacks. On 31 December 1502 Leonardo's friend, Vitellozzo Vitelli, was strangled by Cesare's orders, and two months later Leonardo was back in Florence. The three years which follow were perhaps the most productive of his whole career as a painter.

Fra Pietro da Novellara, in one of his earlier letters, had described how 'two of Leonardo's pupils were doing some portraits and he from time to time put a touch on them'. This had evidently been his practice throughout the later part of his Milanese period and several portraits which puzzle connoisseurs, for example the man in the Brera inscribed *Vita si scias uti longa est*, must be the result of co-operation between pupil and master. In view of Fra Pietro's clear description of Leonardo's workshop method it is obviously difficult to say which pupil has been employed, especially since our evidence for their individual styles is extremely scanty. As I have said, Boltraffio is one of the few whose work affords some clue as to what he may have painted when in Leonardo's studio. Marco d'Oggiono, whose name is linked with his as one of Leonardo's earliest recorded pupils, is known from two monstrous altar-pieces in the Brera, but we cannot trace his peculiarly revolting style in any product of Leonardo's workshop except in his 'Ascension of the Virgin' in the Brera, which may derive in part from a design by his master. Although Vasari tells us that 'there are certain works in Milan that are said to be by Salai, but which were retouched by Leonardo' nothing can be attributed to him on internal evidence, unless it be some childish scribbles on Leonardo's drawings. In despair scholars have been forced to invent imaginary pupils – the master of the Archinto portrait, the pseudo-

Boltraffio, the so-called Gianpetrino. Meanwhile, Leonardo's notebooks contain numerous records of pupils about whom we know absolutely nothing – Bartolommeo, Bonifazio, Lorenzo, Giulio, Galeazzo, Benedetto, Gherardo, Joatti, Arrigo, il Fanfoia. Leonardo's workshop in Milan must have contained craftsmen of all sorts to carry out his multifarious designs for the Sforzas, and many of the pupils mentioned in his notes were apparently machine-makers, locksmiths, glass-cutters, etc. During his years in Florence a great proportion of his pupils must have been painters, but with one or two exceptions, like the Spaniard Fernando de Llanos, we cannot trace their subsequent work: and we must suppose that in Leonardo's studio, with the help and stimulus of the master, their work reached a level of attainment so high as to be unrecognizably different from their independent efforts.

On his return to Florence in 1503, however, Leonardo did execute one portrait entirely with his own hand. This portrait still exists, though hardly as Leonardo would wish us to see it. Before looking at the original we should read Vasari's description.

The eyes had that lustre and watery sheen which is always seen in real life, and around them were those touches of red and the lashes which cannot be represented without the greatest subtlety.... The nose, with its beautiful nostrils, rosy and tender, seemed to be alive. The opening of the mouth, united by the red of the lips to the flesh tones of the face, seemed not to be coloured but to be living flesh.

Red, rosy, tender, it might be the description of a Fragonard. Who would recognize the submarine goddess of the Louvre? (Pl. 67).

How exquisitely lovely the Mona Lisa must have been when Vasari saw her; for of course his description of her fresh rosy colouring must be perfectly accurate. She is beautiful enough even now, heaven knows, if we could see her properly. Anyone who has had the privilege of seeing the Mona Lisa taken down, out of the deep well in which she hangs, and carried to the light will remember the wonderful transformation that takes place. The presence that rises before one, so much larger and more majestical than one had imagined, is no longer a diver in deep seas. In the sunshine something of the warm life which Vasari admired comes back to her, and tinges her cheeks and lips,[11] and we can understand how he saw her as being primarily a masterpiece of naturalism. He was thinking of that miraculous subtlety of modelling, that imperceptible melting of tone into tone, plane into plane, which hardly any other painter has achieved without littleness or loss of texture. The surface has the delicacy of a new-laid egg and yet it is alive: for this is Pater's 'beauty wrought out from within upon the flesh little cell by

67. *'Portrait of Mona Lisa', 1503. Louvre, Paris*

---

11. There is, in fact, quite a lot of colour still left in her cheeks, which might be revealed by cleaning; but who would dare clean her?

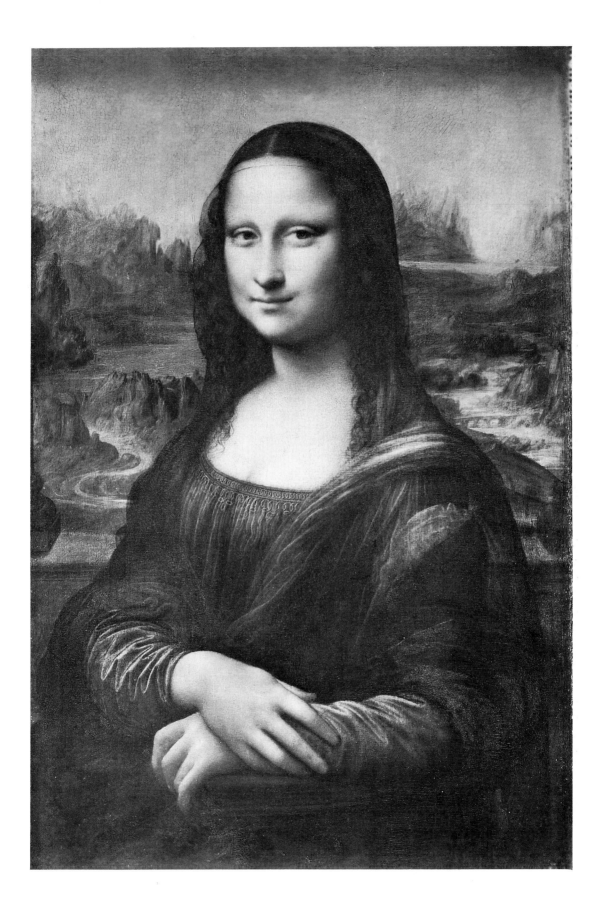

cell' – a phrase which more than any other in that famous cadenza expresses Leonardo's real intention.

Familiarity has blinded us to the beauty of the Mona Lisa's pose. It is so easy, so final, that we do not think of it as a great formal discovery until we rediscover it in Raphael's 'Maddalena Doni' or Corot's 'Dame à la Perle'. Where the romantic overtones are less insistent we are freer to contemplate formal relationships, and we see, in the Raphael for example, how carefully the axes of head and bust and hands are calculated to lead us round the figure with an even, continuous movement. A proof that Leonardo's contemporaries felt the value of this invention is the number of pupils' copies in which the figure is shown undraped. It is possible that Leonardo did a large drawing of this subject in order to realize more fully the implications of the pose, and from this there derive the many pupils' versions, including an accomplished cartoon at Chantilly. At all events, a nude figure in the attitude of the Mona Lisa was well known in France in the early sixteenth century, and formed part of the stock in trade of the Fontainebleau painters on the frequent occasions when they had to portray royal favourites in their baths.

Once we leave these purely historical considerations, we are surrounded by mist and mirage. The English critic, above all, is embarrassed by Pater's immortal passage ringing in his ears, and reminding him that anything he may write will be poor and shallow by comparison. Yet the 'Mona Lisa' is one of those works of art which each generation must re-interpret. To follow M. Valéry and dismiss her smile as *un pli de visage*, is to admit defeat. It is also to misunderstand Leonardo, for the Mona Lisa's smile is the supreme example of that complex inner life, caught and fixed in durable material, which Leonardo in all his notes on the subject claims as one of the chief aims of art. A quarry so shy must be approached with every artifice. We can well believe Vasari's story that Leonardo 'retained musicians who played and sang and continually jested in order to take away that melancholy that painters are used to give to their portraits'; and we must remember the passage in the *Trattato* (para. 135) which describes how the face yields its subtlest expression when seen by evening light in stormy weather. In this shunning of strong sunlight we feel once more the anti-classical, we might say the un-Mediterranean, nature of Leonardo. 'Set her for a moment', says Pater, 'beside one of those white Greek goddesses, or beautiful women of antiquity, and how would they be troubled by this beauty into which the soul with all its maladies has passed.' In its essence Mona Lisa's smile is a gothic smile, the smile of the Queens and Saints at Rheims or Naumburg, but since Leonardo's ideal of beauty was touched by pagan antiquity, she is smoother and more fleshly than the gothic saints. They are transparent, she is opaque. Their smiles are the pure illumination of the spirit; in hers there is something worldly, watchful, and self-satisfied.

The picture is so full of Leonardo's demon that we forget to think of it as a portrait, and no doubt an excellent likeness, of a young Florentine lady of twenty-four. She is often described as Leonardo's ideal of beauty, but this is false, since the angel in the 'Virgin of the Rocks' and the two St Annes show that his ideal was more tranquil and more regular. None the less, she must have embodied something inherent in his vision. How else can one account for the fact that while he was refusing commissions from popes, kings, and princesses he spent his utmost skill, and, as we are told, three years in painting the second wife of an obscure Florentine citizen? We may speculate with Pater on the relationship of the living Florentine to this creature of his thought – 'by what strange affinities has the dream and the person grown up thus apart and yet so closely together'. At least we can be sure that his feeling for her was not the ordinary man's feeling for a beautiful woman. He sees her physical beauty as something mysterious, even a shade repulsive, as a child might feel the physical attraction of his mother. And as often with Leonardo, this absence of normal sensuality makes us pause and shiver, like a sudden wave of cold air in a beautiful building.

Behind the Mona Lisa stretches a circle of rocky spires and pinnacles which sustain the mood of her smile. This is Leonardo's most characteristic landscape, as quintessential as the figure it surrounds, and we may suitably digress to consider his backgrounds in general. From his earliest work he had felt that the only possible background to a picture was a range of fantastic mountain peaks. He had rebelled instinctively against the landscapes taught in Verrocchio's shop, the tranquil undulations of Perugino, or the neat man-made landscapes which his Florentine contemporaries had imitated from Flemish art. To him landscape seems to have represented the wildness of nature, the vast, untamed background of human life; so the resemblance of his mountains to the craggy precipices of Chinese painting is no accident, for the Chinese artist also wished to symbolize the contrast between wild nature and busy organized society. Yet between Leonardo and the Chinese there is also a profound difference. To the Chinese a mountain landscape was chiefly a symbol, an ideograph of solitude and communion with nature, expressed in the most correct and elegant forms which the artist could command. To Leonardo a landscape, like a human being, was part of a vast machine, to be understood part by part and, if possible, in the whole. Rocks were not simply decorative silhouettes. They were part of the earth's bones, with an anatomy of their own, caused by some remote seismic upheaval. Clouds were not random curls of the brush, drawn by some celestial artist, but were the congregation of tiny drops formed from the evaporation of the sea, and soon would pour back their rain into the rivers. Thus, Leonardo's landscapes, however wildly romantic his choice of subject matter, never take on the slightly artificial appearance of the Chinese. To realize the deep knowledge of natural appearance behind them, we have only to compare the background of the 'Mona Lisa', in some ways the most romantic of all, with the caricature of Leonardo's landscape in such a schoolpiece as the 'Resurrection', in Berlin, where the mountains are arranged like the scenery in a toy theatre.

The period of the 'Mona Lisa' is no arbitrary point at which to examine Leonardo's landscapes, because to about this period belong a number of the landscape drawings at Windsor. One of these, a red chalk drawing of a storm breaking over a valley in the Alps (Pl. 68), must date from a few years earlier, and is one of the studies from nature which precede the background of the

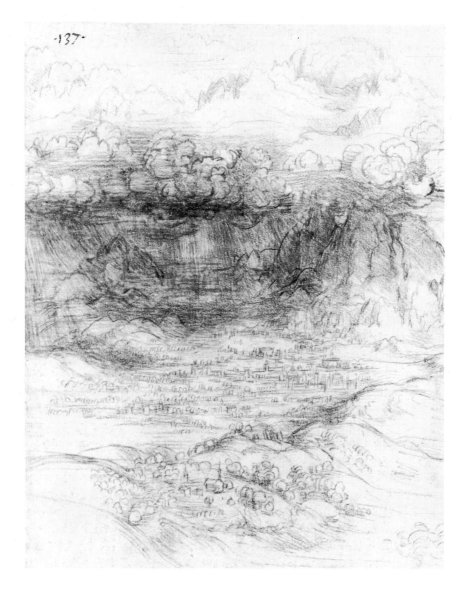

*68. Landscape with a storm in the Alps, c. 1503. Royal Library, Windsor (RL 12409)*

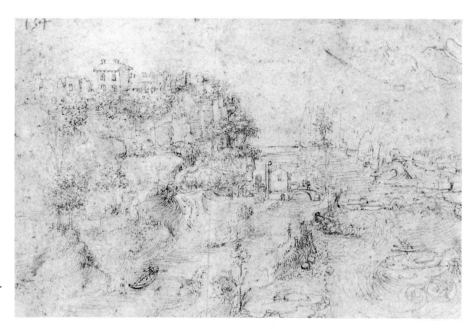

*69. Study of a river and a canal and a castle on a hill, c. 1503. Royal Library, Windsor (RL 12399)*

'Mona Lisa'. The way in which a complex panorama is compressed into a few square inches recalls Turner, though even in such a romantic subject we feel the Italian grasp of formal design beside which a Turner looks unsteady.

The landscape drawings of about 1503 are less romantic. They show the influence of Leonardo's practical pursuits during the preceding years, his map-making for Cesare Borgia, and his studies of watersheds and canalization. Many of them are done from a high point of view – some are almost maps – and contain rivers or canals. The most exquisite are those drawn with short delicate strokes of the pen in a pale ink impossible to reproduce (Pl. 69 and P. 268–9). They have a Japanese fantasy and precision in the spacing of the chief accents, as if Leonardo's vision, in admitting some flavour of actual life into his ideal landscapes, has undergone the same process by which Chinese painting was transformed into the prints of Hokusai and Hiroshige.

The range of Leonardo's interest in nature is further shown by a group of plant studies, done at about the same period as these panoramic landscapes. He drew flowers throughout his life. The grass in the Uffizi 'Annunciation' and the flowers in the 'Munich Madonna' are already the work of someone who understands the inner nature of plant life. Vasari and the Anonimo tell us of a cartoon of Adam and Eve 'in a meadow with an infinite number of flowers' of which not a trace remains; and the second entry on the list quoted on p. 86 is 'many flowers, drawn from nature' – all now lost. The only drawings of plants of this early period are the pages of MS. B, and can be

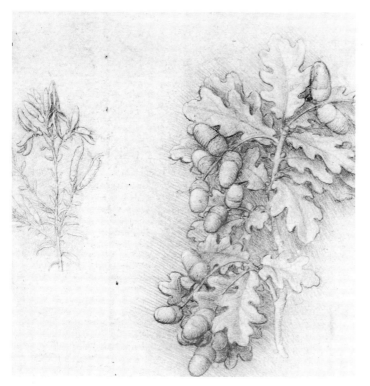

70. *Study of Acorns and Dyer's Greenweed, c. 1506. Royal Library, Windsor (RL 12422)*

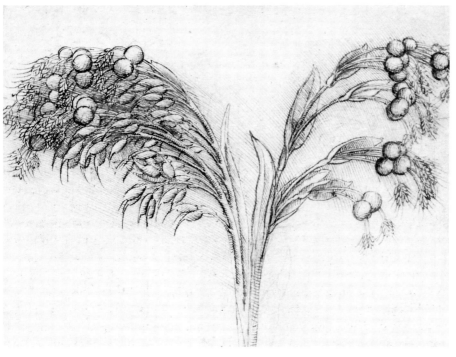

71. *Study of a plant, c. 1506. Royal Library, Windsor (RL 12429)*

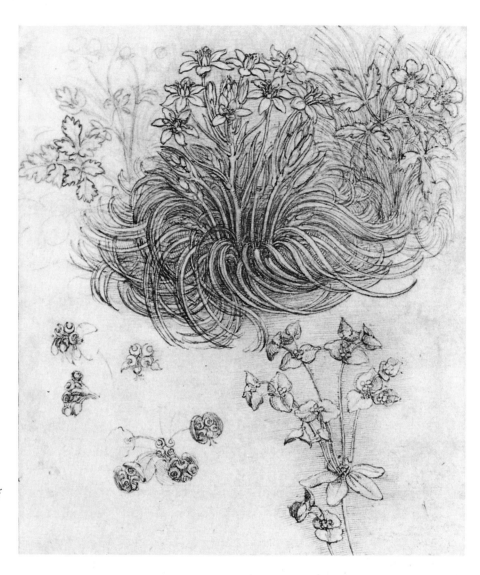

72. *Study of a Star of Bethlehem, Spurge, and other Plants*, c. 1506. Royal Library, Windsor (RL 12424)

connected with the 'Virgin of the Rocks'; to a later period, about the years 1503–6, belong ten studies of flowers and seeds at Windsor (P. 270 to P. 278). Technically, they are amongst Leonardo's most miraculous drawings (Pls. 70 and 71). The majority are in red chalk, on prepared paper, a medium more colouristic than precise; yet Leonardo has given the greatest possible fullness of definition. No one but Watteau seems to have been able to sharpen his chalk to such a fine, firm point, let alone use it. In others, he has added touches with a pen to increase definition. In the finest of all, pen and chalk are equally combined, giving a wide range of tone which might have tempted a less learned draughtsman into facile effectiveness. A masterpiece of this kind is the study of a Star of Bethlehem among swirling grasses (Pl. 72) which combines the rhythmic movement of his hand with the microscopic steadiness of his eye, so that it becomes an essential token of his art when freed from all conscious intentions, dramatic or professional.

As usual it is hard to say how far these studies were made for their own sakes and how far they were preparatory to a picture. That they and others like them were used in a picture is certain. This was the lost picture of 'Leda and the Swan' which, as all the copies show, contained a profusion of flowers and grasses extraordinary even for Leonardo. Both the Anonimo and Lomazzo record that Leonardo painted a 'Leda' which was taken to France

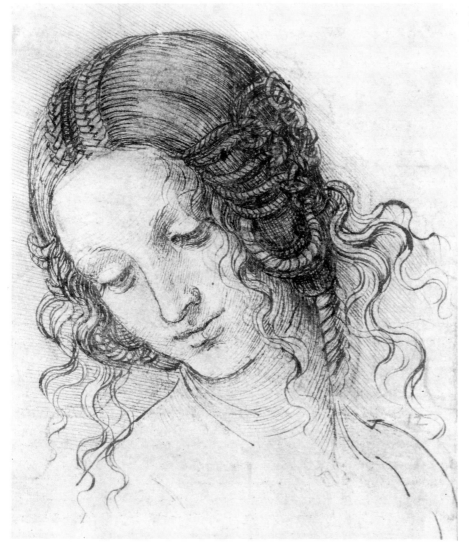

*73. Study for 'Leda', c. 1506. Royal Library, Windsor (RL 12518)*

74. *Raphael after Leonardo, Study of Leonardo's 'Leda',* c. *1506–8. Royal Library, Windsor (*RL *12759)*

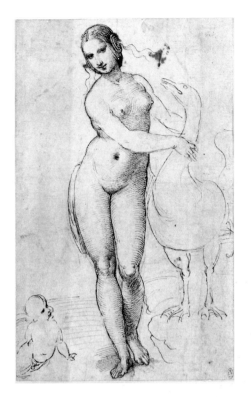

in the sixteenth century. Cassiano del Pozzo who saw it in Fontainebleau in 1625 describes it in detail – 'a standing figure of Leda almost entirely naked, with the swan at her feet and two eggs, from whose broken shells come forth four babies. This piece, though somewhat dry in style, is exquisitely finished, especially in the woman's breast; and for the rest the landscape and the plant life are rendered with the greatest diligence. Unfortunately, the picture is in a bad way because it is done on three long panels which have split apart and broken off a certain amount of paint.' The picture is in inventories of Fontainebleau of 1692 and 1694, but does not appear in them again, and Carlo Goldoni, visiting Versailles in 1775, can find no trace or memory of it. He adds that it is not in the list of pictures destroyed, as he says, from misplaced feelings of devotion, so the tradition that it was burnt by order of Madame de Maintenon because of its indecency is probably without foundation.

Cassiano del Pozzo's description shows that the 'Leda' was one of Leonardo's largest and most important panels and it is worth making some effort to reconstruct it correctly. Our materials for doing so are relatively abundant. In the first place, we have Leonardo's own drawings of the head and bust (Pl. 73),[12] then a pen drawing by Raphael evidently copying Leonardo's

12. At Windsor, nos. 12,515, 12,516, 12,517 and 12,518 (Pl. 74).

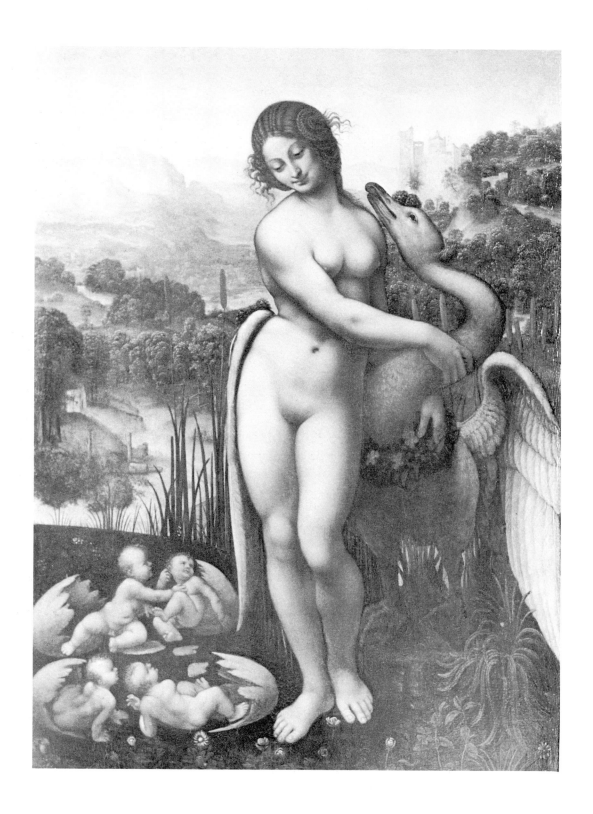

*75. Cesare da Sesto,*
*after Leonardo:*
*'Leda', c. 1520. Wilton*
*House*

cartoon which shows the whole figure and the babies (Pl. 74); a red chalk drawing in the Louvre by a close pupil of Leonardo and numerous painted versions by pupils and contemporaries.

We can divide these copies into two distinct groups. The first, which is represented by Raphael's drawing, the Louvre drawing, a picture by Bugiardini in the Borghese, and a copy formerly in the collection of M. Richeton, shows Leda with her body so far twisted round that her left breast is in profile and the line of her right arm comes almost down to her hip. She seems to be straining away from the swan's bill. The children are not disposed regularly as in the other groups of copies, though the Raphael drawing and the Richeton version contain a baby in roughly the same attitude. Since Raphael's drawing belongs to his Florentine period, this version of the 'Leda' must have been completed before 1504. We may infer that it was no more than a cartoon or large drawing in which the position of the children was only suggested. The other group of copies must derive from Leonardo's picture. All of these are by Milanese and not Florentine artists, and suggest that the original was painted after Leonardo's return to Milan. He evidently felt that the twist of Leda's body in the cartoon had been too violent for a finished painting and modified it considerably. As a result, the dramatic intention of her shrinking movement is lost, and the pose becomes artificial. He also decided on the position of the children, which is the same in all the copies of the painting. Of these the closest to Leonardo is that at Wilton (Pl. 75) which is almost certainly the work of Cesare da Sesto, and so may have been painted in Leonardo's workshop between 1507 and 1510. Cesare has made alterations in the landscape, which is characteristic of his style, but Leda's elaborate coiffure is line for line the same as that in a drawing at Windsor (P. 210).[13] Less close, but still deriving directly from Leonardo's painting, is the ex-Spiridon version which was once claimed as the original. Other versions drift further and further from the original, only the pose of the figure remaining the same.

Even in her final modified form the 'Leda' remains an extreme example of Leonardo's love of twisting forms. As in Indian sculpture, the high full breasts are made the centre of a sequence of curves moving freely in space, and contrasted with the open, frontal axis of the hips. This contrast has its own meaning, but it is interesting to note that Leonardo at an early stage attempted a design even more expressive of his love of contrapposto. This experiment is best seen in a beautiful sketch at Windsor, which is on the same sheet as a study for 'Anghiari' (Pl. 76). Leda is kneeling on her right knee, her left cutting

13. This curious hairdress is a wig, not a plaiting of Leda's own hair. It is clearly shown as such in the Borghese copy and in Leonardo's own drawings, beside one of which (P. 209b) he writes 'this kind can be taken off and put on again without damaging it'. Here again we have a reminiscence of Verrocchio, who seems to have made such wigs for statues in the Medici Palace; cf. the entry in the inventory of Tommaso quoted in M. Cruttwell, *Verrocchio* (London, 1904), p. 86.

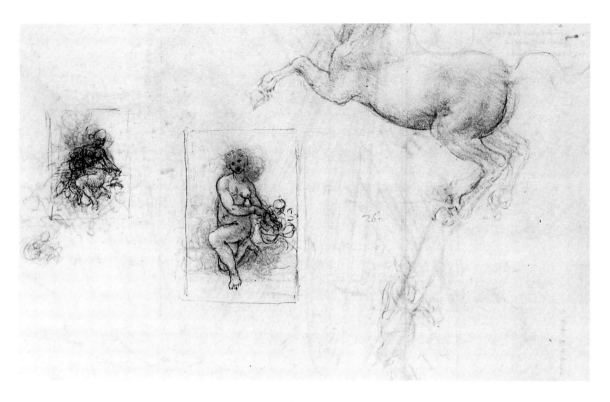

across her body in a counter rhythm to the movement of her shoulders.[14] Two pen and ink drawings at Rotterdam (P. 208) and Chatsworth[15] show how swan and grasses charged the whole composition with a more-than-Indian complexity. Nowhere else does Leonardo give such free rein to his strangely unclassical rhythmic sense.

One more question connected with the 'Leda' remains to be answered. Why did Leonardo choose the subject? It is no answer to say that he wanted to paint a female nude in an attitude of contrapposto. We can be sure that the myth of Leda had some special meaning for him, although at first sight at the furthest remove from his nature. No classical myth is more unblushingly pagan, and Leonardo was the least pagan artist of the Renaissance, never content to enjoy the sensuous surface of life, but searching for the bone beneath the skin. To him, then, the Leda myth could not be what it was to Correggio, an allegory of sensual ecstasy. He saw in it not the joy and beauty of sexual intercourse, but its mystery, and its analogy with the creative

*76. Studies for a 'Kneeling Leda' and of a Horse, c. 1503–5. Royal Library, Windsor (RL 12337r)*

14. The pose of this kneeling Leda was inspired by a Venus Anadyomene in the centre of a Hellenistic sarcophagus representing the transit of the soul, either the version now in the Villa Borghese or one in the Louvre, both of which were visible in Rome in the early sixteenth century.

15. I find it hard to be certain of the authenticity of either. The Weimar drawing is superior and may be an original in a style of which the Chatsworth drawing is an imitation.

*77. Studies of the Urino-genital systems in Woman and Man, c. 1508. Royal Library, Windsor (RL 19095v)*

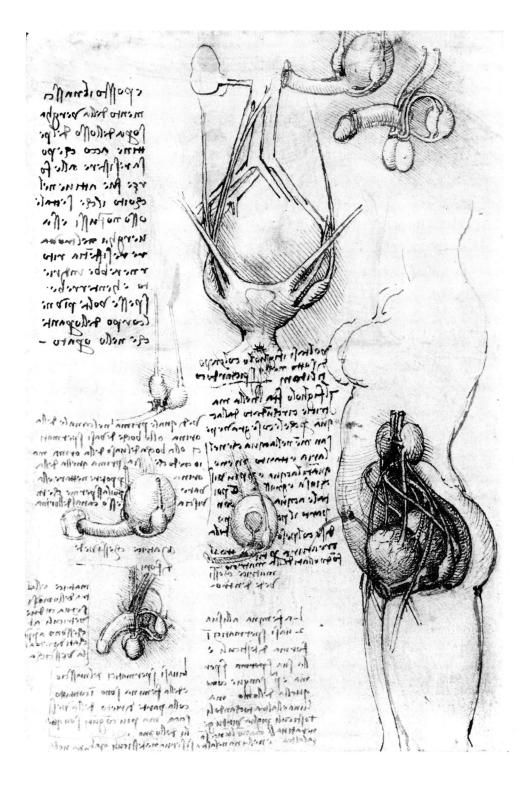

processes of nature. His Leda symbolizes the female aspect of creation. She is a fertility goddess, a Diana of Ephesus, her female attributes emphasized not by monstrous exaggeration, but by ingenuity of pose. The downcast eyes, taken by Lomazzo as a sign of modesty, are dark, secret, remote. Even those elaborate coils of hair seem appropriate to the intricacy of conception. All round this passive figure, nature is bursting with new life, thick grasses writhe out of the earth, thick leaves weigh down the branches; and at her feet, four human babies tumble out of the broken eggs.

That such an interpretation is not fanciful is proved by a study of Leonardo's drawings. The very first sketch for the 'Leda' is on a sheet at Windsor (12,642) on which there is also an anatomical study. Now this study can be related directly to a number of drawings in the Anatomical MS. B, which deal with the problem of generation (Pl. 77). One of these in particular bears a study of female anatomy very similar to the 'Leda' and evidently of the same date. And in the drawing the creative process symbolized in the 'Leda' is examined with scientific detachment.

Leonardo's imagery arouses admiration rather than delight. The intellectual treatment of a theme usually reserved for the emotions is disquieting, even though, as in this case, it displays an intellect of extraordinary subtlety and power. In few of his creations do we feel more clearly the distance which separates Leonardo from common humanity.[16]

16. For a different interpretation of the 'Leda', cf. Solmi, *Scritti Vinciani*, p. 194: '*Leonardo, con arte suprema, aveva saputo infondere alla sua figura tanta grazia e tanto riserbo da acquetare qualunque coscienza più scrupulosa.*'

# CHAPTER SEVEN

# 1503-1508

To realize the amazing productivity of Leonardo during the four years of his residence in Florence, 1503–7, we must remember that a great part of the work done during that period is lost to us. We know it only from literary records and pupils' copies, some of which can be connected with original drawings. Two such lost works, the 'Leda' and the 'Madonna of the Yarn Winder', have already been referred to. These were finished pictures; but for the most part, Leonardo, who hated the labour of painting, was content to expend his unflagging pictorial invention on drawings which were seized upon by the pupils and parasites who surrounded him and turned into saleable pictures. Some of these pupils' copies can be connected with sketches so slight that they can hardly have served as the basis for a finished picture, and since none of them has any indication of squaring, I think that Leonardo himself must have turned them into large drawings or cartoons. This would account for the fact that painters such as Raphael, Piero di Cosimo, and Quentin Matsys borrowed from Leonardo motifs which are only known to us in his smallest scribbles. Of all works of art, cartoons are the most destructible, especially when they have become the common property of a studio; and we are fortunate in having one of these, the Burlington House 'St Anne', more or less intact. Had it not survived we could hardly have guessed at its existence, as it is not recorded in any documents, and only one drawing for it by Leonardo survives. We know that it served as a model for a painting by Luini now in the Ambrosiana, and on the analogy of this connection we may reconstruct several other lost cartoons of a similar type. We may take for example another Luini, the 'Christ among the Doctors' in the National Gallery. This composition, which used to be attributed to Leonardo himself, had a prestige which Luini's unaided work never achieved.

Its origins may be found in a letter from Isabella d'Este of 14 May 1504, in which she asks Leonardo to paint her a youthful Christ 'Of about twelve years old, the age he would have been when he disputed in the Temple'. Isabella's letter refers to a single figure of the youthful Christ, but either her description suggested to Leonardo a composition of Christ in the Temple or he was already at work on such a subject, and Isabella wished him to paint her the central figure alone. In any case, he seems to have carried out the single figure of a Christ bearing the globe, known through numerous copies and two original drawings at Windsor (P. 207), studies of drapery which the copies follow very closely. And, later or earlier, this figure was made the centre of a group of Doctors whose general disposition we know from Luini's free version, and whose physiognomies can be traced in several of Leonardo's drawings. As in the Uffizi 'Adoration' and the 'Last Supper', Leonardo has based his composition on the motif of a central type of innocence and beauty surrounded by embodiments of worldly passions, in this case aged cunning and obstinacy. This was evidently the aspect of the cartoon which most impressed Dürer, for he reproduces it in his own gothic version of the subject painted in Italy in 1505.

Other projects of these years could be traced with equal fullness, both in their origins and their influence. I will mention one that has an interesting bearing on Leonardo's attitude towards the antique: the design of Neptune which Leonardo did for his friend Antonio Segni.[1] This was evidently a highly finished drawing of the kind which, some thirty years later, Michelangelo was to make for his friend Cavalieri. Vasari says it was drawn with such diligence that it seemed wholly alive, and adds: 'In it one saw the ocean troubled, and Neptune's chariot drawn by sea-horses, with fantastic creatures, dolphins and winds; and several most beautiful heads of sea gods.' This final drawing is lost, but two preparatory studies at Windsor show that Leonardo had set himself an unusual problem. Out of compliment to the learned taste of his friend (it was for Segni that Botticelli painted his 'Calumny of Apelles') Leonardo has aimed at a composition in the antique style. The more finished drawing at Windsor recalls an antique gem in the decorative arabesque of sea-horses' heads and tails, which bend round the central figure as if to fill the oval of a cameo (Pl. 78). Leonardo's love of exuberant motion has given this classical idea the character of the Pergamene school; in fact, some by-products of the school, probably sarcophagi, must have been in his mind, and should be remembered when considering the almost contemporary cartoon for the 'Battle of Anghiari'. But in this sketch the violent movement of the Neptune did not seem sufficiently august, and Leonardo has written a

---

1. The motif was taken from a Hellenistic sarcophagus, now in the Vatican, then on the steps of the Aracoeli Church, Rome.

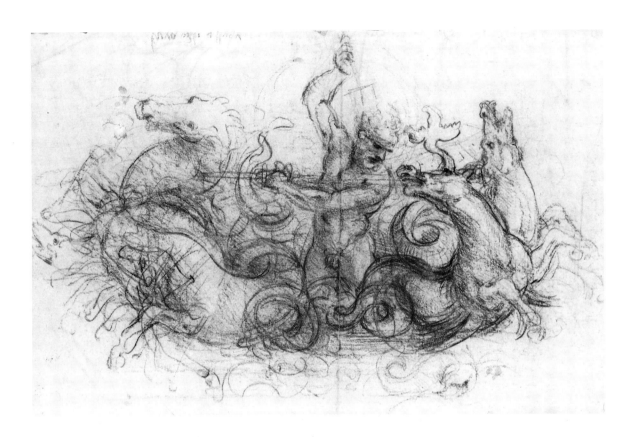

*78. Study for 'Neptune in his Chariot', 1504. Royal Library, Windsor (RL 12570)*

note on the drawing, 'lower the horses', so that the god might attain greater dignity. One, certainly not the final, result of this attempt is to be seen on the other sheet at Windsor (P. 206), where he has drawn sea-horses round the feet of a figure freely copied from Michelangelo's 'David', as if aware that his great rival had a mastery of the antique canon which he could never achieve. It is interesting to remember that in January 1504 Leonardo was one of a committee of artists appointed to consider the placing of the 'David'; and this gives us the date of the Neptune drawing,[2] since it cannot have been much earlier, and in the same year Segni left Florence for Rome. What the final appearance of the drawing may have been we cannot tell. Neither study gives us any indication of how the heads of marine gods, so highly praised by Vasari, were included in the composition. We know that the design was much admired and made the subject of a Latin epigram.[3] It was the first of a kind that long occupied the minds of high Renaissance artists. Raphael's

2. Gaye, *Carteggio*, vol. II, p. 460.

3. It was seen by V. Carducho, *Dialogos de la pintura* (Madrid, 1633), and described as being in the house of Giovanni Gaddi in Pisa.

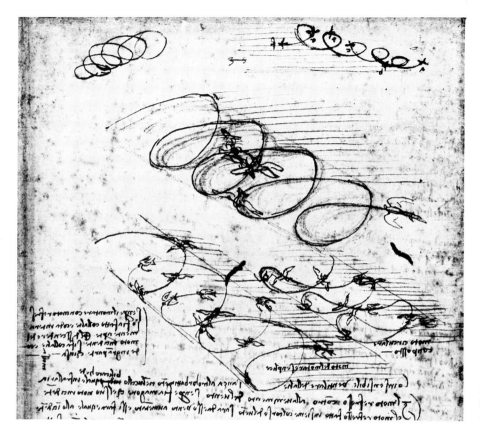

*79. Studies of bird
flight, c. 1505.
Ambrosiana, Milan*

'Galatea', Ammanati's 'Neptune' fountain in the Piazza della Signoria, even
Bernini's 'Trevi' fountain are expansions of the same theme; and a bronze
group by Gian Francesco Rustici (see p. 206)[4] may actually be taken from
Leonardo's drawing and give some idea of its final form.

In addition to Leonardo's immense output as an artist, these years saw
him engaged on some of his most arduous scientific and practical labours.
To 1505 belongs his MS. on the flight of birds, a subject which he continued
to study till his last years. Leonardo was certainly not the first man since
antiquity to try to construct machines by which human beings could fly.
Roger Bacon says that 'an instrument may be made to fly withal if one sit in
the midst of the instrument, and do turn an engine, by which the wings, being
artificially composed, may beat the air after the manner of a flying bird'.
Some such inventions are embodied in Leonardo's earliest studies of flight,

4. Victoria and Albert Museum, formerly Woolbeding House and Cowdray. Cecil Gould, *Burlington
Magazine*, vol. XCIV (1960), p. 289, gives reason to believe that the closest replica of the lost drawing is a
drawing in the Accademia Carrara, Bergamo.

dating from about 1485, which, like the early machines, show that he had
not yet arrived at his experimental approach to every problem. It is characteristic of the growth of his mind that by 1505 he should have gone back to
study from nature the principles of flight (Pl. 79). He assumed, as all early
students of flying assumed, that man would fly in the same way as the birds,
and the manuscript consists almost entirely of small studies of birds in flight.
Not so long ago we should have said that this assumption had been completely
falsified by the invention of the propeller-driven aeroplane. But the growth
of gliding has shown that Leonardo's approach to the problem may yet prove
to be the right one, and students of aeronautics have given more and more
attention to the flight of birds. This book is not concerned with Leonardo as
an inventor, but his studies of flight have a bearing on his art because they
prove the extraordinary quickness of his eye. There is no doubt that the
nerves of his eye and brain, like those of certain famous athletes, were
really supernormal, and in consequence he was able to draw and describe
movements of a bird which were not seen again until the invention of the
slow-motion cinema.

A branch of science more directly related to his painting at this date was
anatomy. During his residence at Florence he stayed in the hospital of Santa
Maria Nuova and the Anonimo tells us that he was given opportunities of
dissection there. Nearly all the drawings in the Anatomical MS. B date from
this period. Many of these are concerned with muscles, especially of the legs
and thighs; and in this way they are connected with the drawings for the
'Battle of Anghiari'. They give some justification to the old belief that
Leonardo studied anatomy in order to make his representation of the figure
more scientific. But in general Leonardo's scientific researches were undertaken for their own sakes, and anatomy was only one manifestation of his
curiosity into the workings of nature. It never became to him, as it did to
Michelangelo, a means of pictorial expression. In fact, he warns the painter
against the abuse of anatomical knowledge: 'O anatomical painter' runs a
note in MS. E, probably written in Rome about the year 1514, 'beware, lest
in the attempt to make your nudes display all their emotions by a too strong
indication of bones, sinews, and muscles, you became a wooden painter.'
The reference to Michelangelo, who at that moment was painting the Sistine
Ceiling, is unmistakable. Leonardo has understood that the true purpose of
Michelangelo's anatomical display is the expression of emotion, but has seen
in it the seeds of mannerism. He goes on to write of anatomical knowledge
used from a purely naturalistic point of view. Michelangelo might have
replied with an exactly analogous criticism of Leonardo's chiaroscuro.

One more of these practical occupations remains to be mentioned, because
it led accidentally to Leonardo's greatest commission. I have mentioned that
while employed by Cesare Borgia, Leonardo met Machiavelli at Urbino. The

two men met again at Imola, and on Leonardo's return to Florence they seem to have become intimate. Each in his own sphere felt the necessity of reconstructing principles on the basis of facts, and brought to the task a great and free intelligence. Machiavelli, moreover, was capable of romantic enthusiasm for unusual abilities; and it was this which made him give all the weight of his position – he was secretary to the republic and friend of the *gonfaloniere* Soderini – to one of Leonardo's most extravagant schemes. At intervals during his life Leonardo had been concerned with schemes involving the management of water. He had drawn plans of canalization for the Sforza at Vigevano, Lomellini, Ivrea, and in Milan itself.[5] He had attempted to drain the marsh at Piombino, and was later to draw plans for draining the Pontine marshes (P. 287). Any student of his drawings will remember that the idea of canalization was always active in his mind. He therefore conceived a plan to end the miserable war between Florence and Pisa which had been dragging on for some years by depriving Pisa of the Arno. Instead the Arno should enter the sea near Stagna and should be navigable as far as Florence. The scheme was first put forward in the summer of 1503 and in August 1504, after a year's discussion, the council decided to adopt it. It is a proof of Leonardo's power of persuasion – *fu nel parlarè*, says the Anonimo, *eloquentissimo* – that the hard-headed Florentine Signoria was ever won round to a scheme which would extend the resources of modern engineering and must then have been wholly impracticable. Some of Leonardo's maps still remain (P. 264), and some drawings of men digging (Pl. 50); but no trace of the canals.[6] The water refused to flow into the new channels, and in October 1504 the work was abandoned.

Leonardo's friendship with Machiavelli was to have a more important result: the commission from the Signoria to paint a great fresco in the Sala del Gran Consiglio of the Palazzo Vecchio. The subject chosen was the victory of the Florentines over the Milanese at the 'Battle of Anghiari': and Solmi believed, on insufficient evidence, I fear, that the description of the Battle drawn up for Leonardo's use and still preserved in the *Codice Atlantico* was in Machiavelli's own hand.

Leonardo began the cartoon in October 1503. By May 1504 the work was so little advanced that the Signoria made an agreement by which it was to be finished in February 1505: and by the end of that year the cartoon actually was finished and Leonardo had begun to paint on the wall. We are told by the Anonimo that he attempted a technical method learnt from Pliny – a

---

5. Cf. Solmi, *Scritti Vinciani*, p. 111.

6. At Windsor. The maps are nos. 12,277, 12,279, 12,677, 12,685. The men digging, nos. 12,644, 12,645, 12,646 and 12,648.

sort of encaustic – and that the result was unsuccessful.[7] The upper half dried
too dark, the lower half melted. The general effect is given fairly well in an
early copy in the Uffizi and as we can see, the painting was not entirely ruined.
In 1513 a special frame was made to enclose it, and Anton Francesco Doni,
in a letter to a friend, dated 17 August 1549, mentions it as one of the things
most worthy to be seen in Florence. 'Having ascended the stairs of the Sala
Grande,' he writes, 'take a diligent view of a group of horses (a portion of
the battle of Leonardo da Vinci) which will appear a miraculous thing to
you.' Even Vasari does not describe it as being in the dilapidated condition
of the 'Last Supper', and he had good reason to make it out as bad as possible
for it was he who finally obliterated Leonardo's work by painting one of his
own feeble and turgid decorations over the top during the general reconstruction of the room in 1565.

The 'Battle of Anghiari' was, in some ways, Leonardo's most important
commission. At the height of his powers he was given a subject ideally suited
to his genius. His work was to occupy a room of state in his native town;
and in the same room the one man who could possibly be considered his
equal was engaged on a similar commission, Michelangelo, who started work
on his cartoon of bathing soldiers surprised at the Battle of Cascina a little
later than Leonardo. Even Leonardo, so little moved by worldly considerations, must have felt that his honour as a Florentine was at stake. The idea
of painting a battle had long been in his mind, and is described in the
Ashburnham MS. I (4 verso), in a dramatic passage too long to quote in full.[8]
As so often happens when painters describe their subjects – Delacroix is
another example – the result is far more 'literary' than modern critics would
suppose. Leonardo's description contains incidents and details which might
seem outside the true scope of painting.

You must make the conquered and beaten pale, their brows raised and knit, and
the skin above their brows furrowed with pain, the sides of the nose with wrinkles
going in an arch from the nostrils to the eyes, and make the nostrils drawn up and
the lips arched upwards discovering the upper teeth; and the teeth apart as with
crying out and lamentation. And make one man shielding his terrified eyes with one
hand, the palm towards the enemy, while the other rests on the ground to support
his half-raised body.... Others must be represented in the agonies of death grind-
ing their teeth, rolling their eyes, with their fists clenched against their bodies and
their legs contorted. Someone might be shown disarmed and beaten down by the
enemy, turning upon the foe, with teeth and nails, to take an inhuman and bitter

7. *Il Codice Magliabecchiano*, ed. Carl Frey (Berlin, 1892), p. 114. The account is full and circumstantial,
but in the book of Antonio Billi (ed. Frey, p. 52) it is said that Leonardo was cheated over the linseed oil
*che gli fu falsato*.

8. This is one of the parts of Leonardo's surviving manuscripts also included in the *Trattato*, para. 145.

revenge. ... You would see some of the victors leaving the fight and issuing from the crowd, rubbing their eyes and cheeks with both hands to clean them of the dirt made by their watering eyes smarting from the dust and smoke.[9]

We may be sure that Leonardo's cartoon included as many of these details as possible, and we know from copies that the man half-raised from the ground, shielding his eyes, was part of the central group. Another feature of this description is his impressionism – his interest in effects of atmosphere.

The higher the smoke, mixed with the dust-laden air, rises towards a certain level, the more it will look like a dark cloud; and it will be seen that at the top, where the smoke is more separate from the dust, the smoke will assume a bluish tinge and the dust will tend to its colour. This mixture of air, smoke, and dust will look much lighter on the side whence the light comes than on the opposite side.[10]

Of this, alas, we have no trace in the copies which have come down to us, and knowing his tendency to make his finished work more and more plastic, it may not have been carried out in the painting. But it is perceptible in the small preparatory sketches for the whole scene, which have survived. These fiery little scribbles show how Leonardo felt his way towards an elaborate composition by first setting down the general sense of the movement, and then condensing the motifs which satisfied him. It is the method he himself suggests in one of the first of his notes on painting. 'These rules', he says, 'are of use only in the second stage (*per ripruova*) of the figure. If you try to apply them to [the first] composition you will never make an end and will produce confusion in your works.'[11] Two of the drawings in the Venice Academy show the main features of what was afterwards to become the standard group, though in more diffuse form (Pl. 80). The horseman on the left who looks back over his horse's haunches, is already a dominant motif. Others contain figures which reappear in several drawings, but not in copies of the Standard group, and from them we can attempt to reconstruct the parts of the cartoon which are lost.

In the choice of poses and in the final composition, Leonardo was much influenced by Bertoldo's bronze relief of a battle now in the Bargello.[12] Bertoldo had been keeper of Lorenzo de' Medici's collection of antiques and the greatest authority on classical art of his time, and for almost a generation he had watched over the youth of Florence drawing antiques in Lorenzo's

9. Richter, para. 602.

10. Richter, para. 601.

11. Richter, para. 18.

12. A more direct influence was a Hellenistic sarcophagus of the Fall of Phaeton, now in the Uffizi, Florence, then on the steps of the Aracoeli Church, Rome.

80. *Studies for the 'Battle of Anghiari'*, c. 1504. *Accademia, Venice*

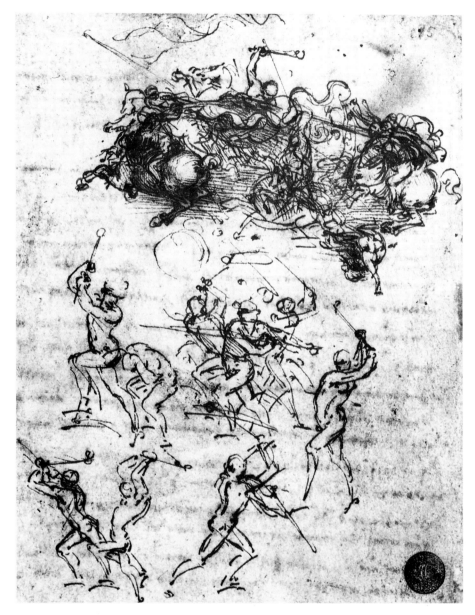

garden. Now to our notions nothing could seem further from classical art than the 'Battle of Anghiari': but that is because we still see the antique through the eyes of Winckelmann and nineteenth-century classicism as something cold, restrained, and static. To the Renaissance it was the exact reverse. They admired in the antique the power of conveying passion and violence, as opposed to the dry and timid movement of their own early painters. Bertoldo's bronze, which is largely taken from a famous antique sarcophagus

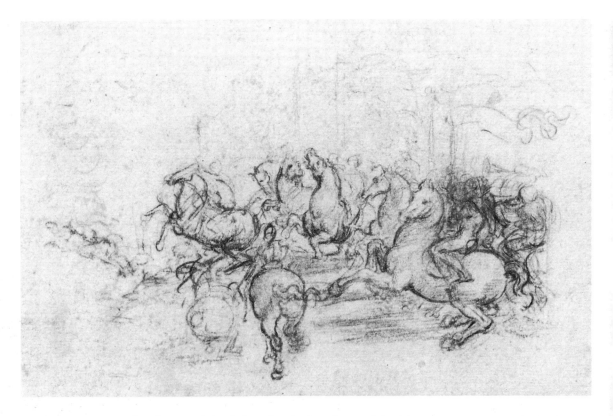

*81. Study for the 'Battle of Anghiari', c. 1504. Royal Library, Windsor (RL 12339r)*

at Pisa, was considered a model of the classical style, and in his cartoon Leonardo no doubt believed that he was approaching the famous battle pieces of Philoxenos.

Our reconstruction of Leonardo's cartoon is conjectural. We have several copies of the central motif, the struggle for the Standard, taken from the wreck of the original painting on the walls of the Palazzo Vecchio; and a number of drawings which show that though the struggle for the Standard was the chief, it was not the only motif of his cartoon. We can guess at the existence of one other group, which included the motif of a wild, galloping horse, known in several studies and in a drawing by Michelangelo, which seems to be a copy of Leonardo's cartoon, and there are hints of a second group, a cavalcade of horsemen in a drawing at Windsor (Pl. 81). Perhaps the struggle for the Standard was to have been the central panel, and the two others were to have been separated from it by windows.

The copy with which we usually illustrate the 'Battle of the Standard', the grisaille by Rubens (Pl. 82), was not made at first hand, for the original painting was obliterated fifty years before Rubens could have seen it, and he may have had no more to go on than Lorenzo Zacchia's meagre engraving. In consequence, his version is inaccurate in many details, and the intention

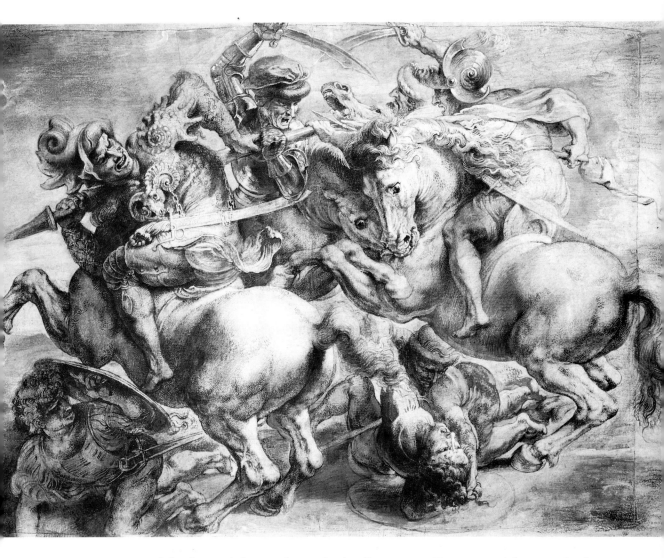

82. *Rubens after Leonardo: part of the 'Battle of Anghiari' 1505. Louvre, Paris*

of the figures is better shown in the direct copy. Yet we are right to study the composition in Rubens' version, because it is by a great artist, and one who has felt so deep a sympathy for Leonardo's design that he has been able to recreate the rhythmic force of the original and to make some appreciation of it possible. We see that the subject gave Leonardo an opportunity of returning to the patterns and problems which had occupied his mind over twenty years earlier in the background of the 'Adoration'. His sense of form had not changed, and for the central group of his new composition he chose the same general design: two prancing horses confronting each other, their haunches and bellies and necks, with tossed-back heads, making the same pattern of energetic curves. But, following the general trend of his development, the

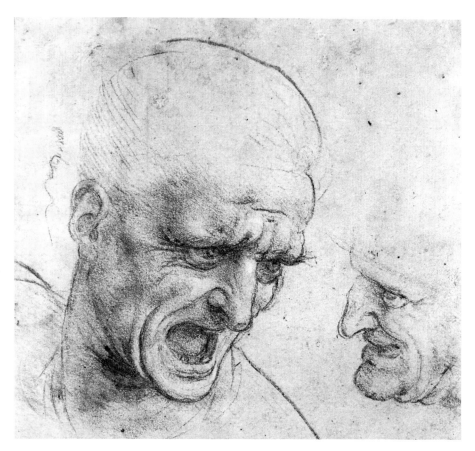

83. *Study of heads of Warriors for the 'Battle of Anghiari', c. 1504. Museum of Fine Arts, Budapest*

composition became far more compact. The free and centrifugal movement of the earlier group was given up for a design almost unbearably close knit and dense. The central group could have been realized in bronze. The small pen and ink sketches for the 'Battle of Anghiari' with their tiny, irresponsible figures, have been developed, by some intellectual process of which we have no record, into the massive complexity of the Standard group.

These battle cartoons of Leonardo and Michelangelo are the turning point of the Renaissance, and a whole book could be written on them – their origins, their purpose, their influence. It is not too fanciful to say that they initiate the two styles which sixteenth-century painting was to develop – the Baroque and the Classical. For the Baroque elements in Leonardo, which I have already stressed, were more forcibly present in the Anghiari cartoon than in any other of his works; and Michelangelo, although he was later to become a prophet of the Baroque, showed in his Cascina cartoon the sort of classicism which formed the mature style of Raphael and Giulio Romano. If, as is inevitable, we compare the work of the two great rivals we must agree

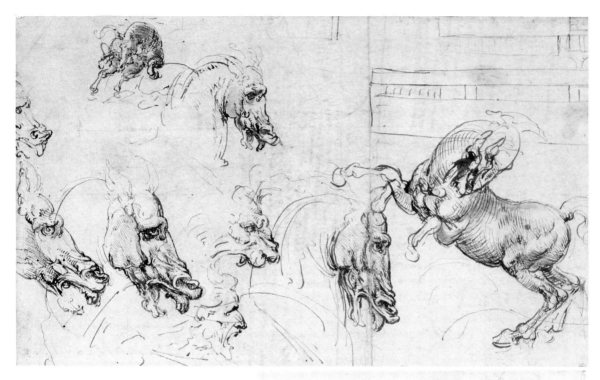

84. *Studies of horses
for the 'Battle of
Anghiari', c. 1504.
Royal Library,
Windsor* (RL 12326r)

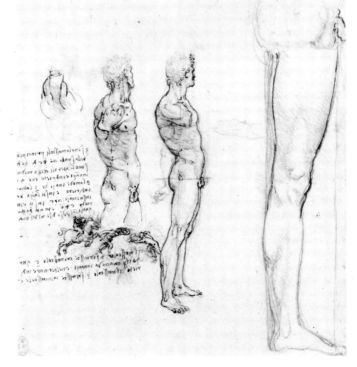

85. *Anatomical
studies of the nude,
connected with
'Anghiari', c. 1504.
Royal Library,
Windsor* (RL 12640)

that this Baroque element has made Leonardo's design much superior in unity. I believe that even Michelangelo felt this; and he seems actually to have copied a part of Leonardo's cartoon – one of the parts not painted on to the wall, and so not shown in later copies, but traceable in Leonardo's drawings. We must also admit, as all contemporaries agreed, that Leonardo excelled in richness of dramatic invention, giving a greater passion to the whole scene and to individual heads (Pl. 83). Of this we can still judge, since several of his studies of the heads survive, and show the fury of slaughter which is so vividly described in his notes on how to paint a battle. Here again we notice one of the apparent contradictions of his nature. The famous military engineer, the inventor of monstrous war-machines, the friend of Cesare Borgia, was by all accounts a man of unusual tenderness, to whom the destruction of any living organism was repulsive. War he referred to as a *pazzia bestialissima*, most beastly madness. We can imagine how these feelings, conflicting with his intellectual interest in war as an art, gave to the Anghiari cartoon an added intensity in the expression of horror.

Contemporaries were also unanimous that Leonardo excelled in the representation of horses. He had so designed the subject as to give this admitted superiority full play and Vasari tells us how these horses played a leading part in the drama, 'for rage, hatred, and revenge', he says, 'are seen in them no less than in the men.' Of this, also, we are in a measure able to judge, as some of his horse studies for the battle have come down to us (Pl. 84).

But when all this had been granted, a Florentine of that date would have decided in favour of Michelangelo, on account of the matchless beauty of his nudes. Leonardo felt this, and during this period made a number of magnificent nude studies. It is impossible to imagine better drawings of the nude than that on Pl. 85; as an actual study of muscular torso Michelangelo could hardly have excelled it, and in fact the heroic pose and treatment shows Michelangelo's influence. But although Leonardo could master the nude when he chose, he was not prepared to make it the main subject of a composition. It gave too little opportunity for his love of fantastic invention, his unexpected imagery – in short for the expression of that anti-classical side of his character to which I have more than once referred. The Anghiari cartoon may have had a classic firmness and coherency; but in spirit, like the 'Adoration', it was a romantic masterpiece – a precursor of Tintoretto, Rubens, and Delacroix. Thus it was outside the main current of its time. Contemporaries could not ignore its marvellous qualities of drawing and design, and we know that it influenced the mannerist painters of the next generation. But Michelangelo with his severe concentration on the nude, his passionate research for noble and expressive form, seemed to offer a firmer and, perhaps, a shorter way to excellence, and it was the 'Battle of Cascina' which captivated the younger artists of the time.

On 30 May 1506, Leonardo was granted leave from the Signoria to return to Milan for three months, at the urgent request of the governor, Charles d'Amboise, Lord of Chaumont; and before the time was out Amboise wrote asking that it might be prolonged 'since we still have need of the master Leonardo to furnish us with a certain work which we have had him begin'. What was the work so urgently required and so discreetly left unnamed? We have not the smallest indication. One possibility is that he was required to finish work on the London version of the 'Virgin of the Rocks' (Pl. 86). It is true that the tone of Amboise's correspondence suggests a more personal interest than he would have displayed on behalf of the Confraternity of the Immaculate Conception. Nevertheless, there is more than literary convenience in favour of discussing the picture at this point.

In 1506 Ambrogio da Predis (acting for Leonardo) and the Confraternity finally agreed to a settlement of their long dispute. After stating that the altar-piece had been commissioned in 1483 and was to have been finished in a year; and establishing that payments had already been much in excess of the sum originally contracted, the judges go on to say:

> Whereas the said altar-piece has not been finished at the said time, and is even now unfinished ... the Master Leonardo and Ambrogio Preda ... are bound and shall be obliged to finish or cause to be finished well the said altar-piece on which is painted the figure of the most glorious Virgin Mary. And this shall be done within the limit of two years from now, by the hand of the said Master Leonardo, provided that he comes to this city of Milan within that time and not otherwise.

This was signed on 27 April; on 30 May Leonardo arrived in Milan. In 1507 and 1508 he was paid 100 lire a year by the Confraternity. We may therefore reasonably suppose that the greater part of the paint visible in the National Gallery picture was put on then. We must, however, admit that when the composition was laid in, presumably at a much earlier stage, Leonardo had already modified its *quattrocento* character. Thus the figures have been made larger in relation to the panel (the National Gallery panel is actually a fraction smaller, but gives the reverse impression) and the distracting motif of the Angel's hand pointing at the Infant John has been suppressed. Probably its Florentine insistence on the Forerunner was distasteful to a body dedicated to the Immaculate Conception. An analogous change has been made in the heads, which have been redesigned under the influence of Leonardo's later theories of painting. The types have lost their gothic freshness and naturalism, but approximate more closely to an ideal. The infant Christ, in particular, has gained in seriousness and a sense of dawning inspiration. Contrary to the best critical opinion of the last fifty years I believe that Leonardo took a considerable share in the execution. Many of the details are drawn with a delicacy quite beyond a pupil, and with

*86. Leonardo and Studio, 'Virgin of the Rocks', largely 1506–8. National Gallery, London*

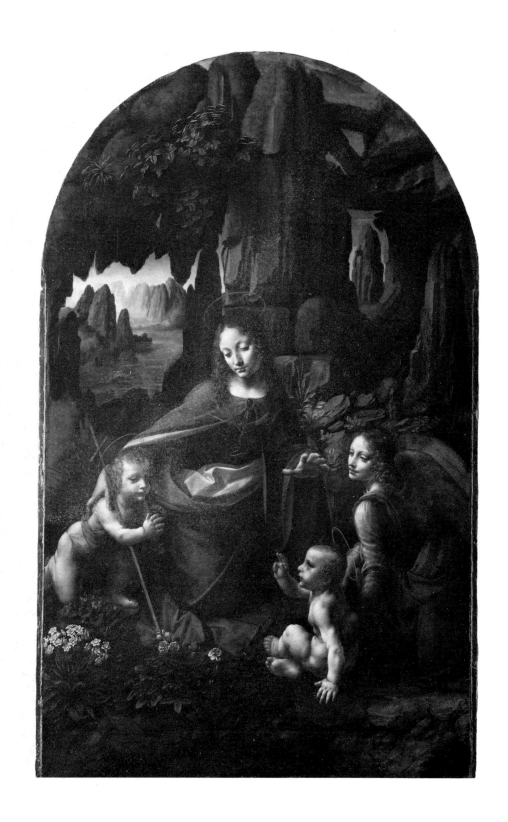

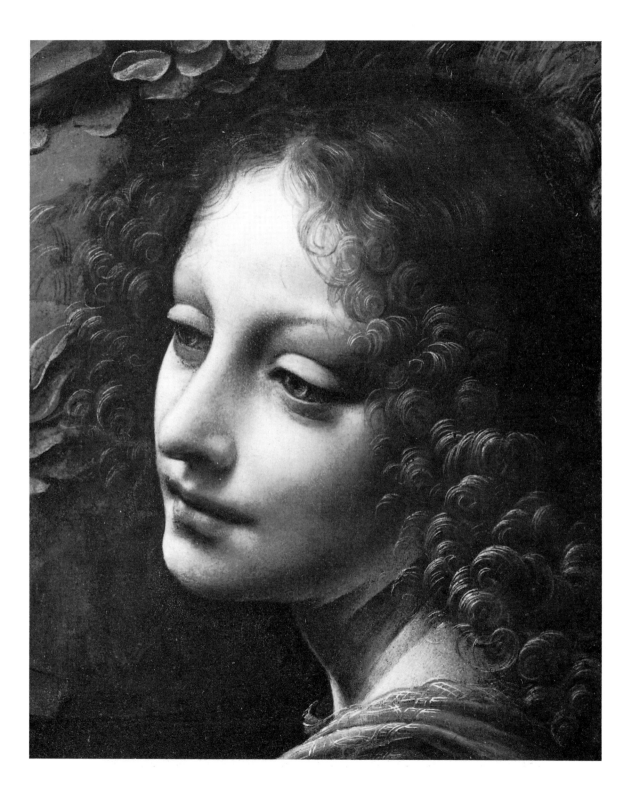

Leonardo's own feeling for living tissue. Unfortunately much of the surface has been damaged by repainting and, even after cleaning, it is hard to say where Leonardo's work ends and a pupil's begins. The most difficult part to explain is the Virgin's head. It is heavy and devoid of inner life: yet the execution is delicate and shows the marks of thumb and palm in the thin paint, which are to be found in all the best passages in the picture.

The angel's head, on the other hand, which departs entirely from the Paris version, is a classic invention of great beauty (Pl. 87); and no one who has looked at it closely can doubt who was responsible for the mouth and chin, and the characteristic curves of the golden hair.

Although much can be said in praise of the National Gallery 'Virgin of the Rocks', it falls far short of the Louvre picture in every kind of beauty and must be partly pupil's work, which pupil we do not know. He is generally supposed to be Predis, owing to the references to his name in the settlement. But these seem to be of an official character. The Confraternity had never shown any enthusiasm for his work; and in fact those passages of the London 'Virgin of the Rocks' which are clearly by a pupil are not at all in the dry, Milanese manner of Predis. The pupil whose style seems to bear most resemblance is the author of a 'Virgin and Child' at Zürich, in which the Virgin's head is almost a replica of that in the London 'Virgin of the Rocks'. The Zürich picture is signed F R L T A, and Suida has suggested that this is the Spaniard Fernando de Llanos, who is more than once recorded as having assisted Leonardo on the 'Battle of Anghiari'.

With the 'Battle of Anghiari' still unfinished Leonardo could not stay away from Florence for long, and when, in September 1506, Charles d'Amboise wrote asking for a prolongation of his visit to Milan, the Signoria sent a stiff answer. 'May your excellency excuse us from coming to an agreement about a day with Leonardo da Vinci who has not borne himself as he ought to have done towards this republic, in that he has received a good sum of money and has made little beginning of a great work which he is under obligation to execute, and has already comported himself as a laggard; with deference to your Excellency.' There is no evidence that Leonardo was in the least disturbed by these accusations, and he continued to work in Milan for another year. His return to Florence in the autumn of 1507 was occasioned solely by a lawsuit with his brothers following the death of his father, and he does not seem to have added another stroke to the 'Battle of Anghiari'. During the whole of the year 1507 Leonardo was working for the King of France and we know that amongst other things he executed a 'Madonna and Child'. Pandolfini, the Florentine ambassador at the Court of Louis XII, who was trying to effect Leonardo's recall to Florence, describes how the King's admiration of him was occasioned by 'a little picture from his hand which has lately been brought here, and is held to be a most excellent work'.

87. *The Angel's head from the 'Virgin of the Rocks'*, c. 1506–8. National Gallery, London

Pandolfini then gives an account of an interview with the King which shows in a vivid way the esteem and affection in which Leonardo was held.

Being this morning in the presence of the most Christian King [he writes], his Majesty called for me and said: 'Your Government must do something for me. Write to them that I want Master Leonardo, their painter, to work for me. And see that your Government are firm with him and command him to serve me at once, and not to leave Milan until I come there. He is a good master and I wish to have several things from his hand.' I then asked his Majesty what works he desired from Leonardo, and he answered, 'Certain small panels of Our Lady and other things as the fancy shall take me; and perhaps I shall also cause him to make my own portrait.'

The King and the Ambassador then went on to speak of 'the perfection and the other qualities of Leonardo'.

His Majesty asked [says Pandolfini] if I knew him. I replied that he was a close friend of mine. 'Then write him some verses,' said the King, 'telling him not to leave Milan at the same time as your Governors are writing to him from Florence,' and for this reason I wrote a verse to the said Leonardo, letting him know the good will of his Majesty and congratulating him on the news.

The letters were written, the Signoria were forced to give up their claim, and Leonardo became in a sense court painter to the King of France. His immediate patron, however, was d'Amboise, who looked after his interest, and had disposal of his pictures. Amongst these were the little panels of Our Lady, which are mentioned in a letter from Leonardo to Chaumont dated in the spring of 1508. 'I send Salai to inform your Excellency', he writes, 'that I am almost at the end of my lawsuit with my brothers and hope to be in Milan by Easter and bring with me two pictures in which are two madonnas of different sizes which I have begun for the most Christian King, or for whoever shall please you.' In an earlier draft of the letter Leonardo wrote 'which are finished' instead of 'which I have begun', and in a letter written shortly after he speaks of them as *condotti in assai bon punto*. Even allowing for Leonardo's usual dilatoriness we may presume that the pictures were finished from the very fact that we have no further correspondence about them, and it is sad to think that both are lost. We have not even the academic consolation of knowing for certain what these Madonnas were like, since no drawings of the subject date from the period. But a picture known as the 'Madonna of the Cherries', which undoubtedly reflects a design by Leonardo, may, on grounds of costume, be dated in these years. All of the numerous replicas are by Flemish artists including Joos von Cleve, which suggests that the picture was sent out of Italy almost as soon as it was painted.

Leonardo seems to have spent the winter of 1507–8 in Florence engaged in

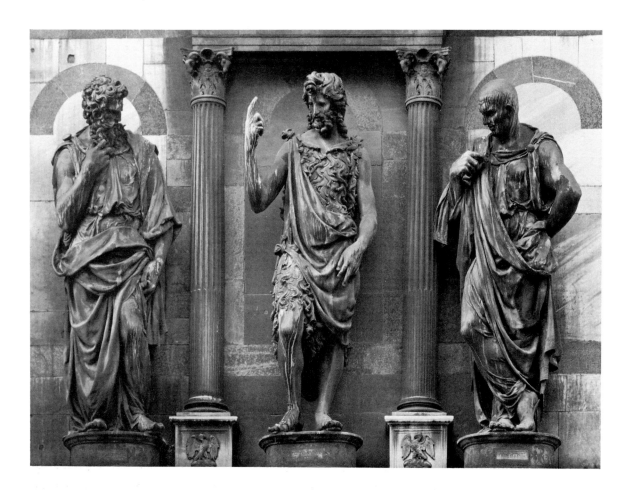

the lawsuit with his brothers, and the British Museum M S. opens with the note, 'begun in March 1508 in the house of Piero di Braccio Martelli'. In the same house lived Gian Francesco Rustici, the sculptor, author of the famous group of the Baptist between a Pharisee and a Levite which stands over the north door of the Florentine Baptistery (Pl. 88).

*88. Rustici, the 'Preaching of St John the Baptist', 1506–11. Baptistery, Florence*

    While Gian Francesco was at work on the clay model for this group, [says Vasari] he wished no one to come near him except Leonardo da Vinci who in making the moulds, preparing the armature, and in short at every point, right up to the casting of the statues, never left him; hence some believe that Leonardo worked at them with his own hand, or at least helped Gian Francesco with advice and good judgement.[13]

Vasari repeats this in his life of Leonardo. 'In statuary he gave proofs of his

13. Vasari, *Lives of the Artists*, 'Life of Rustici' (ed. Milanesi), vol. VI, p. 604.

skill in three figures of bronze which stand over the north door of the Baptistery executed by Gian Francesco Rustico, but contrived with the counsel of Leonardo.' We can see at once that Vasari's statement is correct. In type and gesture the figures are profoundly Leonardesque. The Pharisee stands in the contemplative attitude of the old man in the Uffizi 'Adoration'. The frowning, hairless Levite is very close to the Budapest studies of heads for the 'Battle of Anghiari'. In both, the drapery is so close to the draperies of the various St Annes that it was either executed by Leonardo or taken directly from his drawings, and the pose of St John is a variation of the angel in Leonardo's lost picture which used to belong to the Grand Duke Cosimo. The work of Rustici would therefore seem to be our best guide to Leonardo's sculpture at this period, and it is worth examining a group of small pieces in various materials which have been reasonably attributed to Rustici.[14] These represent struggles of mounted men, and are conceived with a passion and a close-knit complexity of movement which derive from the cartoon of 'Anghiari'. I think it possible that Leonardo himself executed small wax figures of horses with which to build up the composition of his cartoon. Some such practice is suggested by a note beside one of his drawings (P. 202), 'make a little one of wax about four inches long', and this may be the explanation of a small bronze which has been widely accepted as being Leonardo's own work, the horse and rider in the Museum of Budapest. The horse is very like some of those which appear in the studies for 'Anghiari', and reproduces almost exactly the pose and character of a horse on a sheet of studies at Windsor (Pl. 89). But although the Budapest bronze is so Leonardesque in movement, the surface modelling shows a lack of tension hardly conceivable in Leonardo's authentic work, and I am inclined to think that it is the work of a pupil who had before him one of Leonardo's smaller wax models. He has been able to reproduce the character of the original, but with a certain emptiness natural to an enlargement.

One of the few recorded pieces of Leonardo's sculpture is the lost terracotta head of the child Christ which the sixteenth-century painter and theorist Lomazzo describes as being in his own collection.[15] Of this I believe we have a relatively clear record in two red chalk drawings at Windsor (P. 170, 171a). These are studies of a child's head and shoulders in a sculpturesque pose and in each Leonardo has cut off the body with a horizontal line drawn just below the breasts, a device wholly uncharacteristic of him unless he had in mind a piece of sculpture. One of them (Pl. 90) shows the head and shoulders in profile; the child's head is very like that of the infant Christ in the London

---

14. Examples are in the Bargello, Louvre (Camondo Collection), Horne Museum, Florence.

15. Lomazzo, *Trattato* (1st ed.), lib. II, cap. viii, p. 127: '*Arch'io mi trovo un testicciola di un Christo mentre ch'era fanciullo, di propria mano di Leonardo da Vinci.*'

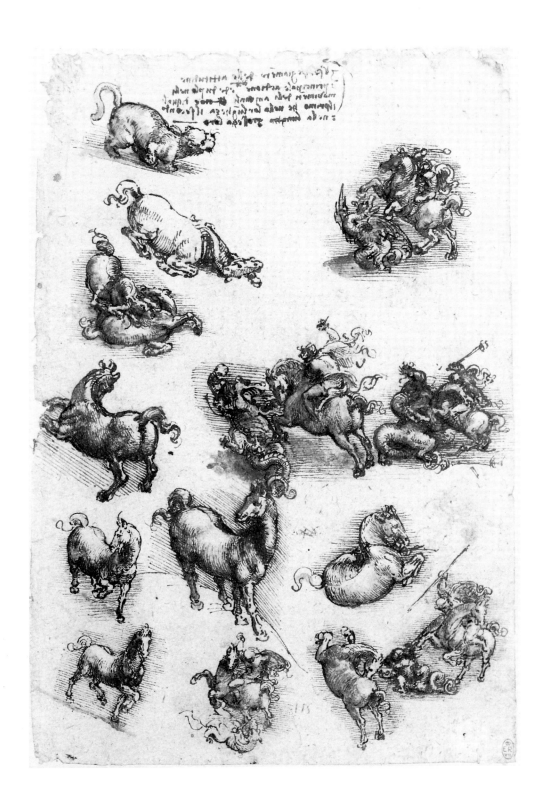

89. *Studies for a St George and the Dragon, c. 1507–8. Royal Library, Windsor (RL 12331)*

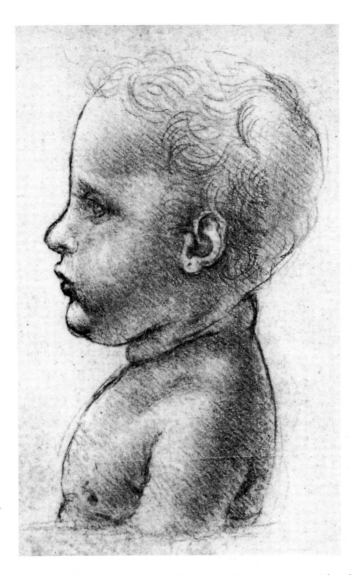

90. *Study for the Bust of a Child, c. 1506. Royal Library, Windsor (RL 12519)*

'Virgin of the Rocks', and the same drawing was evidently used for both; the other (P. 170) shows the child's bust drawn from both back and front in exactly the same pose, further indication that these are studies for sculpture. The handling of the chalk suggests a date about 1500, but the connection with the second version of the 'Virgin of the Rocks' would make the drawings later. These drawings suggest that the terracotta was modelled with that extreme *morbidezza* of surface which must have characterized Leonardo's sculpture. It is precisely the absence of sensitive surface modelling which prevents us from attributing to Leonardo's own hand the wax bust of Flora in the Ehemals Staatliche Museen. This insensitiveness is partly due to the restorations of a sculptor named Lucas, whose son afterwards claimed that his father had fabricated the whole piece. The claim was widely believed at the time, and made the pretext of malicious attacks on Dr Bode, but it cannot be substantiated. Nothing in Lucas's work suggests that he was capable of the noble movement of the 'Flora', and the evidence advanced of his authorship only proved that he had subjected the bust to a severe restoration. The original texture is still visible in the breast, and presumably Lucas reduced the head to its present dull uniformity of surface. Bode was right in seeing this piece as a clear indication of Leonardo's later sculpture, in which he gave plastic expression to the problems of form attempted in the 'Leda' and the later 'St John'. The solution of these problems, in the 'St John' at least, loses something of its clarity through Leonardo's interest in the counter-problem of chiaroscuro, and in the 'Flora', before her restoration, we should, perhaps, have been able to enjoy Leonardo's formal invention with less distraction than in his late painting. In her present condition she is only another of those mutilated documents through which, alas, so much of Leonardo's art must be reconstructed.

# CHAPTER EIGHT

# 1508–1513

I N the summer of 1508 Leonardo returned to Milan, which was to be his headquarters for the next five years. His chief patron was still Charles d'Amboise, Lord of Chaumont, who remained governor of Milan till his death in 1511. Early in his life d'Amboise had been touched by the spirit of the Renaissance, and in Milan he tried to revive or maintain the civilization of the Sforzas. Of this civilization Leonardo had been the greatest glory, and we know that d'Amboise treated him with the utmost consideration. As with the Sforzas he was not simply court painter, but architect, engineer, and general artistic adviser. A few designs for architecture, dating from about this period, are in the *Codice Atlantico* and at Windsor. Among them are plans and elevations of a town house with classical orders and various suggestions for wells and fountains. The British Museum MS. of 1508 also contains his longest writings on architecture, a study of fissures in walls and vaults, which suggest that he was employed in restoring and conserving as well as building. One day he could be deciding on the form of the choir stalls in the Duomo; another, acting as military engineer in the war against Venice; another, arranging pageants for the entry of Louis XII into Milan. It was a variety of employment which Leonardo enjoyed, but which has left posterity the poorer. In these years he also travelled extensively, and although we have many clues as to the course of these journeys we have no hint as to their purpose. They do not seem to be connected with any recorded commission, and it is possible that they were undertaken solely in order to make those observations of nature which were one of the chief interests of his later years. MS. F, dated 22 September 1508 and entitled *Di mondo ed acque*, is the first of a series containing notes on geology, botany, atmosphere, and kindred subjects. Although Leonardo's approach has become more scientific, he still sees with the eye of a painter. His notes on botany describe the ramifications of a tree and the disposition of its leaves, in much the same spirit as Ruskin in the fifth book of *Modern Painters*. Many pages of MS. G are concerned with light striking on trees, the various greens of transparent leaves, and the blue sheen which they reflect from the sky (Pl. 91). The same book contains valuable notes of what Leonardo called *la prospettiva di colore*, the modification of colour by atmosphere; in fact, such observations seem to have been one of the chief motives of his mountaineering expeditions. A drawing at Windsor of the Alps (Pl. 92), one of a beautiful series in red chalk on red paper, contains an elaborate note of the colour of mountain flowers when seen through a great gulf of intervening air at a considerable height. There are also notes on the colour of smoke and mist which remind us of Goethe, and only his dislike of formulas prevented him from anticipating Goethe's principle of translucency. In these writings Leonardo anticipated the impressionist doctrine that everything is more or less reflected in everything else and that there are no such things as black shadows. Meanwhile, his

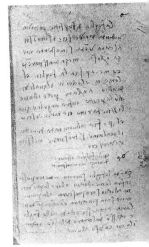

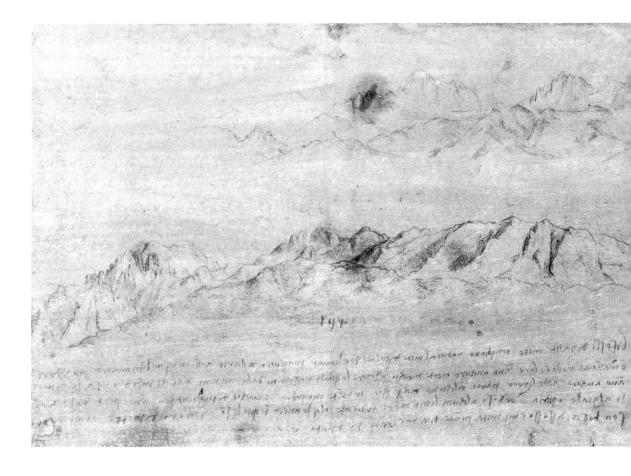

91. *Study of light on leaves*, c. 1513–15. MS. G, Bibliothèque de l'Institut de France, Paris

92. *Study of Alpine peaks*, c. 1511. Royal Library, Windsor (RL 12414)

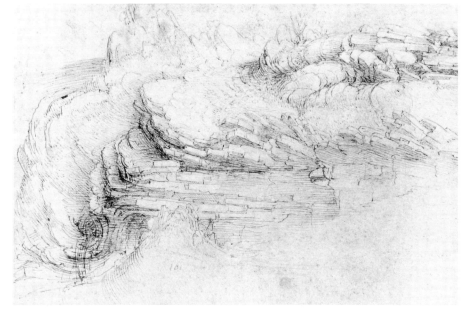

93. *Study of Stratification*, c. 1508, Royal Library, Windsor (RL 12394)

paintings were growing more and more shadowy, so that his last work, the equivocal 'St John' in the Louvre, only just emerges from the darkness.

During these expeditions into the mountains he became interested in problems of geology, and in particular the question of why shells and fossilized marine life can be found high up in mountains many miles inland. The thoroughness, tenacity, and candour with which, in several pages of the Hammer MS., he deals with this problem is an admirable example of his mind at work. He never for a moment admits the idea of a special creation, and he advances decisive arguments against the idea that the shells were carried there by the Flood. Ultimately he assumes that the country has been covered by the sea and sets to work to discover how this can have taken place. Thus his geological observations, taken in conjunction with his studies of embryology and comparative anatomy, show him ready to entertain the whole idea of evolution with a scientific open-mindedness in advance of many distinguished scientists of the nineteenth century.

This study of geology is sometimes quoted as evidence of Leonardo's drift away from art to science; but at every stage Leonardo's researches, however austere, become fused with the texture of his imagination. His study of the earth's bones is no exception. He had always been interested in rock forma-tions, and to about the years 1508–10 belong a series of drawings at Windsor[1]

1. They are nos. 12,389, 12,394, 12,396 and 12,397.

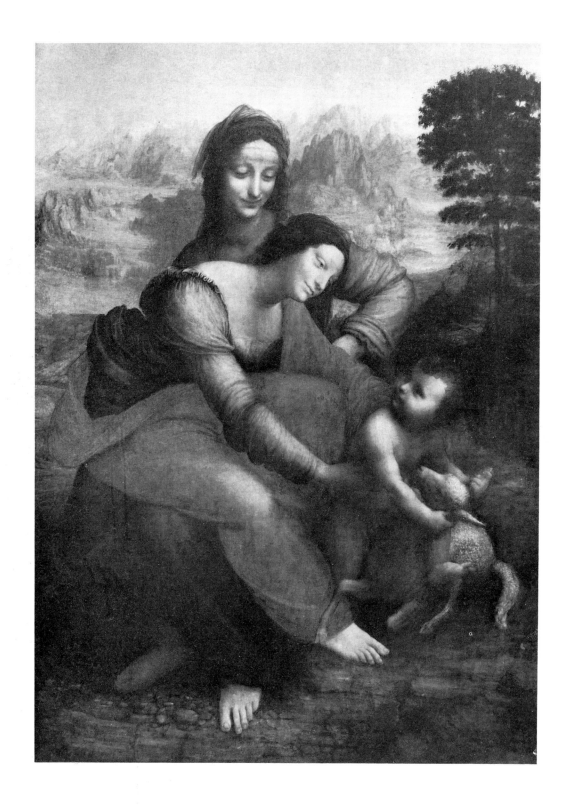

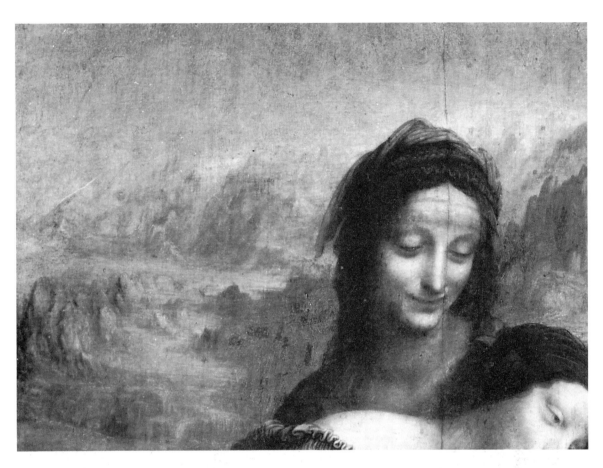

94. The 'Virgin and Child and St Anne', 1508–10. Louvre, Paris

95. Detail of Heads and Landscape from the 'Virgin and Child and St Anne', 1508–10. Louvre, Paris

which show him studying outcrops and disturbed stratification, where the rock has broken through the comfortable humus, and reveals the ancient, grim foundations on which living things have their precarious existence (Pl. 93).

This sense of the world as a planet, seen from a point of distance at which human life is no longer visible, is given final expression in the background of the 'Virgin and Child and St Anne', now in the Louvre (Pl. 94). There are no documents for this work, but the studies for it which have come down to us, no less than the whole character of the composition, suggest a date after Leonardo's return to Milan and perhaps as late as 1510. Only the vast and delicate landscape was coloured by Leonardo's own hand (Pl. 95). The painting of the heads is insensitive and without the fine texture of the Mona Lisa. Parts of it are unfinished – the drapery covering the Virgin's legs, for example, which is no more than an outline. Yet we know how subtle, musical, and close-knit this passage could have been from drawings in the Louvre (Pl. 96) and at Windsor, showing the elaborate preparations he made for all his

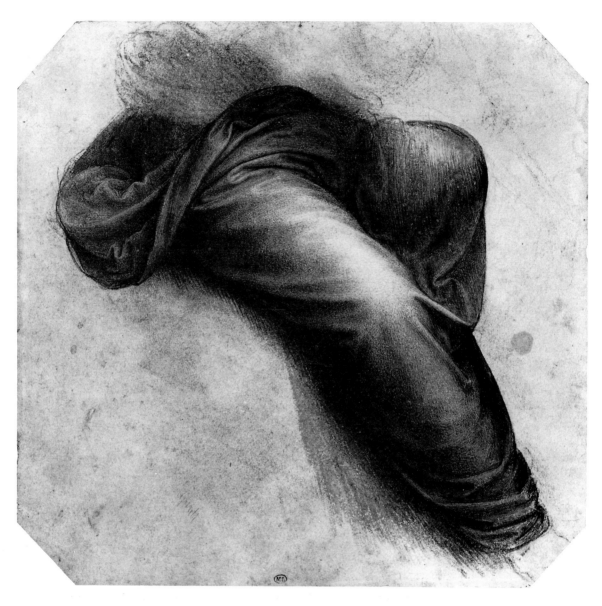

work, although when the time came to use these studies in a picture his inborn distaste for finality forced him to leave it unfinished. Even more interesting than these drapery studies is Leonardo's own drawing for the St Anne's head (Pl. 97). The differences between it and the head in the painting (Pl. 98) are no doubt partly due to Leonardo himself. It was he, for instance, who changed the head-dress in order to give a sharper accent to the pyramidal group, and he may have done something to make her type more regular. But the difference must also be due to the head being painted by a pupil and is

*96. Study of drapery for the 'Virgin and Child and St Anne', c. 1508–10. Louvre, Paris*

an example of a well-known truth, that a great man's pupils are *plus royaliste que le roi*. The conventionally Leonardesque expression of the painted 'St Anne' has a certain charm and an artificial air of mystery, but the human mystery of the drawing is deeper and more subtle.[2]

Despite these alterations the Louvre picture has a force and beauty which no copy could achieve. Critics have objected to the extreme artificiality of the poses, and we are, indeed, very far from the frontal simplicity of early *quattrocento* treatment of this subject. But nothing else in his work shows more clearly his intentions as an artist. The subject had interested Leonardo for many years, as offering the possibility of contrasted interlocking rhythms enclosed within a single shape. Looking at his earlier treatment of this theme we can see how he gradually made his rhythmical sequences more and more complex. In the Burlington House cartoon he has given a maximum of contrapposto to the individual figures of the Virgin and St Anne, but he has kept the whole of the Virgin's figure on one side of the composition and the two heads, although they are looking in opposite directions, are on the same level and give the design a certain formality. Moreover, the two sides of the group are not perfectly thought out. The left-hand side is too characterless and on the right-hand side the intervals between the heads are too regular. In the cartoon of 1501, if we can judge by Brescianino's replica, Leonardo has already succeeded in placing the Virgin's head on a different level and the ascending scale of the heads is more interesting. But he clearly felt that the vertical line in the composition was over-emphatic and in a sketch in the Louvre for his last version of the subject we see how he emphasizes the diagonal line by bringing the Virgin's figure right across the composition (Pl. 99). Finally, he arrives at the solution which we know in the Paris picture. By considerable distortion he has achieved a perfect balance throughout.[3] The design has the exhilarating quality of an elaborate fugue: like a masterpiece of Bach it is inexhaustible. We are always discovering new felicities of movement and harmony, growing more and more intricate, yet subordinate to the whole; and, as with Bach, this is not only an intellectual performance; it is charged with human feeling.

Without the style of Pater this strange blend of mystery and tenderness, human and inhuman, is best left undescribed. But I cannot resist quoting the beautiful, and I believe profound, interpretation that Freud has put on this picture. He imagines that Leonardo must have spent the first years of his life with his mother, the peasant Caterina; but a year after his birth his father

2. I now (1957) disagree with the whole of this passage. I am convinced that the picture was painted almost entirely by Leonardo himself and that the change in St Anne's head was part of the desire for idealization characteristic of his later work.

3. The extent of this can be seen when the figure of the Virgin is isolated from the group, as in Cesare da Sesto's picture in the Poldi Pezzoli.

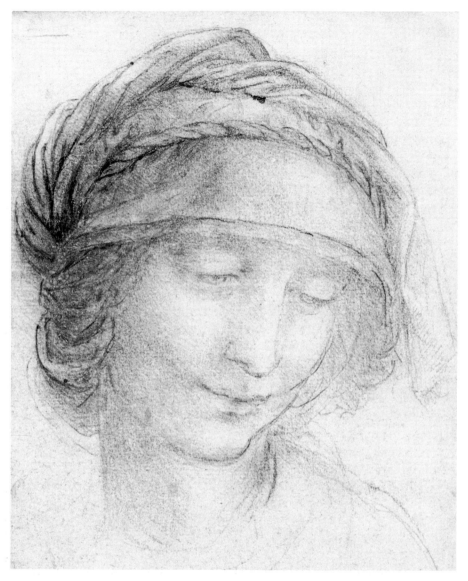

married, and when Ser Piero found that his wife was unlikely to have children, he brought his love child to be looked after by her. In a sense, therefore, Leonardo had two mothers. And it is the unconscious memory of these two beloved beings, intertwined as if in a dream, which led him to dwell with such tenderness on the subject of the Virgin and St Anne. Whether or not this is true in fact, it seems to express the mood of the Louvre picture, and explains the apparent nearness in age of mother and daughter, the strange intermingling of their forms, and their remote, mysterious smiles.

On 10 March 1511, Charles d'Amboise died and the government passed

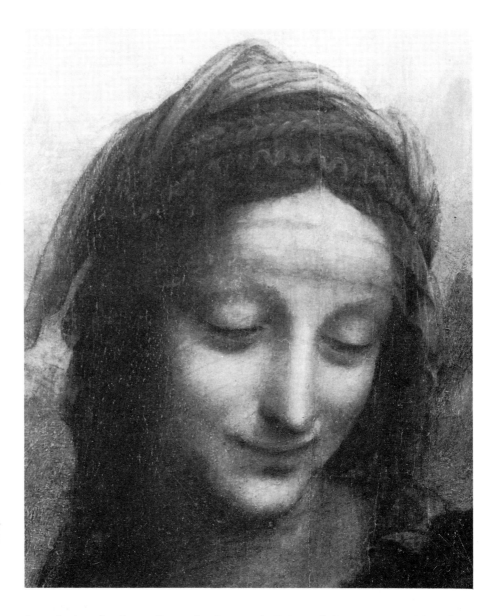

*98. Head of St Anne
from the 'Virgin and
Child and St Anne',
1508–10. Louvre,
Paris*

into the hands of two Generals, Gaston de Foix and Gian Giacomo Trivulzio.
We know that Leonardo undertook to execute an equestrian monument for
the latter and it is reasonable to place in this period the numerous drawings
of horses at Windsor, which on grounds of style and other internal evidence
belong to his second residence in Milan. Superficially these drawings resemble
the studies for the Sforza memorial, and there is a certain irony in the fact
that students have been unable to decide which designs Leonardo made for
his first patron and which for the Sforza's bitterest enemy and conqueror.

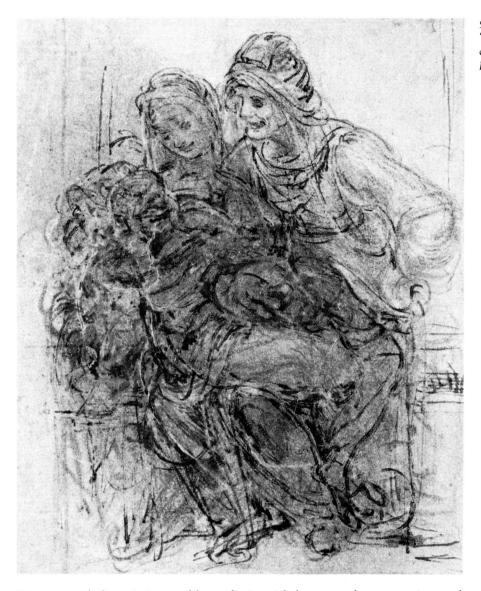

99. *Study for the 'Virgin and St Anne', c. 1508–10. Louvre, Paris*

However, I believe it is possible to distinguish between the two series, and as a result the later project can be studied in detail. It gives us a good opportunity of watching Leonardo at work, inventing and rejecting pose after pose in his effort to achieve something compact and full. The general scheme of the monument is known to us from an elaborate estimate in Leonardo's own handwriting, giving precise measurements and descriptions of every part.[4]

4. *Codice Atlantico*, f. 179a, printed in Richter, para. 725. On the same sheet is a study for the left hand of the Louvre 'St John' which confirms the late date of the estimate.

To begin with there was to be 'a horse as large as life' – that is to say, smaller than the horse for the Sforza memorial – which was to be placed on a high base with a heavy cornice, frieze, and architrave. This base was evidently in an elaborate classical style, since we have estimates for eight columns and eight capitals made of metal. Between them were to be festoons in stone and other ornaments. Set in the base was to be the figure of the deceased, carved in stone, and this figure was to rest on a sarcophagus supported by six harpies with candelabra. Round the base there were to be eight figures which from their price in the specification were evidently to be almost life-size. The relative elaboration of the base is shown by the fact that it accounts for about half the cost of the whole monument, although stone-work was very much cheaper than bronze. A series of drawings corresponds closely with this description (Pls. 100 and 101). They show the heavy cornice and architrave, the classical columns and the tomb with its recumbent effigy; even the figures at the corners are roughly indicated and we see that they were thought of as captives tied to columns. Perhaps as a result of his recent work in Milan Leonardo has laid an emphasis on the architectural side of the monument which was completely absent from the Sforza memorial. He has transferred the motif of a recumbent effigy in the base from the wall monuments common in Northern Italy to a free standing group. In so doing he has changed a *quattrocento* motif into a typically high Renaissance motif. The slaves at the corners recall Michelangelo's projects for the monument to Pope Julius: and some of the studies on a sheet at Windsor[5] are remarkably like that last great monument of high Renaissance sculpture, Alfred Stevens' memorial to the Duke of Wellington in St Paul's. The two main studies show that Leonardo was considering both a prancing horse and a walking horse. Neither satisfied him completely. In the prancing horse the design of the space under the horse's belly still presented difficulties; and the walking horse had to be redesigned with more severely plastic intention. With this end in view Leonardo made a further series of drawings from nature. This is another example of the immense pains – so often lost to us – which Leonardo took about all his compositions. He had been drawing horses all his life with a matchless power of observation. He had studied their anatomy and worked out a theory of their proportions; and at the age of fifty-five he begins again to make detailed and conscientious studies from nature. Superficially these drawings (e.g. P. 95, P. 96) are less attractive than those made for the Sforza monument. The crisp silverpoint, with its sensitive surface quality, is replaced by a slow pen-line, defining a sketch in black chalk. But this deliberation has an extraordinary weight; and it was weight – volume – at which Leonardo

5. I think that some of the sketches on Windsor 12,353 and 12,355 are certainly influenced by Michelangelo, but the question is too complicated to be treated here.

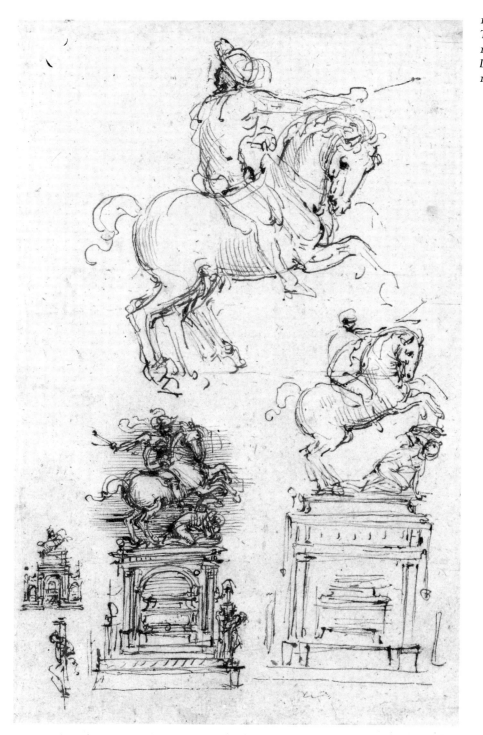

100. *Study for the Trivulzio monument, 1511–12. Royal Library, Windsor* (RL 12355)

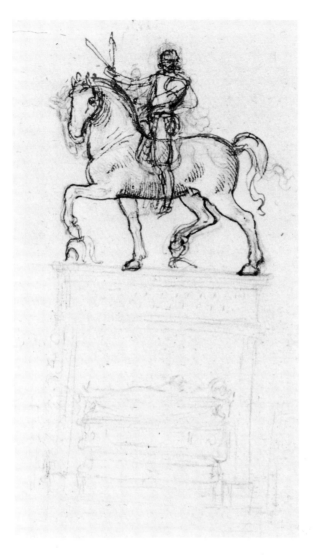

*101. Study for the Trivulzio monument, 1511–12. Royal Library, Windsor (RL 12356r)*

was aiming. These are not simply exquisite drawings from nature; they are studies for a piece of sculpture.

It is worth digressing to notice the differences in pen technique between these drawings, and the earlier studies of horses. The whole system of shading has changed. Instead of diagonals the lines of shading are directed to indicate depth. Thus, a shadow on a cylinder, instead of being made up of graded diagonals, will consist of lines drawn at right angles to the side of the cylinder, following its curves. This is what is known as shading following the form. It is essentially a sculptural style, rejecting the data of sight in favour of a convention based on knowledge. That Leonardo, who was so great a master of impressionistic draughtsmanship, ever adopted this intellectual, classical style is a proof of how much he valued continuity of modelling. This change in the method of shading is one of our best means of dating Leonardo's drawings. There are very few instances of it earlier than 1500, and as time goes on it is used far more openly, with the lines of shading farther apart. Ultimately it is accompanied by cross-hatching, an unlikely system as long as silverpoint was the dominant technique. On the whole, this linear convention was little used by Italian painters.[6] It is a Northern, in particular a German, style, and we cannot reject the possibility that Leonardo was influenced by the prints and drawings of Dürer, which much impressed Italian artists of that date.

In the final series of drawings for the Trivulzio monument[7] two problems were absorbing Leonardo's attention: the filling of the space below the belly of the prancing horse and the position of the rider (Pl. 102). In both he owed much – more than ever before in his life – to the study of classical art. Müller-Walde claims that this was due to the study of an antique equestrian statue at Pavia since destroyed, known as the Regisole, which, to judge from our crude representations of it, was very like the Marcus Aurelius now on the Capitol. Leonardo mentions this statue in a note in the *Codice Atlantico* (f. 147 *recto*). 'The one at Pavia is more praised for its movement than anything else – the imitation of antique things is more praiseworthy than that of modern – one cannot have beauty and utility together, as may be seen in men and fortresses – the trot has almost the quality of a free horse – where natural liveliness is lacking, it is necessary to make accidental liveliness.' I have quoted the entry in full because besides referring to the Regisole, it is a good example of Leonardo's way of jotting down his thoughts, and shows how his aesthetic ideas had moved away from the naturalism of the *quattrocento*. It also shows that this increased interest in the antique was not limited to the statue at Pavia. In fact, most of his later drawings for the Trivulzio monument seem to derive from classical reliefs or gems, and even show the rider transformed into a nude and laurel-crowned hero. The relation of the rider to the horse was a problem of design which, in his work on the Sforza monument, Leonardo had disregarded. It was always referred to simply as *il cavallo*: the rider was to be cast separately and added later. Such a haphazard procedure was foreign to Leonardo's later ideal of perfection, and in sketches for the Trivulzio monument the rider is always indicated, his position varying with minute variations in the pose of the horse. These variations – a barely perceptible raising or lowering of the head or fore-leg which gives a slightly

*102. Studies for the Trivulzio monument, 1511–12. Royal Library, Windsor (RL 12360)*

6. The cross-hatching of sculptor's drawings, familiar in the numerous drawings attributed to Bandinelli, but probably going back to Donatello, is of a different kind.

7. These are Windsor 12,359, 12,344, 12,342, 12,360, 12,354. I give these numbers in what seems to me to be the chronological order of the drawings.

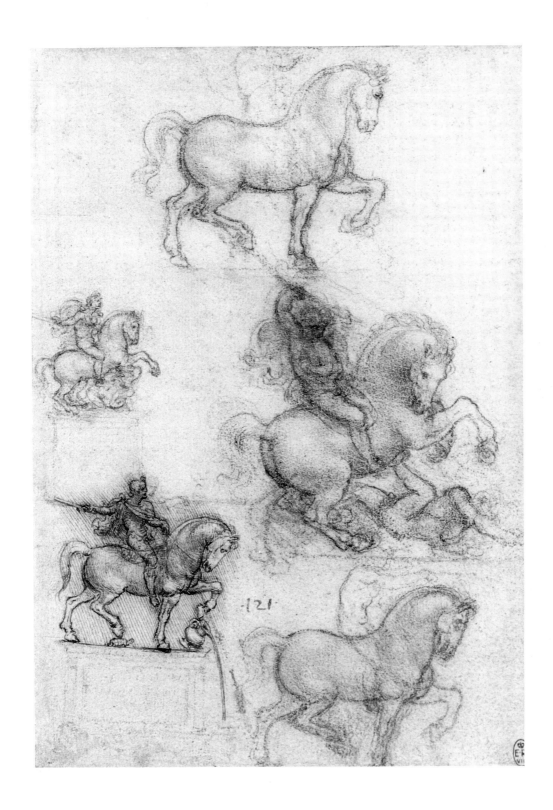

·121·

different movement to the whole – cannot be described in detail, but may be understood from one example. Was the rider's arm to be pointing forwards or backwards? At first, following the precedents of 'Gattamelata' and the antique, he is pointing forwards (Pls. 101 and 102). But Leonardo found this rather stiff, and in Pl. 102 he experiments with what I may call an open pose, the rider pointing rhetorically backwards. The idea is worked out with a walking horse in a small sketch on P. 99; but not to his satisfaction, as he continues to experiment with the closed form, trying to give it movement by making the rider point forwards though looking backwards (P. 100), or lean forwards energetically (Pl. 102, lower drawing). An interesting example of the relation of horse and rider is the pen and ink drawing also on Pl. 102. Here we feel at once that the open pose is too open, and we wonder how Leonardo came to make such a mistake until we notice that in the original chalk drawing the rider is leaning forwards, and it was only when he came to ink the drawing in that Leonardo makes him point backwards, without altering the pose of the horse's neck. We do not know which pose Leonardo would have selected finally, but it may be some indication that on a sheet at Windsor, 12,347, with instructions for casting the statue written at this time, an illustrative sketch shows the rider in the open pose.[8] Similarly, in the project for the prancing horse, he tries several variations on the motif, familiar in classical reliefs, of the conquered foe crouching beneath its hooves, and in one drawing actually turns the trampled man on his back so that his legs, pressed against the horse's belly, form a counter-rhythm to the rider's upraised arm. Although more closely knit than the first Sforza designs, this, too, has an intricacy unsuitable to large-scale sculpture, and probably Leonardo never intended to carry out the design of the prancing horse; at least, one of his drawings of it (Pl. 102) seems to belong to a later date than the rest of the series, and can never have been intended for use. It is Leonardo's last word on a subject that had interested him all his life, and is worth comparing with Michelangelo's last word on one of his problems, the composition of two nudes, as we see it in a drawing in the Ashmolean of Samson slaying a Philistine. The similarity of the two drawings is obvious and rather touching since it would have been equally distasteful to either artist. Both have learnt in old age to avoid outlines and to present their subject through interior modelling, suggested by mysterious blots and blurs. This is what Cézanne meant when he praised a picture by saying that it was *dessiné dans la forme*.

The studies for the Trivulzio monument, both by the way in which the black chalk is used and by the watermark of the paper, help us to date a series of beautiful drawings for masquerade costumes (Pl. 103). These drawings are

8. This used to be connected with the Sforza monument, but the handwriting above shows that it is for the Trivulzio.

like one another in style and conception and were probably all for the same masquerade, but which we cannot say. It must have taken place in 1511–12. The use of pen and ink on two of them seems to make them too late for Louis XII's residence in Milan in 1509: and the connection with the Trivulzio drawings is proof that they were not done for the masquerades which we know him to have directed in France. Nevertheless, these drawings have a subtly French flavour. The elegant artifice of the costumes, no less than the sentiment, recalls that silvery, lunar reflection of the Italian Renaissance which we see in the châteaux of the Loire; and two of the figures wear corselets of straps and ribbons, elaborately crossed and plaited in a style which suggests that typical product of the French Renaissance, St Porchaire faience. Perhaps they do so for the simple reason that Leonardo's own inherent love of interlaced movement influenced the trend of French design. But we may also feel in these masqueraders something remote from the Italian spirit of the time, something dreamlike, as if seen through the eyes of a man to whom the golden life of the Renaissance was a distant, fanciful dream. For this reason they are remarkably like the drawings of the English Pre-Raphaelites, although the finest Burne-Jones would look thin and lifeless by comparison, and under the fluttering diaphanous skirts of Leonardo's masqueraders we catch sight of muscular legs, anatomically perfect and very different from the wooden, dainty limbs of Rossetti. Most magical of all these costume pieces (if such it be) is the figure of a woman standing beside a little waterfall, pointing into the distance with a glance and a gesture of mysterious invitation (Pl. 104). This should be Leonardo's last drawing, just as *The Tempest* should be Shakespeare's last play. In it he returns to the inspiration of his youth, the tradition of Fra Filippo and Botticelli,[9] and presents it with the depth and mastery of age. It is the figure which had haunted him all his life, his angel, his familiar, transfixed at last. Unlike the 'St John' in the Louvre, where a similar creature of his imagination is almost smothered in the labour of painting, this drawing is built of touches as broken and evasive as the latest Titian. We cannot imagine it being done part by part. A puff of wind had blown away the mist, and revealed this goddess, as stately as an elm, as subtle as a gothic Virgin.

The studies for the Trivulzio memorial and the masquerade costumes must be the last works Leonardo executed for his French patrons in Milan. In June 1512 an unholy alliance of Spaniards, Papal mercenaries, and Venetians took over the government of the city, and Milan, which had been steadily declining as a centre of civilization, became completely disorganized. The poets, artists,

9. P. Mellor has shown convincingly that Leonardo was inspired by Botticelli's illustrations to Dante, and that this figure represents Matelda as she appears to Dante in canto XXVIII of the *Purgatorio*; cf. *Actae Historiae Artium*, II, 3/4 (1955), p. 135.

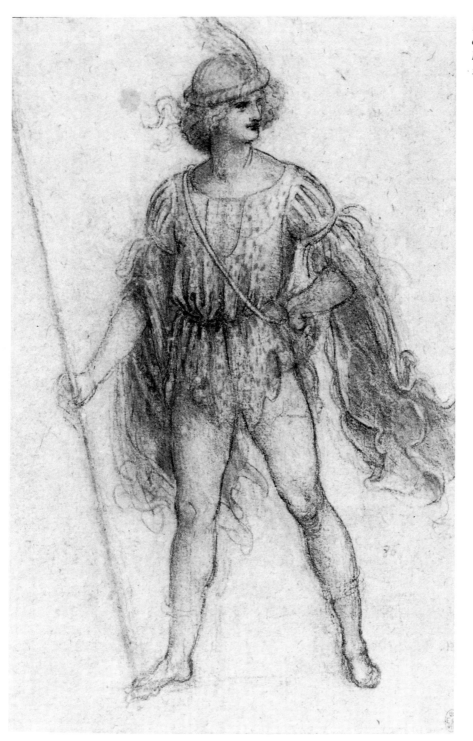

103. 'Masquerader',
c. 1512. Royal
Library, Windsor (RL
12575)

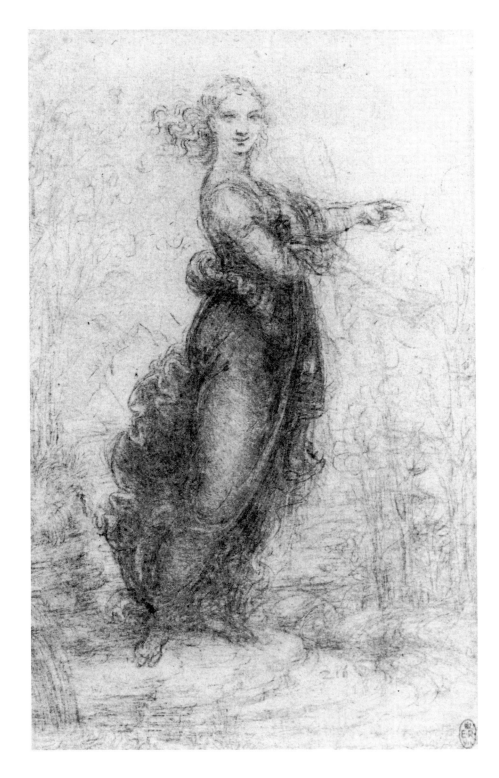

and men of learning who at first hoped to find in the French occupation some afterglow of the Sforza patronage had already turned their hungry eyes elsewhere, and chiefly to Rome, whither Leonardo himself was soon to follow them. But for another year he remained in Milan, or near by at Vaprio, in the house of his exquisite new friend and disciple, Francesco Melzi.

One of his occupations during this year must be noticed, since it provides us with our last dated evidence of his style of drawing. This is his study of anatomy. In 1510–11 he met Marc Antonio dalla Torre, the greatest anatomist of his time, who, according to Vasari, helped Leonardo in his anatomical researches. But of this help Leonardo's dated notebooks give no evidence. As we have seen, he was already studying anatomy in 1489 when Marc Antonio was only seven years old. By 1500 his researches had been carried far beyond anything necessary for the science of painting, and Leonardo had begun to cut deep into the central problems of biology by studying the processes of generation. A famous anatomical drawing representing the coition of a man and a woman shows the strange detachment with which he regarded this central moment of an ordinary man's life. It must date from about 1497. A few years later he was at work on the same subject, and symbolizing it, as we have seen, in the 'Leda'. A large manuscript at Windsor, known as the Anatomical MS. A, bears the inscription 'in the spring of this year, 1510, I hope to have completed all this branch of anatomy'. The greater part therefore dates from the year 1509, before the meeting with Marc Antonio, and proves that Leonardo cannot have learnt anatomy from the younger man. This manuscript contains a number of drawings of *écorché* figures, beautiful in themselves and useful as dating Leonardo's pen technique (Pl. 105). We see his system of shading following form carried almost to the point of mannerism. The line is dry and wiry, seldom betraying any feeling or vivacity, a sad, scientific style, compared to the beautiful anatomical drawings of 1489: yet the masquerade costumes of the same date show that Leonardo had not lost the magic of his touch when he chose to release it. This manuscript deals chiefly with musculature, but as a whole his later anatomical studies show him interested less in the mechanical than the organic side of his subject. A whole notebook dating from about 1512 is devoted to embryology, and he makes what must be one of the first drawings of a child in the womb (Pl. 106). When we remember the tenderness and delicacy of feeling which all early authorities attribute to Leonardo we can realize some of the noble and passionate curiosity which drove him to make such a terrible dissection, and to draw it with such a lucid and purposeful touch. His last anatomical manuscript, dated 9 January 1513, deals with the heart (Pl. 107). It is characteristic that although he investigates the action of the heart and arteries with great thoroughness, he never brings himself to propose the circulation of the blood as a formulated theory. The manuscript is written with a blunt pen

*105. Studies of the anatomy of the shoulder, 1510. Royal Library, Windsor (RL 19003r)*

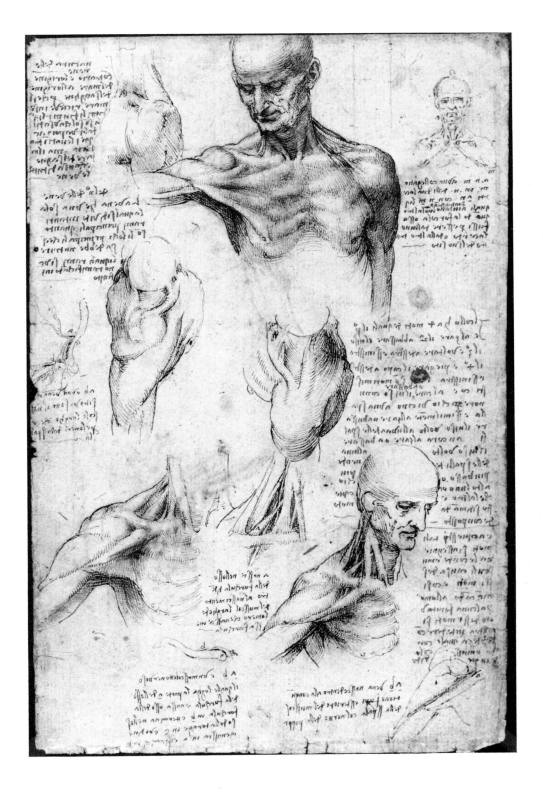

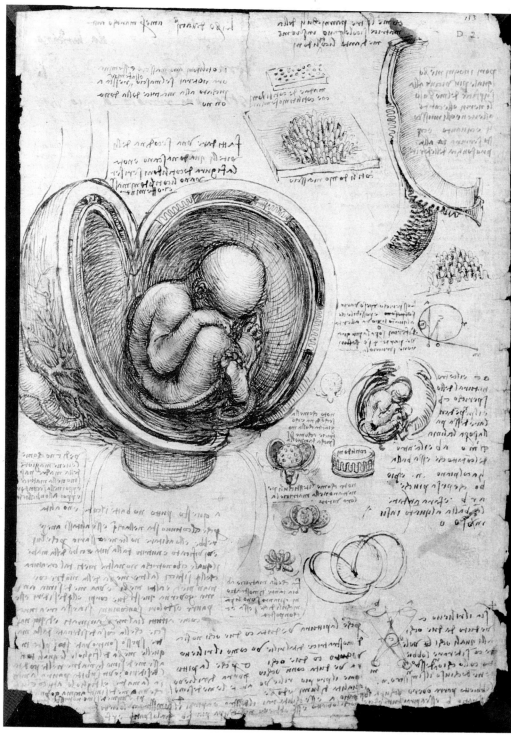

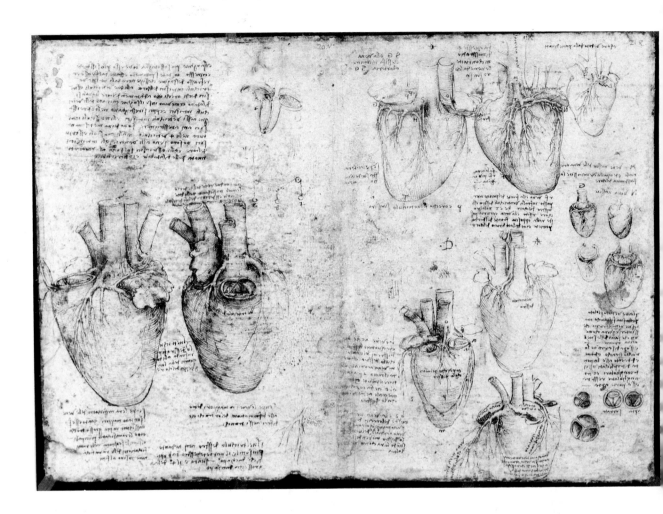

106. *An embryo in the womb*, c. 1512. Royal Library, Windsor (RL 19102r)

on coarse, blue-grey paper, and the illustrative drawings have a deliberate carelessness of touch as though Leonardo were denying himself the comeliness of his earlier style (Pl. 108). This is the technique of nearly all his latest drawings. It is not attributable to any physical decay, for we have neat writing of a later date: rather it seems to reflect the pessimism and the disillusion of old age, which rejects material beauty even if it consist in a dexterous line or a finely-turned cadence of verse.

107. *Studies of the anatomy of the heart*, 1513. Royal Library, Windsor (RL 19073v & 74v)

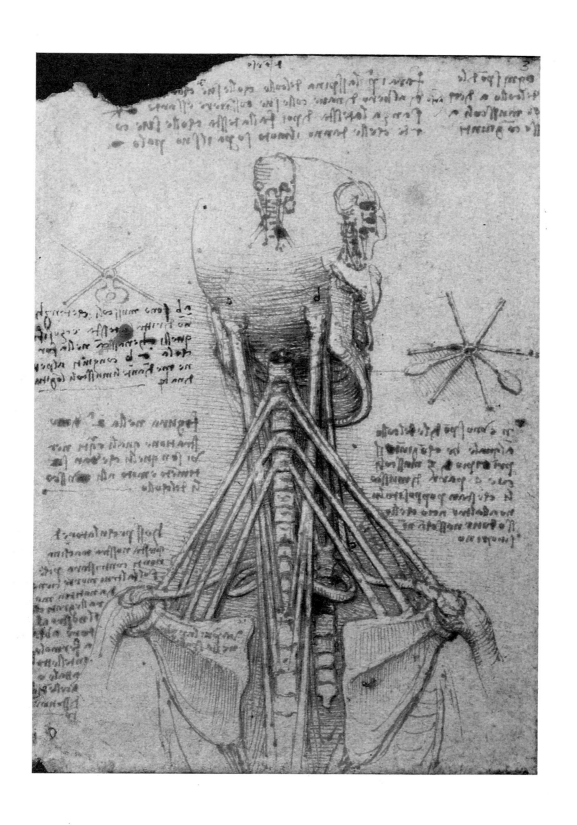

# CHAPTER NINE

# 1513-1519

*108. Schematic study of the anatomy of the neck and shoulders, c. 1513. Royal Library, Windsor (RL 19075v)*

'ON the 24th of September 1513,' says Leonardo, 'I left Milan for Rome, with Giovanni Francesco de' Melzi, Salai, Lórenzo, and il Fanfoia.' Like many other artists he was attracted by the notorious liberality of Giovanni de' Medici, who, in the preceding March, had become Pope Leo X. After stopping in Florence, Leonardo arrived in Rome towards the end of the year and was installed in rooms in the Belvedere of the Vatican, specially prepared for him by Giuliano de' Medici, the Pope's brother: so the favour which Lorenzo the Magnificent withheld from Leonardo was given to him by Lorenzo's sons. Giuliano, weak and unstable though he was, combined interest in art and science in a manner which should have made him an ideal patron for Leonardo. But there seems to have been a fate against his relations with the Medici,[1] and contemporary documents give us a sad picture of Leonardo's life in Rome. The solitary old exquisite, who had lived for so long according to his fancy remote from the world, found himself quartered among half the leading artists of Italy, crowding, criticizing, jockeying for positions. Raphael, with his troupe of ambitious youths, must have been frequently in the Belvedere to study the fragments of sculpture collected there, but we ask in vain if he visited the master from whom he had borrowed so freely. Worse of all, Michelangelo was in Rome, having gained by his work on the Sistine ceiling a position of unassailable authority. No wonder that Leonardo felt too weary to engage with such formidable rivals, and withdrew further into a melancholy and mysterious solitude. Vasari gives an account

1. In a note written at about this date, C.A., 159, *recto* C, he writes '*Li medici me creorono e desstrussono*'. This may refer to doctors, but Calvi is strongly of the opinion that it refers to the Medici, Calvi, *Archivio Storico Lombardo*, Anno XLIII (1916), facs. iii, p. 417.

of his occupations worth quoting at length, since it shows how his scientific researches appeared to the eyes of his contemporaries.

He formed a paste of a certain kind of wax, as he walked he shaped animals very thin and full of wind, and by blowing into them, made them fly through the air, but when the wind ceased they fell to the ground. On the back of a most bizarre lizard, found by the vine-dresser of the Belvedere, he fixed, with a mixture of quicksilver, wings composed of scales stripped from other lizards, which, as it walked, quivered with the motion; and having given it eyes, horns, and beard, taming it, and keeping it in a box, he made all his friends, to whom he showed it, fly for fear. He used often to have the guts of a wether completely freed of their fat and cleaned, and thus made so fine that they could have been held in the palm of the hand; and having placed a pair of blacksmith's bellows in another room, he fixed to them one end of these, and, blowing into them, filled the room, which was very large, so that whoever was in it was obliged to retreat into a corner; showing how, transparent and full of wind, from taking up little space at the beginning they had come to occupy much, and likening them to virtue. He made an infinite number of such follies, and gave his attention to mirrors; and he tried the strangest methods in seeking out oils for painting, and varnish for preserving works when painted.

It is interesting to notice that the story of Leonardo frightening his friends with a counterfeit dragon which occurs at the beginning of the *Life*, is repeated, in a different form, at the end. We cannot doubt that it is true and typical. But the only part of Vasari's account which can be confirmed is the reference to mirrors. Leonardo was probably at work on optical toys, such as the camera obscura, which during his Roman visit had occupied the attention of his precursor, Leon Battista Alberti, over eighty years earlier.[2] It seems that Leonardo had been given the services of a craftsman to carry out his designs, named Giorgio Tedesco. This man gave him infinite trouble and we have several drafts of long and angry letters on the subject which Leonardo addressed to his patron, Giuliano de' Medici. Giorgio was dissatisfied with his pay, worked for others, would not follow Leonardo's drawings, would not learn Italian, and went off shooting in the ruins with members of the Swiss Guard. Worst of all, he came under the influence of a fellow-countryman known as Giovanni degli Specchi, a manufacturer of mirrors who had his workshop in the Belvedere. This man was jealous of Leonardo's influence with his patron and engineered a quarrel over their accommodation. Finally, he found a means of reporting Leonardo's studies of anatomy to the Pope and having them stopped. It is ironical that the first instance of ecclesiastical interference with Leonardo should be due to Leo X. And I may here digress to contradict a belief, once commonly upheld, that Leonardo wrote back-

2. Cf. L. B. Alberti, *Opere Volgari*, ed. Bonucci, vol. I (5 vols., Florence, 1843–9), p. cii.

wards in order to conceal his thoughts, and did not publish his conclusions for fear of ecclesiastical persecution. This is completely unhistorical. In Leonardo's time the Church allowed far more dangerous and directly subversive opinions than his to go unchecked. His scientific researches were carried out with full cognizance of religious institutions. His dissections were made in ecclesiastical hospitals such as Santa Maria Nuova in Florence. If his notebooks contain occasional gibes at the clergy these are less frequent and less severe than in most literature of the period. Leonardo wrote backwards because he was left-handed, and he did not publish his researches because he could not bring himself to try to put them in order. We have, in fact, no evidence that Leo X was concerned with Leonardo's opinions except in this instance, but Vasari records that the Pope was distressed by his dilatoriness. 'It is said that a work being given him to execute by the Pope, he immediately began to distil oils and herbs in order to make a varnish: whereupon Pope Leo exclaimed "Alas! This man will never do anything, for he begins by thinking about the end before the beginning of the work. *Oimè! Costui non è per far nulla, da che comincia a pensare alla fine inanzi il principio dell'opera.*" '

Constitutional dilatoriness, an inability to carry anything through from beginning to end without the intervention of a thousand experiments and afterthoughts, had always been part of Leonardo's character, and we must recognize it as a disease of the will similar to that which ruined the magnificent intellect of Coleridge. *Di mi se mai fu fatta alcuna cosa* – tell me if anything was ever done – this was the first sentence which flowed from Leonardo's pen in any vacant moment. *Di mi se mai, di mi se mai*, again and again, dozens of times, we find it on sheets of drawings, among scribbles or mathematical jottings, or beside the most painstaking calculations, till it becomes a sort of refrain, and a clear symptom of his trouble. With Leonardo, of course, the shrinking of the will was only intermittent and was largely cancelled by the superhuman energy of his mind. But during those years in Rome it seems to have taken a hold on him, and almost the only record of his activity is a note in which he mentions his *De Ludo Geometrico* 'finished on the 7th day of July, at the 23rd hour, in the study made for me by il Magnifico' (Giuliano). Innumerable drawings in the *Codice Atlantico* – one sheet alone contains ninety-three – show us the nature of these geometrical games, and leave us lamenting the waste of Leonardo's time and ingenuity. For these figures have as much to do with geometry as a crossword puzzle has to do with literature.

A drawing at Windsor, which dates from these years, seems to symbolize his state of mind (Pl. 109). It shows an old bearded man seated in profile, his head in his hand gazing into the distance, with an air of profound melancholy. His nutcracker nose and sharply turned-down mouth remind us of the old

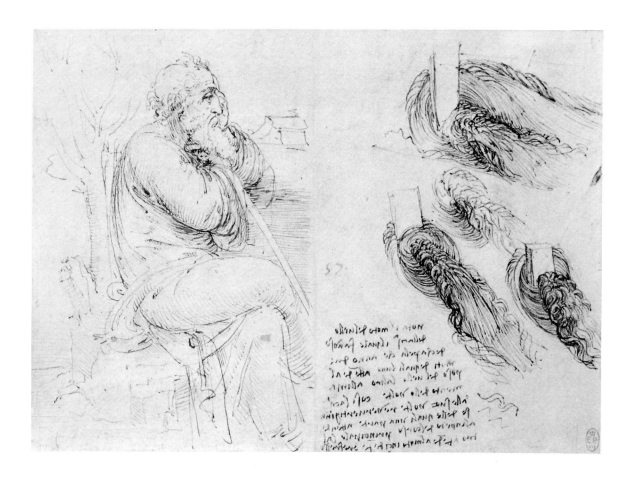

men in Leonardo's unconscious scribbles, but his curling beard and large deep-set eye recall the likenesses of Leonardo himself. Even if this is not strictly a self-portrait we may call it a self-caricature, using the word to mean a simplified expression of essential character. Opposite him on the sheet are studies of swirling water and a note comparing its movement to that of plaited hair; and although these studies were not intended to have any connection with the old man, for the sheet was originally folded over, they are like the projection of his thoughts. For of all Leonardo's interests the most continuous and obsessive was the movement of water. At various times in his life he had been able to turn this obsession to semi-practical ends by applying himself to problems of canalization and irrigation. But the quantity of his notes on the subject – it forms one of the largest and most disheartening sections of his written work – and the quality of his drawings show a passion with no relation to practical life. Some of his studies of swirling water are amongst the most direct expressions of his sense of form, springing from the

*109. An old man meditating and studies of water, c. 1513. Royal Library, Windsor (RL 12579r)*

*110. Studies of water, c. 1510. Royal Library, Windsor (RL 12660v)*

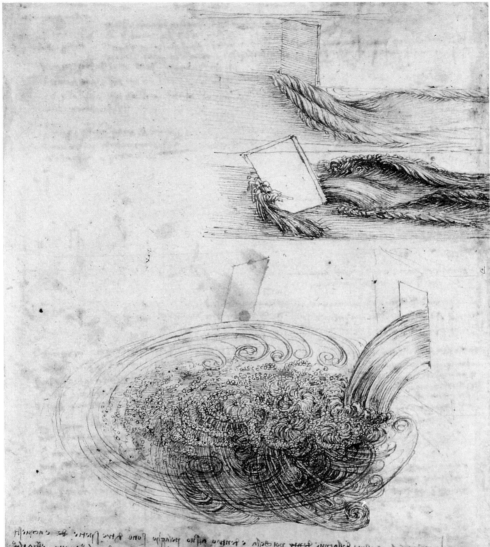

same mysterious source of his love of knots and tendrils. A sheet at Windsor shows water taking the form of both hair and flowers, racing along in twisted strands, and pouring from a sluice so that it makes dozens of little whirlpools, like a cluster of ferns with long curling tendrils (Pl. 110). His superhuman quickness of eye has allowed him to fasten on the decorative aspects of the subject, since confirmed by spark photography, and we must take these drawings of water as genuinely scientific. But as he gazed half hypnotized at the ruthless continuum of watery movement, Leonardo began to transpose his observations into the realm of the imagination, and to associate them with an idea of cataclysmic destruction which had always haunted him. Here for once he seems to have been touched by contemporary emotions, for the last years of the fifteenth century saw a series of prophetic writings, foretelling the destruction of the world by flood. These prophecies, which form a branch of the apocalyptic writings accompanying the Reformation, were condemned by the Church, but in spite of official opposition, they took an extraordinary hold on the popular mind and we are told that many made preparation for the catastrophe, sold their houses, and fled to the hills, so that in parts of Germany whole villages were deserted. It is revealing that Leonardo, who often expressed his contempt for vulgar superstition, should have allowed his mind to dwell on these prognostications of a deluge. They correspond with his own deepest belief: that the destructive forces of nature were like a reservoir, dammed up by a thin, unsteady wall, which at any moment might burst, and sweep away the pretentious homunculi who had dared to maintain that man was the measure of all things. By a curious chance, an artist who in some ways, resembled him, Albert Dürer, was also influenced by the idea of a deluge.

In the year 1525 [says Dürer], between Wednesday and Thursday after Whitsunday during the night, I saw this appearance in my sleep, how many great waters fell from heaven. The first struck the earth about four miles away from me with a terrific force, with tremendous clamour and clash, drowning the whole land.... I was so frightened when I awoke that my whole body trembled and for a long while I could not come to myself. So when I arose in the morning, I painted above here as I had seen it. God turn all things to the best.

Dürer's water-colour drawing[3] shows a column of black water, without weight or movement, standing over a peaceful landscape, while the other waterspouts hang like dark aprons in the distant sky. It is a conception at the furthest remove from Leonardo. Compared to Dürer's account of his dream, his very natural fear for his own safety, his pious prayer to God,

3. A. Rosenthal in *Burlington Magazine*, vol. LXIX (1936), p. 82.

Leonardo glories in the triumph of natural forces and dwells with gusto on every detail of destruction. His descriptions of the Deluge are found as early as the Ashburnham Codex of 1494 and as late as MS. G, but the most famous of them is on a sheet at Windsor, 12,665, where, on the pretext of instructing the painter how to represent a storm (the sheet is headed *come si deve figurare una fortuna*) Leonardo gives free rein to his imagination. Parts of his passage are literary and dramatic.

You might see on many of the hill-tops terrified animals of different kinds collected together and subdued to tameness, in company with men and women who had fled there with their children. The waters which covered the fields were strewn with tables, bedsteads, boats, and various other contrivances made from necessity and the fear of death, and on these were men and women with their children, weeping, terrified by the fury of the winds which, with tempestuous violence, rolled the waters under and over and about the bodies of the drowned. Nor was there any object lighter than the water which was not covered with a variety of animals, among them wolves, foxes, snakes, and others which, having come to a truce, stood together in a frightened crowd seeking to escape death.

You might have seen assemblages of men who, with weapons in their hands, defended the small spots that remained to them against lions, wolves and beasts of prey who sought safety there. Ah! what dreadful noises were heard in the air rent by the fury of the thunder and the lightnings it flashed forth, which darted from the clouds dealing ruin and striking all that opposed its course. Ah! how many you might have seen closing their ears with their hands to shut out the tremendous sounds made in the darkened air by the raging of the winds mingling with the rain, the thunders of heaven, and the fury of the thunder-bolts.

Other parts of his description are more closely connected with his studies of moving water, and dwell on that aspect of the Deluge which appealed to his sense of form.

Let there be first represented the summit of a rugged mountain with valleys surrounding its base, and on its sides, let the surface of the soil be seen to slide, together with the small roots of the bushes, denuding great portions of the surrounding rocks. And descending ruinous from these precipices in its boisterous course, let it dash along and lay bare the twisted and gnarled roots of large trees turning up their roots; and let the mountains, as they are scoured bare, discover the profound fissures made in them by ancient earthquakes. The base of the mountains may be partly covered with ruins of shrubs, and these will be mixed with mud, roots, boughs of trees, and with all sorts of leaves thrust in with the mud and earth and stones. Into the depth of some valley may have fallen the fragments of a mountain, damming up the swollen waters of its river; which, having already burst its banks, will rush on in monstrous waves; and the greatest will strike upon and destroy the walls of the cities and farmhouses in the valley. Then the ruins of the high buildings in these cities will throw

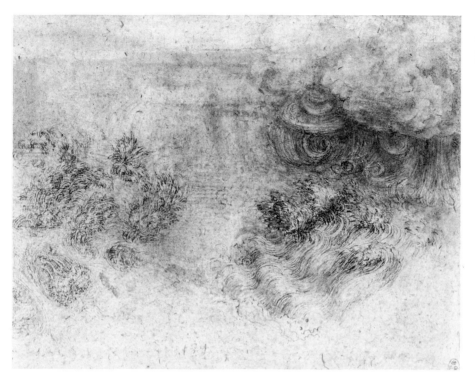

111. *The beginning of the deluge*, c. 1514. *Royal Library, Windsor* (RL 12379)

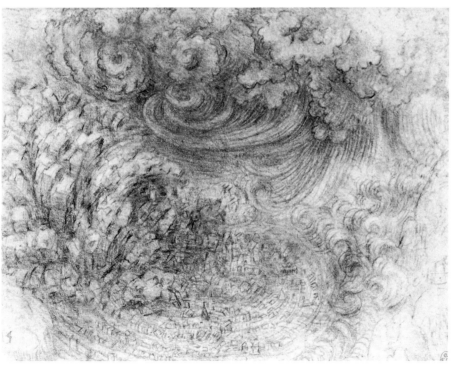

112. *A mountain falling on a town*, c. 1514. *Royal Library, Windsor* (RL 12378)

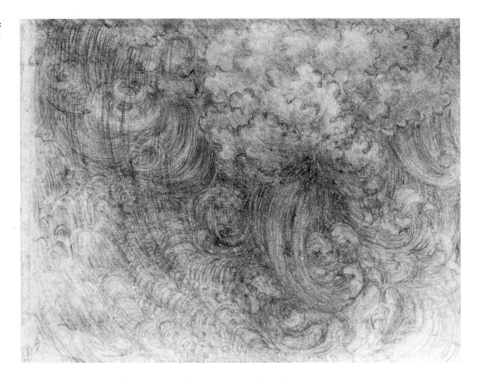

113. *The deluge at its height*, c. 1514. *Royal Library, Windsor* (RL 12383)

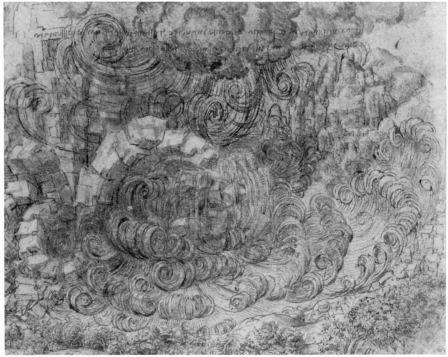

114. *The deluge formalized*, c. 1514. *Royal Library, Windsor* (RL 12380)

up a great dust, rising up in shape like smoke or wreathed clouds against the falling rain. But the swollen waters will sweep round the pool which contains them, striking in eddying whirlpools against the different obstacles, and leaping into the air in muddy foam; then, falling back, the beaten water will again be dashed into the air. . . .

The drawings at Windsor in which Leonardo illustrates these visions are the most personal in the whole range of his work (Pls. 111 to 114). They express, with a freedom which is almost disturbing, his passion for twisting movement, and for sequences of form fuller and more complex than anything in European art. They are so far from the classical tradition that our first term of comparison might be one of the great Chinese paintings of cloud and storm, for example, the Dragon Scroll in the Boston Museum. Only in Oriental art do we find a similar mastery of the convention, by which forces and directions are reduced to visible linear curves. Yet, as with his landscape, closer study shows that Leonardo's scientific attitude has given his drawings a character fundamentally different from Chinese painting. By profound research into movement of water he has learnt to give his lines of force a logical as well as an expressive significance. In these drawings Leonardo has filled the atmosphere with the cascades and currents which he had studied in moving water. He explains how such atmospheric currents can be made visible. 'Let the air be darkened,' he says, 'by heavy rain whose oblique descent driven aslant by the rush of the winds will fly in drifts through the air like dust.' In another passage he writes: 'A mountain falling on a town will fling up dust in the form of clouds; but the colour of the dust will differ from that of the clouds,' and beside it the note, 'A stone falling through the air leaves on the eye which sees it the impression of its motion, and the same effect is produced by the drops of water which fall from clouds.' The scientific care with which these appalling catastrophes are studied has an almost comic effect. 'If heavy masses of great mountains fall into vast lakes, a great quantity of water will be flung into the air, and its movement will be in a contrary direction to that of the object which struck the surface, that is to say, the angle of refraction will be equal to the angle of incidence.' This fusion between science and fantasy is even more surprising when, as in Pl. 114, some drily scientific observations on the nature of rain are barely legible through the turmoil of universal destruction. Through what strange inhibition did Leonardo attempt to hide from himself the true motive of these drawings? Was it pride in a science which might still look with detachment at the annihilation of humanity; or was it a kind of reserve which prevented him from betraying his innermost feelings in words, even though they were expressed in line?[4] For these drawings come from the depths of Leonardo's

4. Freud notes the prosaic brevity with which Leonardo records the death of his father, and, as Freud surmises, his mother.

soul. In them he has used his scientific knowledge as Michelangelo came to use his understanding of the human body, distorting it to express his sense of tragedy. If in the lovely drawing of a pointing woman he is Prospero, in these Deluges he is Lear:

> Blow, winds, and crack your cheeks! rage! blow!
> You cataracts and hurricanoes, spout
> Till you have drencht our steeples, drown'd the cocks!
> You sulphurous and thought-executing fires,
> Vaunt-couriers to oak-cleaving thunderbolts,
> Singe my white head!

*115. The deluge with wind gods and horsemen, c. 1513. Royal Library, Windsor (RL 12376)*

The drawings probably belong to a single period, but some sort of chronological sequence can be established in which the treatment becomes gradually more personal. The earliest is a large study of horsemen assailed by a tornado (Pl. 115), which is like an illustration to the *Trattato*, and even includes a

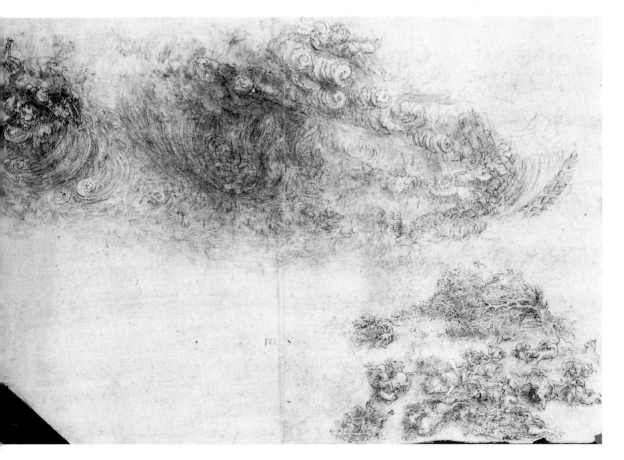

wind god in the clouds, a conceit far from the spirit of the later drawings.[5] An apocalyptic intention first appears in the pen and ink drawing (P. 288), in which terrified little figures cower beneath a rain of fire. Then come drawings like Pl. 111 where the fury of the elements is released, but the scene is comparatively restricted and within the bounds of possibility. In Pl. 112 the Deluge is at its height, and we see the motif, often alluded to in Leonardo's description, of a mountain undermined by the gigantic spouts of rain falling on a town and annihilating it. But even more appalling is Pl. 113, where the Deluge has carried all before it, so that no sign remains of human life or vegetation. This is the climax of the series. There follow several drawings in which Leonardo has grown so absorbed in the elaboration of curvilinear patterns that the scenes lose some of their dramatic force. In Pl. 114, for example, the linear convention is used so openly that the deluge has become merely decorative; the water-spouts are as powerless as the petals of a chrysanthemum, and the collapsing mountain is made of a child's bricks. Yet compared with the waves of a Japanese screen Leonardo's composition is infinitely richer and more complex. It has a quality of inexhaustible suggestion only possible in the work of a man to whom the subtlety of natural appearances was perfectly familiar.

On grounds of style and spirit, these drawings must belong to the uneasy years of residence at Rome. During that period the Pope seems to have consulted him on a scheme for draining the Pontine marshes,[6] and in a drawing at Windsor (Pl. 116), representing a bird's-eye view of the land in question, the treatment of hills and trees is very similar to the foreground of the deluges. It is suggestive that in the margin of that description of a tempest which most closely conforms to the drawings is the note, 'The wave of the sea at Piombino is all foaming water'; for it was at Piombino that Leonardo had been employed in another great effort to drain marshy land.

In the same years – 1514–15 – I would place Leonardo's last surviving picture, the Louvre 'St John' (Pl. 117). It is usually said, on no evidence, to have been painted in France, but if this were the case we could hardly account for the numerous contemporary Italian copies. No doubt Leonardo had been working on the subject for years and the actual date of its execution as a picture can never be established. The 'St John' is the least popular of Leonardo's works. Critics have found it so little to their taste that they have called it the work of assistants. This is certainly false. The 'St John' is a baffling work, but every inch of it smells of Leonardo. Even if we dislike it we must admit its power to trouble the memory, both as image and design. The initial

---

5. Curiously enough this practice is recommended in L. B. Alberti's *della Pittura*, ed. Janitschek (Vienna, 1877), p. 131, which, as noted on p. 128, was well known to Leonardo.

6. Cf. Solmi, *Scritti Vinciani*, p. 299 *et seq.*

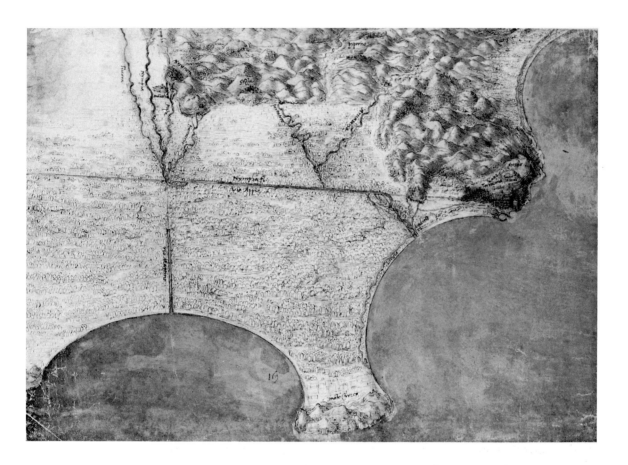

*116. Scheme for the draining of the Pontine Marshes, 1513–16. Royal Library, Windsor (RL 12684)*

cause of our uneasiness is iconographic. We are aware, from the little reed cross which he holds, that this extraordinary creature is intended to represent St John, and our whole sense of propriety is outraged. Every critic has laboriously pointed out that this is not a satisfactory presentation of the Baptist, and we must try to answer the question why Leonardo, who attached so much importance to the interpretation of a subject, has created an image almost blasphemously unlike the fiery ascetic of the Gospels. To a certain extent, the answer is to be found in the origin of the design. At the end of his second Florentine period, Leonardo became interested in the subject of an angel. There is a rough sketch of it on a drawing in Windsor dateable *c.* 1505 (P. 203), and we know that he finished the picture, for Vasari describes it as being in the cabinet of the Grand Duke Cosimo – 'a head of an angel raising its arm in the air so that it is foreshortened from the shoulder to the elbow, the other arm being laid on the breast, showing the hand.' A figure corresponding to this description has come down to us in several paintings which are clearly replicas of a Leonardesque original (Pl. 118). We can see

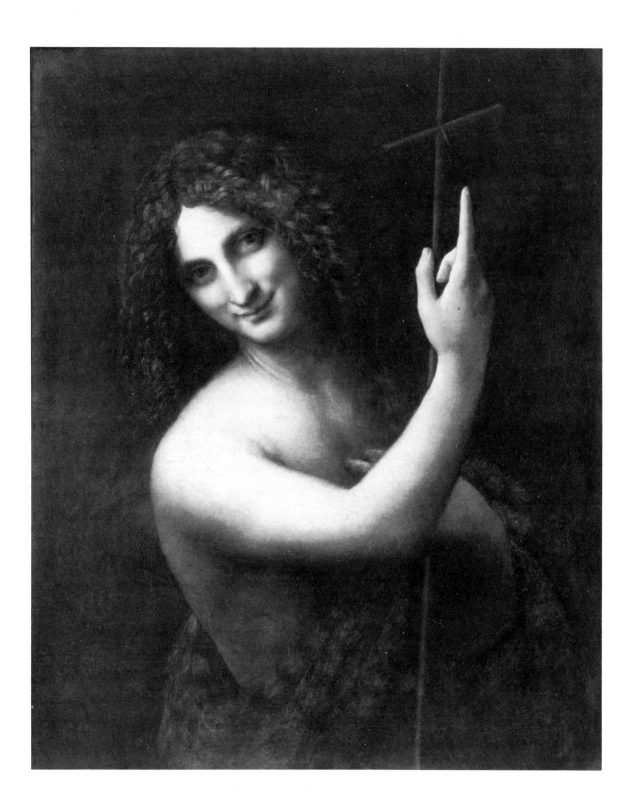

117. 'St John the
Baptist', c. 1515.
Louvre, Paris

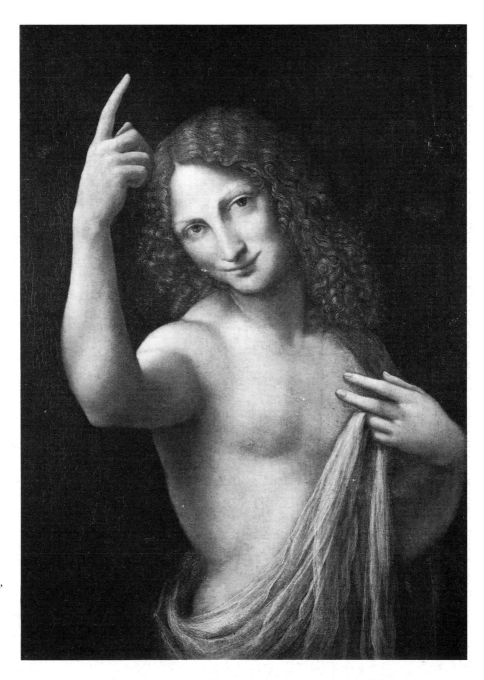

118. Leonardo (after),
'Angel of the
Annunciation', c.
1505–7. Öffentliche
Kunstsammlung,
Basel

that this angel was very like the St John in general conception, but with the
one important difference, that the St John's right arm is bent across his breast
so that his hand points upwards over his left shoulder. The angel's arm is
seen in foreshortening, the hand and index finger pointing upwards; and from

this gesture we see that he is an Angel of the Annunciation. Leonardo, with an audacity which is almost disturbing, has shown us the Announcing Angel from the point of vision of Our Lady. We can imagine what complex ideas Leonardo might have wished to express in this strange conception; for the Annunciation can be made to imply that union of flesh and spirit, human and divine, which he wished above all to express. Just as the forces of nature, subject to material analysis up to a point, became suddenly incomprehensible, so the Angel of the Annunciation, though taking human shape, was the agent of a mystery; and mystery to Leonardo was a shadow, a smile and a finger pointing into darkness.

As an Angel, then, this figure is understandable; and if it shocks us, that is largely because we have taken for granted the pagan notion that an angel must be a type of fair-haired physical beauty, fragile or lusty as the taste of the period shall demand. It is less easy to understand how this image could be converted, with a single change of gesture, into a St John, and I must confess that some years ago, when art was supposed to consist in the arrangement of forms, I believed that Leonardo made this alteration for purely formal motives: that he bent the arm across the figure in order to achieve a denser and more continuous volume. It is true that the St John looks much more solid than the Angel, but we can be sure that Leonardo would not have varied the pose solely for that reason. Between the two figures there is more than a formal connection. They are, in fact, the two messengers announcing the birth of Christ. The Angel points upwards to God; St John points over his shoulder – 'there is one that cometh after me'.[7] Even this difference does not quite dispose of our difficulties, because the type and expression which can be understood in an Angel may seem to us inconsistent in a St John. And here we must assume that Leonardo had formed of St John a curiously personal conception which we must interpret as best we can. Of several possible interpretations I offer the following which is at least in keeping with Leonardo's spirit. St John the Baptist was the forerunner of the Truth and the Light. And what is the inevitable precursor of truth? A question. Leonardo's St John is the eternal question mark, the enigma of creation. He thus becomes Leonardo's familiar – the spirit which stands at his shoulder and propounds unanswerable riddles. He has the smile of a sphinx, and the power of an obsessive shape. I have pointed out how this gesture – which itself has the rising rhythm of an interrogative – appears throughout Leonardo's work. Here it is quintessential. The design has the finality of a hard-won form rendered in an intractable material. Leonardo, who could give life to every pose and glance, has subdued his gifts as if he were working in obsidian.

7. As a matter of fact St John points upwards, but iconographers have usually interpreted the turn of his body as implying a figure behind him.

The Louvre 'St John' being the most idiosyncratic of Leonardo's works, was also the most influential; and part of our distaste for it is due to the large number of pupil's copies which it recalls: for to most people the Milanese school is like the Cheshire cat – only the smile remains. Of these monotonously smiling figures I will mention only one, because it occurs in all early literature as an original Leonardo. This is the so-called 'Bacchus' in the Louvre which, reversing the role of Heine's pagan gods, is really a converted St John the Baptist. As such he is described by Cassiano del Pozzo, who saw him at Fontainebleau in 1625; he adds, 'it is a most delicate work but does not please because it does not arouse feelings of devotion.' Presumably for this reason some painter was told to add a crown of vine leaves and change the cross into a thyrsis: and in the 1695 inventory *St Jean dans le désert* is crossed out and *Baccus dans un paysage* written instead. These alterations no doubt involved complete repainting, and were probably accompanied by a transference from panel to canvas; as a result the 'Bacchus' makes a poor impression and has been rejected from the canon of Leonardo's work by all serious scholars. But the original design was due to Leonardo and has been preserved in a highly finished red chalk study in the Museum of the Sacro Monte at Varese (Pl. 119), which, in spite of retouching seems to me an authentic drawing of about the period 1510–12. It shows St John completely nude, with a clear, articulate, muscular body, in contrast to the smooth fleshy limbs of the Louvre Bacchus. Whether Leonardo himself did a painting from this drawing we shall never know. Probably he left the execution to Cesare da Sesto, who was working closely with him at this date, and whose style is still perceptible in the Louvre picture.[8]

'The magnificent Giuliano de' Medici,' Leonardo notes, 'left at dawn on the 9th day of January 1515, to marry a wife in Savoy; and in the same day the King of France died.' For a year after this his movements are obscure, though we know that he was still attached to the household of Giuliano.[9] Then on 17 March 1516, Giuliano died, and soon afterwards Leonardo must have accepted an invitation from Francis I to settle in France. The King seems to have treated him with the greatest liberality. He gave him the manor of Cloux, near Amboise, and asked nothing in return but the pleasure of his conversation, which he enjoyed almost every day. Of this we have first-hand evidence from Cellini, who twenty years later heard Francis say 'that he did believe no other man had been born who knew as much as Leonardo, both in sculpture, painting, and architecture, so that he was a very great philosopher'. Free to talk, experiment, and dream at will, it is not surprising that Leonardo seems to have produced practically nothing during his stay in

8. A Cesare of the same design is the small 'St John' in the collection of Lord Crawford.

9. H. Horne (trans.), *Leonardo*, p. 42.

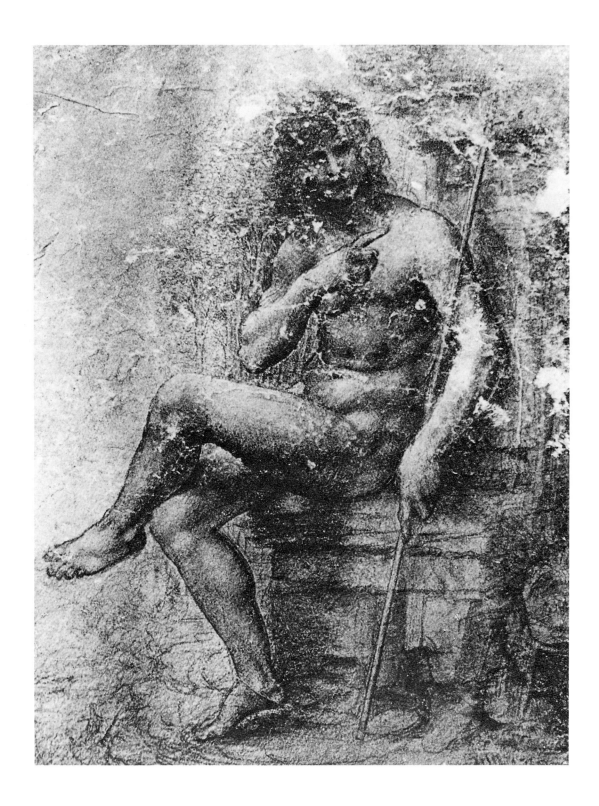

*119. Study for 'St
John the Baptist', c.
1510–12. Formerly
Museum of the Sacro
Monte at Varese*

France. We have a number of notes and drawings which show him interested
in canalizing the Loire to Romorantin, and in town planning,[10] and from
these we can date certain architectural drawings (Pl. 120), including a fine
study of a turreted fortress in the *Codice Atlantico*.[11] It is arguable that the
style of French châteaux architecture as we see it, for example, at Chambord,
derives from these drawings, and an ingenious attempt has been made to
show that he designed the staircase of the Castle of Blois on the plan of a
nautilus shell. Such a procedure would be characteristic of Leonardo, but
unfortunately there is no evidence for it, except the well-known evidence
that Shakespeare was a Scot – that the ability of the design warrants the
assumption.

Apart from architecture, all attributions of drawings to the period of his
residence in France must be pure speculation, because we have no certain
evidence of Leonardo's activity in France, no dated drawings and only one
documented commission; and this commission has not come down to us, for
it was the lion filled with lilies recorded by Vasari and Lomazzo as being
one of Leonardo's most ingenious works.[12] The lion is also mentioned
independently in contemporary records of a Masquerade at the Château of
Blois. These court descriptions do not mention the name of Leonardo, but
their account of the lion exactly corresponds to that of Leonardo's biographers. The lion took several steps forward and seemed to attack the King,
when its head opened disclosing a great bank of lilies against a blue background. Much of an earlier Leonardesque spirit seems to survive in this fancy
of his old age, the spirit which made him the inventor of emblem and elegance
to the Sforza court.

On 10 October 1517 Leonardo was visited by the Cardinal Louis of Aragon
whose secretary Antonio de' Beatis has left us an interesting and puzzling
account of him. He says that Leonardo showed the Cardinal

three pictures; one of a certain Florentine lady, done from the life, at the instance of
the late Magnificent, Giuliano de'Medici; the other of St John the Baptist, as a Young
Man; and one of the Madonna and the Child, which are placed in the lap of St Anne,
and all of them most perfect: but indeed, on account of a certain paralysis having
seized him in the right hand,[13] one cannot expect more fine things from him. He has
instructed a Milanese disciple, who works well enough; and although the aforesaid
Messer Leonardo is not able to colour with that sweetness which he was wont,
nevertheless he works at making designs and giving instructions to others. This

10. For example, British Museum M S. 270 *verso*.

11. In the *Codice Atlantico*, f. 43 v.a. For these architectural projects for Francis I, cf. L. H. Heydenreich
in *Burlington Magazine*, vol. XCIV (1952), pp. 277 ff.

12. Cf. Solmi, *Scritti Vinciani*, p. 339, *et seq.*

13. *Destra*, presumably meaning his working hand, although Leonardo was left-handed.

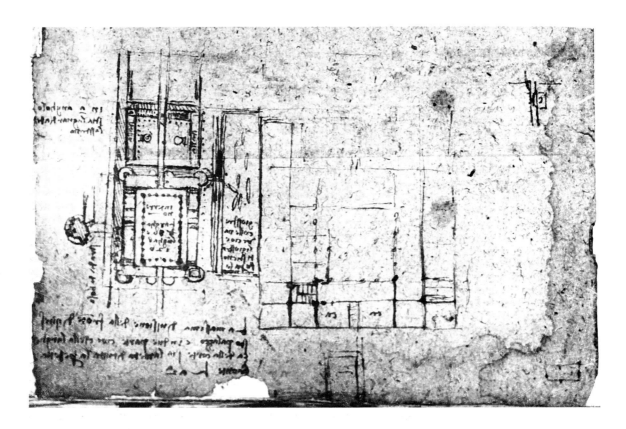

*120. Plan for a Royal Palace at Romorantin, 1516–18. Ambrosiana, Milan*

gentleman has compiled a particular treatise of anatomy, with the demonstration in draft not only of the members, but also of the muscles, nerves, veins, joints, intestines, and of whatever can be reasoned about in the bodies of men and women, in a way that has never yet been done by any other person. All of which we have seen with our eyes; and he said that he had already dissected more than thirty bodies, both men and women of all ages. He has, also, written concerning the nature of water, and of divers machines, and other things, which he has set down in an endless number of volumes, and all in the vulgar tongue.

The 'St Anne' and the 'St John' are easily recognizable as the pictures now in the Louvre. But the portrait of a Florentine lady cannot be the 'Mona Lisa', which was certainly not done at the instance of 'the late Magnificent, Giuliano de' Medici'. This must have been a work in Leonardo's late style, and no replica of such a picture exists to give us any hint of what the original was like. De' Beatis's description of the notebooks inspires confidence in his veracity, and makes it more than ever difficult to know how we should interpret his account of Leonardo's paralysis. That Leonardo was paralysed in an ordinary sense is demonstrably untrue, since we have plenty of manuscripts of a later date than October 1517, including a sheet in the *Codice*

*Atlantico*, inscribed 'in the Palace of Cloux at Amboise, 24th June, 1518'. On these the writing, sometimes blunted by the roughness of the paper, is still beautifully clear and firm. It is true, however, that the lines of shading in the drawings of water are rather more ragged than formerly, and we may conjecture that Leonardo's paralysis did not affect his fingers, but prevented him from moving his arm with any freedom. This would account for the statement that he was still able to make designs; and if he could draw, the inability to colour with that sweetness which had cost him so much pains would not greatly distress Leonardo. Of these designs, as I have said, we have no solid evidence; but on grounds of style I would attribute to the French period some drawings handled even more broadly than the masquerade costumes: such for example as the head of an old man at Windsor, 12,500, where the broken touch no less than the feeling of grave authority recall the late self-portraits of Titian (Pl. 121). Leonardo's own self-portrait, the red chalk drawing at Turin (Pl. 122), is in a fine, clear style which must indicate an earlier date. He has represented himself as being of a great age, but we know that Leonardo looked older than his years. De' Beatis speaks of him as being more than seventy, though actually he was only sixty-four at the time, and the self-portrait may date from about 1512 when Leonardo would be sixty. This is the only authentic likeness of Leonardo. The numerous portraits in profile are copies which gradually come to approximate more and more to the idealized representation of a sage. But even the self-portrait is, to my mind, remarkably unrevealing. This great furrowed mountain of a face with its noble brow, commanding cavernous eyes, and undulating foot-hills of beard is like the faces of all the great men of the nineteenth century as the camera has preserved them for us – Darwin, Tolstoy, Walt Whitman. Time, with its spectacle of human suffering, has reduced them all to a common level of venerability.

Leonardo died in the Castle of Cloux on 2 May 1519, leaving to his friend and pupil, Melzi, the great store of drawings and manuscripts through which we should be able to form a clear conception of his character. But in spite of this mass of material his image changes like a cloud. Leonardo is the Hamlet of art history whom each of us must recreate for himself, and although I have tried to interpret his work as impersonally as possible, I recognize that the result is largely subjective. Certain things in his art are clear and definable; for example, his passionate curiosity into the secrets of nature, and the inhumanly sharp eye with which he penetrated them – followed the movements of birds or of a wave, understood the structure of a seed-pod or a skull, noted down the most trivial gesture or most evasive glance. But even in his art there are chords which seem to be left unresolved. One of these I have stressed throughout, the conflict between his aesthetic and his scientific approach to painting, the former deeply, even extravagantly romantic,

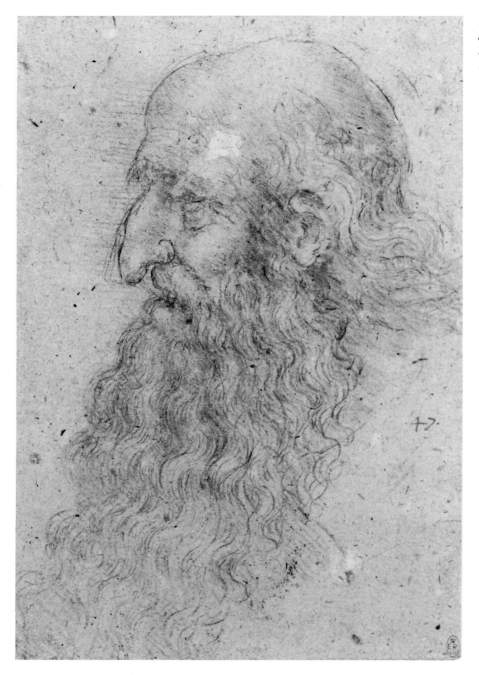

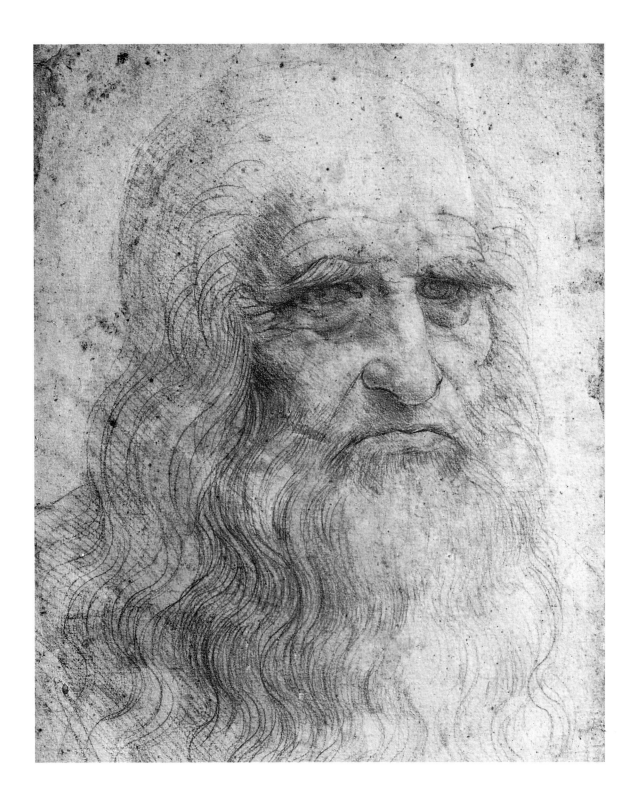

comparable to such painters as El Greco and Turner; the other, found in the composition of the 'Last Supper', forming the foundation of later academism.

Even more bewildering is the contrast between his drawings and his notebooks. In all his writings – one of the most voluminous and complete records of a mind at work which has come down to us – there is hardly a trace of human emotion. Of his affections, his tastes, his health, his opinions on current events we know nothing. Yet if we turn from his writings to his drawings, we find a subtle and tender understanding of human feelings which is not solely due to the efficiency of the optic nerve. In his contemplation of nature, this human understanding seems to have been gradually swamped; and here, perhaps, is a hint of some unifying principle in all Leonardo's work. From the first he is obsessed by vital force and finds it expressed in plants and creatures; then, as his scientific researches develop he learns the vast power of natural forces and he pursues science as a means by which these forces can be harnessed for human advantage. The further he penetrates the more he becomes aware of man's impotence; his studies of geology show that the earth has undergone cataclysmic upheavals of which ordinary earthquakes are but faint and distant echoes; his studies of embryology point to a central problem of creation apparently insoluble by science. The intellect is no longer supreme, and human beings cease to be the centre of nature; so they gradually fade from his imagination, or when they appear, as St Anne or St John, they are human no longer but symbols of force and mystery, messengers from a world which Leonardo da Vinci, the disciple of experience, has not explored though he has earned the right to proclaim its existence. *La natura è piena d'infinite ragioni che non furono mai in esperienza.*

# LIST OF DATES

1483    25 April. Contract with Leonardo and Ambrogio and Evangelista da Predis for the 'Virgin of the Rocks', other paintings and polychroming of the altar-piece of the Milanese Confraternity of the Immaculate Conception in San Francesco Grande in Milan.

1487    July–January 1488. Payments for model of tambour of Milan Cathedral.

(c. 1488    MS. B. Portrait of Cecilia Gallerani.)

1489    2 April. MS. Anatom. B (Windsor 19,059r.) (early anatomical drawings, e.g. skulls).

1490    13 January. Designs for the 'Festa del Paradiso' to celebrate the Sforza–Aragon wedding.

23 April. 'On the 23 of April 1491 I commenced this book and recommenced the horse' (MS. C, 15v.).

21 June. In Pavia with Francesco di Giorgio.

22 July. 'Day of the Magdalene'. Salai joins Leonardo, aged ten (MS. C, 15v.).

23 July. Leonardo brands Salai a 'thief, liar, obstinate, glutton' for stealing money from him.

(c. 1491    MSS. Ash. II and A. Description of storms, battles, and profiles.)

1491    17 May. Scheme for casting the Sforza horse (MS. Madrid II, 157v.).

1492    10 July. MS. Ash. I, 34v.

1493    1 January. MS. Madrid Iv. (written left to right).

26 January. Organizes a *festa* for a joust at the palace of Galeazzo da San Severino.

16 July. Notes about a horse, a *morel fiorentino* (i.e. still at work on the Sforza monument) (Forster III, 88r.).

November. Full-size clay model for the horse exhibited.

1494    MS. H. (Allegories.)

2 February. Description of hydraulic engineering at Vigevano (MS. H², 65v.)

14 March. MS. H¹, 41r.

(1495–6    MS. Forster II, description of the 'Last Supper'.)

1497    January. Still at work on the 'Last Supper'.

29 June. 'Last Supper' nearing completion, and Ludovico il Moro gives instructions for Leonardo to start on the 'other wall'.

28 September. MS. Madrid I, cover.

(c. 1497    MS. I.)

1498    Sala delle Asse.

2 October. Ludovico gives Leonardo a vineyard.

(c. 1498–1500    MS. M.)

1499    May. Sends 600 gold florins for safe keeping to the Hospital of Sta Maria Nuova, Florence.

1 August. 'I wrote ... on motion and weights' (CA, 104r–v).

December. Leonardo leaves Milan.

1500 February. In Mantua. Draws portrait of Isabella d'Este.

13 March. In Venice.

April. Returns to Florence.

1501 3 April. Novellara's letter to Isabella d'Este describes a cartoon for a Virgin and St Anne and portraits (? or copies) done by his pupils which Leonardo touches up.

14 April. Letter from same describes Leonardo at work on the 'Madonna of the Yarnwinder'.

1502 With Cesare Borgia as his *architecto e ingegnero generale*, maps. MS. L.

At Urbino (30 July), Pesaro (1 August), Cesena (10 August), Porto Cesenatico (6 September).

1503 March–June. Legal documents in Milan relating to the dispute over the payment and completion of the 'Virgin of the Rocks'.

22 July. Notes regarding the Arno Canal (MS. Madrid II, 1v.).

October. Begins cartoon for the 'Battle of Anghiari'.

1504 25 January. Consulted as to the best position for Michelangelo's 'David'.

1 April. First monthly payment of 15 gold florins for the 'Battle of Anghiari'.

24–27 May. Isabella d'Este requests Leonardo to paint a young Christ.

9 July. Death of Leonardo's father, leaving ten sons and two daughters.

1 November. Observations of coloured shadows at Piombino (MS. Madrid II, 125r.).

November. Engineering schemes at Piombino (MS. Madrid II, 24v. and 25r.).

25 December. Solution to a geometrical problem (MS. Madrid II, 118r.).

1505 6 June. A storm interrupts his work on the 'Battle of Anghiari' (MS. Madrid II, 2r.).

12 July. MS. Forster I, 3v.

1506 4–27 April. Arbiters in Milan rule that Leonardo should be required to finish the 'Virgin of the Rocks' within two years for 200 lire.

30 April. Executors exclude Leonardo from his father's will on the grounds of his illegitimacy. A legal action is started.

30 May. Obtains leave from the Signoria of Florence to return to Milan for three months.

August and September, letters from Charles d'Amboise asking that his leave may be extended.

1507 March. Brief return to Florence.

27 April. His Milanese vineyard, which had been confiscated, is returned to him.

26 August. An instalment of 100 lire paid for the 'Virgin of the Rocks'.

September. Returns to Florence.

22 September. Studies of bird flight (MS. Trn., 18v.).

(1507–08 MS. D, 'On the Eye'. Intensive work on anatomy.)

1508 22 March. MS. Arundel, 1r.: 'begun in Florence in the house of Piero da Braccio Martelli on the 22nd day of March'.

July. Leonardo in Milan.

July–April 1509. Records of his salary from the French king, Louis XII, totalling 340 scudi and 200 francs.

18 August. 'Virgin of the Rocks' in place in its altar-piece, and the Confraternity agrees to facilitate the making of a copy.

MS. F, 1r.: 'begun at Milan on the 12th day of September' (used till 1513).

23 October. Final payment of 100 lire for the 'Virgin of the Rocks'.

October. Lends Salai 13 scudi to make up his sister's dowry.

1509  30 April. Solution to a geometrical problem (Windsor 19,145).

1510  Winter. MS. Anatom. A: 'In the winter of this year . . . I expect to complete all this anatomy' (Windsor 19,016r.).

1511  January. MS. G, 1v.

    18 December. A fire started by the Swiss invaders is depicted on a landscape drawing (Windsor 12,416).

1513  9 January. MS. Anatom. C. ii (Windsor 19,077v.) bold drawings on blue paper.

    15 March. In Milan as the guest of Prevostino Viola.

    30 April. Barrier erected in the Council Hall in Florence to protect the unfinished 'Battle of Anghiari'.

    24 September. Leonardo leaves Milan with Melzi, Salai, Lorenzo and Il Fanfoia (MS. E,1r.).

    October. In Florence.

    1 December. In Rome, in the Belvedere of the Vatican. MS. G (notes on landscape).

1514–16 In Rome, but making frequent journeys.

1514  7 July. Working in the studio in the Belvedere granted to him by Giuliano de' Medici (CA, 90v–a.).

    25 September. In Parma with Giuliano de' Medici (MS. E 80r).

    27 September. 'On the bank of the River Po at S. Angelo' (MS. E, 96).

1515  January. 'The Magnifico Giuliano left Rome on the 9th day of January 1515, just at daybreak to marry his wife in Savoy; and on the same day there occurred the death of the King of France' (MS. G, cover).

1516  3 March. Solution to a geometrical problem (CA, 230 v-b).

    August. Notes measurements of S. Paolo, Rome.

(1516–17 Goes to France).

1517  22 May. Ascension Day at Amboise, May at Cloux.

    10 October. Shows the Cardinal of Aragon three pictures – a portrait of a Florentine lady done for Giuliano de' Medici, a young St John the Baptist and the 'St Anne'.

1518  24 June. 'St John's day, 1518, at Amboise in the palace of Cloux (CA, 249r–b). (Geometrical researches.)

1519    23 April. Last will and testament.
       2 May. Death.
       1 June. Melzi writes to Leonardo's brothers expressing his sorrow.
       12 August. Buried at Amboise.

# BIBLIOGRAPHY

A SHORT LIST OF BOOKS ON LEONARDO

Referred to in the text and likely to be of use to the general reader. (Additions to Clark's bibliography are marked *. A small quantity of additional literature has been selected in keeping with Clark's intentions, and annotated accordingly.)

AMORETTI, CARLO. *Memorie storiche vita ... di Leonardo da Vinci*, Milan, 1804. (The first biography of Leonardo to make use of documents.)

ANONIMO. *Il Codice Magliabecchiano*, ed. Carl Frey, Berlin, 1892. (Also known as the Anonimo Gaddiano. One of the most reliable early sources of information for Leonardo, especially during his Florentine years.)

BERENSON, BERNARD. *The Drawing of the Florentine Painters, classified, criticized and studied as documents in the history and appreciation of Tuscan art* (with a copious *catalogue raisonné*), 2 vols., London, 1903. (The author's aim is implied in the title.)
'Leonardo da Vinci, an Attempt at a Revaluation' in *The Study and Criticism of Italian Art*, Third Series, London, 1916, pp. 1–37

BIBLIOGRAFIA: ETTORE VERGA. *Bibliografia Vinciana 1493–1930*, Bologna, 1931. (Useful in spite of bad index and numerous inaccuracies.)
LORENZI, ALBERTO and MARANI, PIETRO. *Bibliografia Vinciana 1964–1979*, Firenze, 1982.* (This continues the bibliographies published in successive volumes of the *Raccolta Vinciana*.)
GUERRINI, MAURO. 'Bibliografia leonardiana 1972–1985', *Raccolta Vinciana*, XXII, 1987, pp. 389–573.

BODMER, HEINRICH (ed.). *Leonardo: des Meisters Gemälde und Zeichnungen*, herausgegeben und eingeleitet von Heinrich Bodmer. Klassiker der Kunst series, Stuttgart, 1931. (The most convenient collection of reproductions with notes containing accurate information.) A more recent and readily available survey of Leonardo paintings is provided by L. D. Ettlinger and A. Ottino Della Chiesa, *The Complete Paintings of Leonardo da Vinci* (Harmondsworth, 1985).\*

BOSSI, GIUSEPPE. *Del 'Cenacolo' di Leonardo da Vinci*, Milan, 1810. (The first serious study of Leonardo as an artist. Through a famous review by Goethe it made Leonardo known in Germany and England.) Goethe's review is now available in *Goethe on Art*, ed. J. Gage (London, 1980).\*

BRIZIO, ANNA MARIA (ed.). *Scritti Scelti di Leonardo da Vinci*, 2nd edn, Turin, 1966.\*

BROWN, DAVID ALLAN. *Leonardo's 'Last Supper': the Restoration*, National Gallery of Art, Washington, 1983–4. (The best account in English of the latest restoration.)\*

CALVI, GIROLAMO. *I manoscritti di Leonardo da Vinci dal punto di vista cronolico, storico e biografico*, Bologna, 1925. (New edition introduced by A. Marinoni (Busto Arsizio, 1982).\*) (A masterpiece of scholarship, fundamental for the chronology of the manuscripts.)

CLARK, KENNETH. *A Catalogue of the Drawings of Leonardo da Vinci in the Collection of His Majesty the King at Windsor Castle*, Cambridge, 1935. (Second edition in collaboration with Carlo Pedretti, *The Drawings of Leonardo da Vinci in the Collection of Her Majesty the Queen at Windsor Castle*, 3 vols. (London and New York, 1968).\*)
'A Note on Leonardo', *Life and Letters*, II, February 1929, pp. 122–32\*
'Leonardo and the Antique' in C. D. O'Malley (ed.), *Leonardo's Legacy*, Berkeley and Los Angeles, 1969, pp. 1–34.\* (This volume also contains valuable essays by other authors, including E. H. Gombrich on the water drawings.)
'Mona Lisa', *Burlington Magazine*, CXV (1973), pp. 144–50\*
'Leonardo e le curve della vita', XVII, *Lettura Vinciana* (Vinci, 1977), Florence, 1979\*

FREUD, SIGMUND. *Eine Kindheitserinnerung des Leonardo da Vinci*, Vienna, 1910 (*Leonardo da Vinci and a memory of his childhood*, London, 1957\*)

GIOVIO, PAOLO. 'Leonardo Vinci Vita', in G. Tiraboschi, *Storia della Letteratura Italiana*, vol. VII, Venice, 1796

GOULD, CECIL. *Leonardo: The Artist and the Non-Artist*, London, 1975\*

HEYDENREICH, LUDWIG H. *Leonardo da Vinci*, London, 1954. (A well-balanced account of Leonardo's total achievement.)

HORNE, HERBERT (trans.). *The Life of Leonardo da Vinci by Giorgio Vasari*, London, 1903. (The best translation of Vasari with notes containing out-of-the-way information.)

KEELE, KENNETH. *Leonardo da Vinci's Elements of the Science of Man*, London and New York, 1983.\* (An introduction to Leonardo's scientific thought through his anatomical researches.)

KEMP, MARTIN. *Leonardo da Vinci: The Marvellous Works of Nature and Man*, London and Cambridge (Mass.), 1981*

LOMAZZO, G. PAOLO. *Trattato dell'arte della pittura*, Milan, 1584. (This volume and the same author's *Idea del tempio della pittura*, contain important information which the author must have had direct from Francesco Melzi, Leonardo's favourite pupil and heir.)

MCCURDY, EDWARD. *The Mind of Leonardo da Vinci*, London, 1928

MALAGUZZI VALERI, FRANCESCO. *La Corte di Ludovico il Moro*, vol. II, *Bramante e Leonardo*, Milan, 1915

MARINONI, AUGUSTO. *La Matematica di Leonardo da Vinci*, Milan, 1982.* (The drawing together of researches on Leonardo's mathematics by a major scholar who has contributed widely to Leonardo studies.)

MARINONI, AUGUSTO (ed.). *Leonardo da Vinci. Scritti Letterari*, Milan, 1974.* (A useful selection with valuable interpretative essays.)

MÖLLER, EMIL. 'Salai und Leonardo da Vinci', in *Jahrbuch der Kunsthistorischen Sammlungen in Wien*, 1928, pp. 139–61
'Wie sah Leonardo aus?' in *Belvedere*, XLIV, 1926, pp. 29–46

MÜLLER-WALDE, PAUL. *Leonardo da Vinci, Lebensskizze und Forschungen über sein Verhältnis zur Florentiner Kunst und zu Rafael*, Munich, 1889. (An early work which does not do justice to the author's great powers and shows his weakness as a connoisseur.)
'Beiträge zur Kenntnis des Leonardo da Vinci', in *Jahrbuch der Königlichen Preussischen Kunstammlungen*, VIII, IX, X, 1897, 1898, 1899. (Eight articles of great value, especially with reference to the Equestrian monuments and the 'Leda'. For patience, observation and a scholarly sense of method they have not been surpassed.)

MÜNTZ, EUGENE. *Léonard de Vinci: L'artiste, le penseur, le savant*, Paris, 1899 (*recte* 1898). (Out of date from the point of view of connoisseurship, but useful for reproductions, and for social conditions in Milan, etc.)

PACIOLI, LUCA. *De Divina Proportione*, Venice, 1509. (The author was intimate with Leonardo and records valuable details about his work. The illustrations were designed by Leonardo.)

PATER, WALTER. *The Renaissance*, London, 1893. (ed. D. L. Hill, Berkeley, Los Angeles and London, 1980.*) (The famous essay on Leonardo on pp. 103–35 was reprinted from an article in the *Fortnightly Review* for 1869.)

PEDRETTI, CARLO. *Leonardo da Vinci: Fragments at Windsor Castle*, London, 1957. (Important evidence for dating the drawings.)
*Leonardo da Vinci on Painting: A lost book (Libro A)*, California, 1964. (Invaluable study of the *Trattato della Pittura*.)
*Leonardo da Vinci: A Study in Chronology and Style*. London, 1973.* (The only book in English that synthesizes for the general reader some of the researches of this important and prolific Leonardo scholar, though it does not do full justice

to his encyclopedic grasp of Leonardo's written legacy. See also *Leonardo* (Bologna, 1979).*)

*Leonardo da Vinci: The Royal Palace at Romorantin*, Cambridge (Mass.), 1972.* (The early chapters also contain a valuable outline of Leonardo's previous architectural work.) See also *Leonardo Architect*, London, 1986.

PEDRETTI, CARLO AND KEELE, KENNETH. *Leonardo da Vinci: Corpus of Anatomical Drawings in the Collection of Her Majesty the Queen*, 3 vols., New York, 1979–80.* (Contains facsimiles, transcriptions and full-scale commentaries on the Windsor anatomical drawings first catalogued by Clark in 1935.)

POGGI, GIOVANNI (ed.). *Leonardo da Vinci: la 'Vita' di Giorgio Vasari, nuovamente commentate e illustrata con 200 tavole*, Florence, 1919. (A thorough piece of scholarship, giving the chief documents in a convenient form.)

POPHAM, A. E. *The Drawings of Leonardo da Vinci, Compiled, Introduced and Annotated*, London, 1946; 2nd edn, London, 1964. (The most complete selection, with judicious notes.)

POPP, ANNY E. (ed.). *Leonardo da Vinci: Zeichnungen*, herausgegeben von Anny E. Popp, Munich, 1928. (The best short study of the drawings, and the first to understand the importance of chronology.)

RETI, LADISLAO (ed.). *The Manuscripts of Leonardo da Vinci . . . at the Biblioteca Nacional of Madrid*, 5 vols., New York, 1974.* (Contains facsimiles, transcriptions and commentaries on the re-discovered manuscripts, unknown to Clark when he wrote his monograph.)

*The Unknown Leonardo*, London, 1974.* (An uneven collection of essays which contains some of the material from the Madrid Codices in convenient form. Later issued in three separate volumes as *Leonardo the Artist, . . . the Scientist,* and *. . . the Inventor* (London, etc., 1981).*)

RICHTER, JEAN PAUL. *The Literary Works of Leonardo da Vinci*, compiled and edited from the original manuscripts. Revised edition. 2 vols., London, 1939. (See also Carlo Pedretti's *Commentary* 2 vols. (Oxford, 1977),* containing a great deal of important reference material. A shorter anthology is also available in Irma A. Richter (ed.), *Selections from the Notebooks of Leonardo da Vinci* (Oxford, 1977).*)

ROSCI, MARCO. *The Hidden Leonardo*, trans. J. Gilbert, Oxford, 1978*

SÉAILLES, GABRIEL. *Léonard de Vinci: L'artiste et le savant*, Paris, 1892. (This remains the best introduction to Leonardo's thought. It formed the basis of Paul Valéry's well-known *Introduction à la méthode de Léonard de Vinci*, trans. by T. McGreevy as *Introduction to the Method of Leonardo da Vinci* (London, 1929),* which, however, misinterpreted Séailles's conclusions.)

SEIDLITZ, WALDEMAR VON. *Leonardo da Vinci, der Wendpunkt der Renaissance*, 2 vols., Berlin, 1909. (The fullest and, on the whole, the best life of Leonardo, but better for life than art.)

SIRONI, GRAZIOSO. *Nuovi documenti riguardanti la 'Vergine delle Rocce' di Leonardo da Vinci*, Milan, 1981.* (Contains transcriptions of the new 'Virgin of the Rocks' documentation. Sironi's own interpretation of the documentation as a whole is questionable.)

SOLMI, EDMONDO. *Leonardo: (1452–1519)*, Firenze, 1900. (One of the best accounts of Leonardo's life, but wholly inadequate as an account of his art.)

'Le fonti manoscritti di Leonardo da Vinci', in *Giornale storico della letteratura italiana*. Suppl. 10–11, Turin, 1908, and LVIII, 1911, pp. 297–357. (Though far from exhaustive, the first systematic attempt to find how far Leonardo's manuscripts are transcribed from other sources. Supplemented by the same author in the same journal for 1911.)

*Scritti Vinciani*, Florence, 1924

SUIDA, WILHELM. *Leonardo und sein Kreis*, Munich, 1929. (An adventurous book in which a few unconvincing attributions are more than counter-balanced by some valuable discoveries.)

TONI, G. B. DE. *Le piante e gli animali in Leonardo da Vinci*, Bologna, 1922

TRATTATO. *Trattato della Pittura* di Leonardo da Vinci, prefazione di Angelo Borzelli, Lanciano, 1914. (This is the Italian edition used by Clark.) The standard critical edition is in German, *Das Buch von der Malerei*, herausgegeben von Heinrich Ludwig (Vienna, 1882). (See also *The Treatise on Painting*, 2 vols., ed. A. McMahon (Princeton, 1956),* containing facsimile and translation.)

WASSERMAN, JACK. *Leonardo da Vinci*, New York, 1975*

ZUBOV, VASILIJ. *Leonardo da Vinci*, trans. D. Kraus, Cambridge (Mass.), 1968.* ( A perceptive, thematic analysis of Leonardo's philosophy.)

# INDEX

In the following index, 'Leonardo da Vinci' is abbreviated to 'L.'